Sheena + The Bra Lounge!

Thank you so much
for your support of our
Breast Cancer fundraiser.

I hope you enjoy
my story.

Tim

TAKEN
—TO MY—
KNEES

**MY JOURNEY AFTER A
BREAST CANCER DIAGNOSIS**

*Kim Rideout
2013*

KIMBERLEY RIDEOUT

authorHOUSE®

AuthorHouse™
1663 Liberty Drive
Bloomington, IN 47403
www.authorhouse.com
Phone: 1-800-839-8640

Published by AuthorHouse 04/03/2013

ISBN: 978-1-4817-3566-7 (sc)
ISBN: 978-1-4817-3564-3 (hc)
ISBN: 978-1-4817-3565-0 (e)

Library of Congress Control Number: 2013905903

Cover photo by www.tracykuhl.com

This book is printed on acid-free paper.

To
Cliff, Kelsey, and Kayla
for loving me through it

and

in loving memory of
Jane Rideout
(November 22, 1937–March 29, 1995)
for giving me the strength to fight.

.

Contents

Foreword

Dear Mom,

Where to start? You are the most kind-hearted, inspirational woman in my life. They don't even make fictional characters like you. You know why? Because there is nothing this world could throw at you that you wouldn't walk away from without a smile on your face. After everything we have gone through, from those teenage years from hell to where we are now, this letter could go on for a while, but I just wanted to let you know that I appreciate everything you've done for me.

I appreciate the lesson I learned from a bag of clothes being thrown at me.

I appreciate the time you bought me the exact same charm I bought you when you were having a rough time.

I appreciate when you brought me to the emergency room when I got macaroni and cheese stuck in my teeth after my wisdom teeth surgery.

I appreciate the best Christmas ever and how you and Dad made it that way.

I appreciate the time I got sick all over the house and you had to take a dive to clean it up.

I appreciate your courage on amusement park rides.

I appreciate your laugh and how sometimes I wish I didn't inherit it; it's a laugh that can light up the whole room.

I appreciate your honesty, even though it's not what I want to hear sometimes.

I appreciate your strength and faith, which sometimes gets me through the day.

I appreciate your patience with everything I do.

I appreciate the look you give me when we are fighting, and I can't help but laugh or smile; it really breaks the tension.

This letter could be a million pages long, but I just want to let you know that I love you and that I'm thankful for every day I have a mother as great as you.

Love,

Kay

Cancer, such a disgusting word. But it never seems to be a word that affects you directly; it's always your friend's mother's friend. I guess that the world had something else in store for my family. My mother is my inspiration. She is my heart, my soul. The year of 2012 has been the toughest year of our lives, and I am happy to say it has finally come to an end.

—Kayla Rideout

When I found out Mom was sick, I didn't know what to think. I was scared, upset, but most of all mad. It's hard to accept that someone you love has to go through something so life changing. It was so hard to see her not be able to do the things she loved like spending countless weekends camping or gardening. I can't explain the relief of that last treatment and for a clean bill of health. I am thankful for everyone who helped my mom throughout the months of treatment.

—Kelsey Rideout

Preface

I never set out to write a book. But then again, I never set out to get breast cancer. On March 14, 2012, I found out I had breast cancer, and my life took a completely different course than the one I had planned for myself the day before. My life changed forever; I changed forever.

In the early days of my diagnosis, my friend Bonnie gifted me with a journal along with instructions to start writing what I was feeling. I believe that one gesture was the beginning of what is now this book. I started writing and didn't stop. I wrote when I was sad, I wrote when I was happy, I wrote when I was sick, and I wrote when I was feeling well. I wrote on my deck in the middle of the afternoon, and I wrote at night by the light of a single lamp while everyone in my world was sleeping. My journal was always at my side, and when I filled it, I purchased another, then another, and then another. Over the course of seven months, I filled four journals. My words were full of fear in the early days, with enough pain and sadness to last a lifetime.

After each treatment, I sent out an update to those closest to me, often summing up the events that were diarized in my journals, and without fail someone would write me back and tell me I needed to write a book. The seed was planted, and I finally decided to give it a try.

When I started to write, my intent was to summarize this time in my life and to share those feelings and experiences with those closest to me. It was my way of saying thank you to those who had stood beside me, supported me, and loved me through the darkest time of my life thus far.

I wanted to let people know that words are powerful and that I appreciated every single e-mail, phone call, and text I received. The words of encouragement kept me going more than anyone can ever appreciate. The visits, short or long, showed me that they remembered me. The hugs confirmed their love.

I will never forget anything and everything that was done, said, or expressed. Thank you just doesn't seem enough to say.

I am who I am because of the beautiful souls who surround me. I am as strong as I am because of the strength that surrounds me.

If you, the reader of this book, come away with anything after finishing my story, I hope it is encouragement to be kind and to love. You never know when that simple statement will make a life-changing difference in someone's life, when that hug will breathe enough strength to help someone get through another minute, or when that card dropped in the mail will set that person's mood for the day.

Despite the challenges you face, the world looks so beautiful when you are surrounded by love.

I also hope that if you are a recently diagnosed breast cancer patient you can read my words and know that breast cancer is not a death sentence. You are not a victim. You, like me, can survive!

Acknowledgments

First and foremost, I want to thank my husband, Cliff. He stood beside me through it all, loving me unconditionally even when I couldn't love myself. He let me draw on his strength when I was fading and held me up when I stumbled. Thank you for being my biggest cheerleader and my best friend. Thank you for giving me the will to fight and then fighting right alongside me. I will love you forever.

To my daughters, Kelsey and Kayla, my life would not be worth living without each of you. I marvel in your accomplishments daily and am so proud to be your mom. I love you both more than you will ever know. You will only appreciate the depth of that love when you have your own children. I am so excited to be here to watch your lives as they unfold into the exciting futures I know are in store for you.

To my mother-in-law, Jane Rideout, who lost her fight with cancer many years ago, thank you. You gave me a gift while fighting your own battle that served me well in my journey. You taught me that love conquers all, life is worth fighting for, and to never lie down and give up. You represented grace, resilience, and courage in your fight, and I tried each day to follow in your shoes and to be as brave as you were. I miss you.

To my sister-in-law Peggy and my brother-in-law Dyrick there are no words to say just how much your kindness has meant to me. From the moment you found out about my diagnosis, you started making your travel plans, needing to be here to help me in whatever way you could. Your visit gave us the strength to keep going and showed us that our love transcends the miles that separate us.

To my dear friend Juanita Dwyer, who also made a trip across the country to be with me in the early days of my treatment, I will forever be in your debt for all you did for me. How do you thank someone who one minute can make you laugh so hard you cry and then shave your head the next? I love you, my friend.

To my friend Bonnie Rattai, who was literally with me from the first moments of my story, thank you. You gave me strength at a time when I didn't think I had any. I will never forget your kindness. I am so happy we found each other.

Tracy Thody, you were my rock, my confidant, my sister. Thank you for helping me through some of my darkest moments. I honestly don't know if I could have done it without you in my corner. Thank you for seeing me through.

Tammy Dodge, you kept it all real for me, kept me from losing my mind, explained all the clinical details, and made me so happy to have a best friend who is a nurse. I love you more than I can say.

Simone Ullrich, you prayed for me when I forgot how to pray. When I needed more than prayers, you made me laugh loud enough to be heard around the neighborhood. You are such a beautiful friend.

Linda Zazula, you are the coach every woman needs in her corner. You loved me through every day, tied up my gloves, and sent me back into the ring even when I was so tired I wanted to quit. How can I ever repay that kind of support? Thank you for laughing and crying with me.

Krista Dezall, thank you for never giving up even when things got confusing. I always felt your love and look forward to making some new wonderful memories. I love you.

To my brother, Brian, and his wife, Pearl, thank you for all your support even when you were going through your own hell on earth dealing with your own breast cancer diagnosis. While I wish neither of our families had to go through the trials we have faced this year, I am so happy we have come through it as survivors.

To my dad, thank you for giving me your wonderful gift of storytelling. It has served me well in writing this book. To my mom, I am happy I inherited your fantastic sense of humor. It has helped me during many of the darkest moments. I love you both more than words can say.

To my extended family, and to Cliff's family, thank you all for your support, your love, and your concern in whatever forms they were delivered.

To all my friends, near and far, thank you. For all the cards, for the hundreds of e-mails I received, for the twenty-seven flower deliveries that made it to my door, for all the gifts of books, food, and scarves, and for everything in between—thank you. Not one gesture of kindness went unnoticed, and I will be forever thankful.

To my medical team. Dr. Roxana Nechifor - thank you for your kindness and your professionalism and for making me feel like I was your only patient every time I was in your office. Dr. Paul Hardy - I am so thankful for your skills as a surgeon as well as your kindness. Nurse Krista Rawson - you were my nurse but I will always consider you my friend first. Thank you for seeing that I was a wife and mother long before I became a cancer patient of yours. I will never forget your kindness and your friendship.

To my co-workers at Farm Credit Canada (FCC) and my boss Spencer Higginson, you guys rock! Thank you for sticking by me, for supporting me through the Run for the Cure, and for holding my job until I was well enough to return to work. Thank you for everything.

To Tracy Kuhl of Tracy Kuhl Photography, all I can say is thank you. You made me feel beautiful at the lowest point in my life and marked that period for eternity with such beauty. Thank you for being a master at your craft.

To all those of you who encouraged me to write a book and who believed I could write something special even when I had doubts, thank you. Your faith in me is what made this possible, and for that I will be forever grateful.

Introduction

February 2010

We were so excited. Cliff and I were heading out on a long-anticipated vacation to Mexico, just the two of us, kind of like the honeymoon we never had. We were booked into a five-star hotel right on the beach and had been looking forward to this getaway since the previous fall. We had never been away on vacation with just the two of us before and could not wait to hit the runway, arrive at the hotel, and do all those things honeymooners do.

As we broke over the hill just outside Red Deer on our way to Edmonton, we cracked open a bag of candy we had purchased to eat on the way. *That's funny* … I thought. "Here, honey, have one of these. Does it taste weird to you?"

Cliff took the candy I offered and popped it into his mouth. "Tastes okay to me," he said.

And off we went. We arrived in Edmonton an hour or so later and checked into our hotel, where we would spend a few hours before our 5:00 a.m. departure. We were so excited. Well, I was so excited and bouncing off the walls. Cliff is famous for saying he is excited on the inside. Christmases, birthdays, vacations—he always has the same demeanor. But I know he was looking forward to the trip. Later in the evening, I was hungry. It was freezing cold outside, and neither of us wanted to warm up the car to head to the nearest store, so we hit the vending machine on our floor. It didn't have a big selection, but we each made our choices and headed back to the room.

I opened up my bag of peanuts and poured them into my mouth

after offering a few to Cliff, who started to cough as soon as the first one hit his tongue. Chili pepper peanuts and I hadn't even blinked. *Weird,* I thought, as I could hardly tolerate black pepper. *I must be getting a cold.* And then I remember thinking that I hoped I didn't get sick while we were in Mexico.

We arrived at the airport in the morning, all excited and ready for our vacation to start. We met up with a friend's aunt and uncle, who were traveling on the same flight, and we visited with them before we boarded, on route to the vacation of our dreams. Our flight was uneventful, and when the tires hit the runaway south of the border, we were among the first up after the seat belt sign turned was off, ready to get going and get started on having fun.

Our hotel was everything we had dreamed of, including the swan towels on the bed and the heart made out of rose petals. We dropped our bags, pulled a drink out of the fridge, pulled on our shorts, and headed out to walk along the beach. I was feeling kind of off at that point, and Cliff commented on how clammy my skin was. We chalked it up to the moisture in the air, which was unlike the dry Alberta winter we had just escaped. Our first night was all we had dreamed it would be, and we were excited for morning so that we could explore more and get a feel for the resort in the daylight.

Morning arrived, and I knew something was wrong when I woke up. The right side of my face felt funny and stiff, and I thought perhaps I had eaten something the night before and was having an allergic reaction, so I told Cliff I was going to visit the gift shop and see if they had any Benadryl. As I walked back to my room, I knew something was really wrong. When I arrived, I could not feel the right side of my face. *What is happening to me?* I thought. *Am I having a stroke?*

Cliff and I quickly gathered up our passports and headed to the front desk to ask about seeing a doctor, and luckily there was one on the resort grounds at the time. We were shown to his office, and after an examination, he determined that I was suffering from Bell's palsy. At that point, complete and total paralysis had set in from my hairline to my ear and down to my collarbone on the right side of my face. My face drooped on the right side, and I could not close my mouth or my eye. I looked like someone who'd had a stroke.

The doctor recommended that we stay in Mexico, as he did not recommend air travel. He felt the cabin pressure would be too much on my ear at that early stage, and he said the best thing for Bell's palsy was to relax and sleep. What better place to do that but on vacation? I wanted nothing more than to go home.

We stayed the week in Mexico in the shade. I was advised to not drink any alcohol, eat only familiar foods (for me that was bread), and stay out of the sun. Because I was unable to close my eye, I could not walk on the beach because the wind blew sand in my eye, and the doctor did not recommend covering it. I could not swim for the same reason. When I slept, I would wake to Cliff's hand on my back, his way of reassuring himself that I was breathing.

We managed to make the best of it and actually made some very good memories. We found a secluded pool with a covered cabana, where we spent our days relaxing.

This is what I wrote a short time after while still recovering from Bell's palsy:

Just imagine ... waking up one morning on vacation in a country where you don't speak the language ... being all alone with just your husband and feeling something is wrong. Then watching the side of your face lose all movement over the period of hours, relying solely on the broken English from a local doctor and the Internet, diagnosing yourself as having Bell's palsy, and praying every day it is not something much worse.

Just imagine ... You go to the dentist for a filling ... Remember that feeling of numbness, not being able to feel your face? Now extend that numbness from your hairline to your neck. Every time you try to eat something, you bite your lip, tongue, or cheek because they have no sensation. Drinking with a straw becomes commonplace, trying not to result in a mini shower every time.

Just imagine ... trying to smile when you physically can't. Place your hand on one side of your face, with the heel of your hand at your mouth. Then push in just enough to make it uncomfortable but not to hurt. Then pull down. That is how Bell's palsy feels. Uncomfortable? You bet … Now try to smile … Imagine how tiring that is day in and day out.

Just imagine … not being able to close your eye for what seems like forever. Hold your eye open with your fingers and go for a short walk around your house. Amazing how much wind you create when you are walking, isn't it?

Just imagine … not being able to remember what it feels like to kiss or be kissed.

Just imagine … jumping out of bed every morning and rushing to the mirror with hope that a smile will be shining back.

Just imagine … being so grateful for all the blessings in your life and the wondrous anticipation you would feel with each little improvement and waiting for your healing to be complete so that you can once again smile as big on the outside as you feel on the inside!

That is life with Bell's palsy, my friends.

During my recovery from Bell's palsy, I kept thinking, *This is the worst thing that has ever happened to me.* Little did I know what I was in store for two short years later.

> *To be a person is to have a story to tell.*
> ——Isak Dinesen

This is my story.

Chapter 1

The Diagnosis

Out of difficulties grow miracles.
　　—Jean De La Bruyere

March 14, 2012

I was waiting to have my forth mammogram in eight months and didn't expect today to be different from any other. As I sat in the waiting room, I mentally went over the list of things I had to do that evening. I was leaving in the morning to head to Toronto to visit my brother, Brian, and his family. Brian's wife had recently been diagnosed with breast cancer, and I was heading there for the weekend to visit them, help out a little with their three small children, and spend some much overdue time with them.

I have a history of breast infections, and I'd had a couple of surgeries in the past couple of years to remove infections, but there had never been any sign of cancer or cancer cells. Other than a great aunt on my mother's side, there was no history of breast cancer in my family, and my doctors over the years had constantly reassured me that the infections I had would not lead to breast cancer.

Mammograms had become so routine for me. I'd had one in July, August, and November of the previous year, and they had all come back clean. This appointment was no different, and I had actually forgotten to even tell Cliff I was going until that morning. I'd had a doctor's appointment the day before, on March 13, and my new doctor ordered the tests because of another flare-up I was experiencing. I was a little anxious about the mammogram, as I was afraid that the infection I was dealing with might break during the compression of the mammogram, and my past experience was that they always tended to hurt more when I had an active infection. My doctor had ordered a mammogram, ultrasound, and a possible biopsy, and I was not concerned, as I'd had these done many times in the past. Routine.

The infection was in my right breast, the same as so many times before, and while I was not nervous, I was anxious to get this appointment over with, as I had things to do and was supposed to meet Cliff for supper.

While I sat in the waiting room waiting for my name to be called, I busied myself texting my girlfriend.

Bonnie (1:43): Have you left for your apt yet?

Me (2:19): Still here now. Sweating!

Bonnie (2:19): Sweating? Why? Nerves?

Me (2:20): Yeah. I know it will be fine but your nerves always play games on you!

Me (2:21): I am the youngest woman here! Everyone else's got grey hair!

Bonnie (2:21): Yeah I know. It will be fine though. Let me know when you're done.

Me (2:22): Will do.

I was called into the room shortly after. The technician completed the mammogram pictures on my right breast and then came around to position me to take pictures of my left breast.

I said, "I don't think you need to do that breast. The concern is in my right breast."

"Oh, we will do both," she answered.

Little did I know that her decision to do both breasts possibly saved my life. To this day, I don't know why she did both, if it was routine or if it was a fluke, but I am so grateful that she did. That decision to take a look at my left breast set into motion a series of events that changed my life forever.

Once we were done, she told me to collect my things and wait in the waiting room until the radiologist took a look. Again, routine. I collected my clothes, held my gown together, and returned to the waiting room, all the while hoping this wouldn't take too long. I still had to have the ultrasound done and a possible biopsy. I looked at my watch and noted that the afternoon was ticking away, and my list of things to get done before my flight in the morning still sat in my purse, untouched.

Me (2:49): Mammogram done. Waiting on radiologist to read to see if I need another. Then off to ultrasound. That hurt!

Bonnie (2:50): I bet. Did it pop like you thought it would?

Me (2:52): No. She didn't compress as much as normal hoping not to break it. But may have to get redone if radiologist can't see enough because it wasn't so compressed.

Bonnie (2:53): Hopefully it worked out good enough. When is your ultrasound?

Me (2:54): They will send me to the other side when my mammogram is read and I am cleared.

I looked up as my name was called, and the technician asked me to come back in. When I entered the room, she said the radiologist wanted more pictures taken. *Okay,* I thought. At this point I was not too concerned, as this had happened before, and I always thought it was better for them to be diligent.

As I moved toward the machine, I positioned myself so that she could place my right breast on the screen; however, the technician came up behind me and said, "It is the left breast we need to take another look at."

My left breast? Full stop. The hair stood up on the back of my neck. *Why?* I thought, but I couldn't speak. My mouth went dry. *The left breast?*

There is nothing wrong with the left breast! As I tried to settle the panic I felt moving up my chest, I noticed that she seemed very nervous herself. *My left breast?* As I held onto the machine, she kept apologizing for causing me discomfort as the machine squished my breast tissue, but I didn't even feel it. I was concentrating on holding on, physically and mentally. My hand was so wet with sweat that I was afraid I would slip, causing me to move and ruin the pictures. She said she had to do several different images of the breast and kept pulling and tugging on my breast to get it in the exact position. I kept thinking, *My left breast. Why my left one? There is nothing wrong with my left breast.*

Once we were done, she asked me to once again return to the waiting room and told me they would let me know if they had all the images they needed. Sitting in the waiting room, I could not meet anyone's eyes. I was scared. Everyone there seemed old enough to be my mother or my grandmother. Women went into the exam rooms, came out with their clothes on and smiles on their faces, and left the building. The TV droned on in the background. I could hear laughter, but all that was registering with me was the blood I could hear rushing through my ears. Every time a door opened, I looked up to see if they were looking for me.

Eventually, the technician who took my pictures came back out and bent down to speak to me as I remained in my seat in the waiting room. I searched her face but could not read anything from her expression; however, her body language told a different story, and I knew there was something wrong. I took some deep breaths and silently told myself to remain calm as she advised me that they would be calling me in for the ultrasound shortly. I kept myself busy by continuing my texting with Bonnie, not revealing my worry but using our communication as a way to keep my mind occupied.

Me (3:10): Just had more pictures taken. OMG I could cry.

Bonnie (3:13): Well hopefully that will be it!

Me (3:13): Another reason to have small boobies.

Bonnie (3:14): They won't be able to get a hold of mine!

Me (3:15): I have heard that it is harder when you are smaller because they have to pull more. Either way, it is uncomfortable.

Bonnie (3:16): I have no idea but either way it doesn't sound like a picnic.

Me (3:23): Now off to ultrasound. No more squishing.

Me (3:23): Two people in front of me.

Bonnie (3:24): You are going to get home at regular time. When do you fly out?

Me (3:25): Tomorrow at noon. At this rate I will be home by 5:00. Wondering if they will still do the biopsy today. They are running behind.

Bonnie (3:26): Hopefully eh? They haven't said anything about not doing it?

Me (3:26): No

Bonnie (3:27): Well I hope they get it all done for you. Then you will get all of the results.

Me (3:28): Yup. Me too. They are moving me to the other side now.

Looking back through the text messages, I know I'd been waiting about twenty minutes, but at the time it had seemed like hours. Finally I heard my name called, and I walked down the hall. Little did I know that when I retraced my steps in an hour, my world as I knew it would be no more.

I entered the room where the ultrasound equipment was, put my clothes and purse on the table, and lay down as instructed. I took deep breaths while staring at the ceiling as I waited for the exam to begin. I'd had this technician in the past, and she was always very friendly and carried on a conversation while she worked; however, this time I noticed right away that she was different, very businesslike in her instructions, and she offered no small talk at all.

Once I was settled on the bed, she applied the gel they use to complete the ultrasound to my breast and quickly scanned over my right breast. Within seconds, she focused her attention on my left breast, and I noticed how fast and precise she was in the location that she targeted. She knew exactly what she was looking for and where it was. I watched her face, I looked at the screen, and then I stared at the ceiling. Cyst? Infection? What? Right away I started making deals with God. I kept looking back at the screen, trying to see what she was seeing, but it all looked the same to me. Could it be possible that it was nothing? Was I borrowing trouble? *Oh God, please let it be nothing*, I pleaded in my mind.

I am not sure how long the ultrasound took, but I remember my heart pounding and the hair on the back of my neck standing up. I knew something was wrong, I knew this was not good, and I knew something terrible was about to happen. You know that little voice inside your head that tells you something is wrong? It was screaming at me. The conflicting emotions were gut-wrenching, knowing something was wrong while praying it was nothing. *Please, it has to be just a cyst that they want to check out.* I kept making deals with God. *Please let it be a cyst.*

Once the technician finished taking pictures, she said she was going to talk with the radiologist and would be back in a minute and for me to remain where I was. It did not go unnoticed by me that she failed to make eye contact as she prepared to leave. The door closed, and I was alone. Alone with all those frightening thoughts. What was happening, and how was this happening? Was I going to have to have surgery? I'd just had a mammogram in November. Surely there couldn't be anything there. But what if there was? What was it? So many thoughts and I was so scared. I lay on that examination table, the lights down low, with just a sheet over my body, and I started to shake. I felt the tremors start in my stomach and move up and down my body, and I pulled the sheet up to my chin, hoping to get some warmth from it. After finding none, I folded my arms across my chest and hugged tightly as I squeezed my eyes closed.

The door opened, and the technician as well as the radiologist entered the room. I took note that once again she did not look at me, but he did, and I knew right away that the news he was about to deliver was not good. He kind of smiled, but it was a sad smile, and I knew he was going to tell me something I didn't want to hear. I believe I already knew. My heart started to pump again, and I wanted to jump off the bed and run out of the room. I did not want to hear what he was going to say.

Please God! my mind screamed. *No!*

He greeted me with a hollow hello. Then he came to my side and took the ultrasound wand and grazed it over my left breast. He placed the wand down after a slight nod like he had confirmed what he had already seen. I heard him take a deep breath, and I looked over his shoulder at the technician, but she was busy with the machine and didn't meet my gaze.

He started talking. I listened, but I didn't listen. *Is he really saying what I think he is saying?* Lump? Suspicious? Left breast? Breast carcinoma? Lymph node involvement? Surgery within a week? Carcinoma? Carcinoma was cancer; I knew that. Cancer? *Oh my God, cancer!*

I felt tears running out of my eyes and down my cheeks. I was still lying down, and I remember wondering why he didn't have me sit up. I felt so vulnerable right then, lying on my back with a thin sheet over my breasts. The tears were just streaming out of my eyes, but I wasn't making a sound. Cancer? He kept talking softly, and I once again caught a glimpse of the technician, and she was crying too. Cancer.

Finally I spoke. "Are you telling me I have breast cancer?" I needed to be clear on what I was hearing, but I didn't want the answer.

"Yes, Kimberley. You have breast cancer."

My world changed forever. Breast cancer. Full stop.

I took a deep breath and choked back the sobs that were in my throat. The shaking had returned, and I felt like I was going to throw up. I was drowning in my silent tears. I felt so alone.

"What do I tell my husband? What do I tell my girls?" I asked. "How do I tell my family that I have breast cancer?"

He told me to tell them everything, that a lump had been found and needed to be removed, that there was concern with a lymph node as well, and that we needed to have surgery within a week. *A week! This is serious. This cannot be happening.*

"I am leaving tomorrow to go to Toronto to see my brother and his family. His wife has breast cancer. I am going to see them and spend some time with their children. I haven't seen them in a long time. My brother is expecting me," I rambled on.

"I know, but perhaps you should think about putting that off for now." He knew. They had talked in the office before he came to see me. He knew of my plans. I remember wondering how that conversation between him and the technicians had gone. Was it something like, "Poor girl. You better tell her today. She is leaving town tomorrow"?

Cancer.

How do I tell my family, my friends that I have cancer? And why won't this water stop coming out of my eyes? I was not making a sound, but it kept running. No sobs, no screams of disbelief. Just silence. The river of blood rushing through my ears was so loud that I wondered if they could hear it.

The radiologist reached out and touched my shoulder and said he was sorry. The water ran faster. I couldn't see. I needed to sit up, but I was naked from the waist up. I felt like I was going to drown.

The radiologist then said, "We caught it early. Remember, that is good. If you had waited until your routine screening in July, we would be having a very different conversation right now."

"Thank you for finding it," I managed to say. From the very first moments, even through the panic and fear, I was thankful. I was thankful that we were not having that "different conversation."

"But how can you be sure? Don't we need a biopsy first?" I asked. Maybe I'd heard him wrong. Maybe he meant it was suspicious and that he thought it was cancer but was not certain.

"I am sure it is breast cancer. But yes, a biopsy will be done to confirm my findings," he replied. He did not offer me any hope and was calling it as he saw it. Now I am thankful that he didn't give me any false hope, but at the time I would have grabbed it if he had dangled in front of me.

We talked for a while longer. I am not sure how long. All I remember was how kind he was, as was my technician. He took his time, talking slowly and explaining everything in detail, and he asked me several times if I had any more questions before he left. He left me with instructions to call my family doctor first thing in the morning. He told me he would be sending her his report as soon as he returned to his office and she would take over from there.

The technician, how I wish I could remember her name, sat on the bed with me and held me as I started to cry once he left the room. Tears had been flowing from almost the minute the radiologist walked into the room, but now I started to cry.

Cancer … Oh My God, I have breast cancer. No, this can't be happening. Breast cancer! Me! No no no!

She held me while I cried, and then I thought, *I have to go home. I have to figure this out.* She talked to me, and while I will always remember her kindness, I cannot remember a word she said. Just her kindness and genuine concern. Then she left me alone to dress and told me to take as much time as I needed.

As I dressed, I went into automatic drive. The tears stopped, and I knew I needed to get out of the building fast. As I opened the door to leave the examination room and peered out, I was thankful that the halls were deserted and the waiting room was empty. It was closing time. As I took a step outside the room, I was surprised to find I could not feel my legs; it felt like they were just swinging from the knees. *Please do not let me fall,* I thought. *Just get to the car, and I will be okay.* As I walked down the hall on legs I couldn't feel, I kept focusing on the corner in front of me. *Make it to that corner and then the next corner. Then you will be at the front door.*

As I opened the front door, I looked down the front steps and wondered if I could make it down without falling. Somehow I did, and the next thing I knew I was in my vehicle. I put my head on the steering wheel and started to cry once again, deep wrenching sobs of disbelief. *Breast cancer. Me! No!*

I needed to talk to someone, and my hands shook as I dialed the number for my friend Tammy. She was a nurse. She would know what to do. She would have the answers. As it rang, I wanted to scream, "Pick up!" I kept thinking, *Pick up, Tammy. Please pick up. You will know what to do.* It went to her voice mail, and at the sound of her voice, I started to cry once again. I knew I could not leave her a message. I couldn't speak. I could not scare her by trying to leave a message. How sad she would be that she didn't pick up. A lump had formed in my throat, and I couldn't swallow. I hung up. Then I tried my friend Tracy. She would come get me. She was always there when I needed her. As it rang, I knew it would go to voice mail as well. *My dear friends, where are you when I need you the most?* I thought

I started the car and drove home. It was a miracle that I made it home without having or causing an accident. I have no recollection of the drive. I should never have driven. I could not feel my legs, I could not see through the tears that flooded my eyes, and my hands shook so badly that I wonder how I ever was able to hold onto the steering wheel. But I needed to get to the safety of my home. Then I could figure this out.

The next thing I knew, I was home, and as I threw the vehicle into park, I knew I had an angel watching over me that day, guiding me home safely.

Suddenly I remembered my trip to my brother's house. *What do I do about tomorrow?* I knew I couldn't travel to Brian's now. I needed to see my doctor. Surgery within a week, the radiologist had said. A week! I needed to tell Cliff and the girls. *How do I tell everyone? Do I wait until I see the doctor? Cancer! Breast cancer! This cannot be happening. No, this cannot be happening,* I kept thinking. The lump that had formed in my throat was still there, only growing larger as the minutes ticked by. I sat on the couch as my phone buzzed with texts coming in.

I had my first panic attack on the couch at that moment, though it took me a few months to identify those episodes as panic attacks. I tried to slow my heart rate and breathing. *Am I having a heart attack on top of all of this?* I wondered. *What is happening to me? How do I begin to deal with this? What do I say? Who do I tell? I do not want to hurt my family like this,* I kept thinking. *I don't want this to be happening.*

Call my doctor. I needed to call my doctor. I found her number and talked to the secretary. I told her briefly what was going on, and she said she would have Dr. Nechifor call me back. I fell back on the couch. *Oh my God, oh my God. What do I do? How do I make this right?* I was scared. Within minutes, Dr. Nechifor called back, and I knew immediately from the tone of her voice that she had read the report already.

She asked me what the radiologist had told me, and I told her he told me I had breast cancer. There … I said it. "I have breast cancer." My voice cracked, and I fought so hard not to cry, but I lost the battle and started to sob as we made an appointment for me to come in the next morning, and she asked me if I needed anything to help me cope. Right then I should have said, "Yes, right away." But I said no, I would be okay, and I hung up the phone.

I picked up my phone and noticed several texts from a couple of friends wondering how my appointment went.

Bonnie (4:18) You done yet? Just finished with Shaw. Going to get Shaye from school.

Bonnie (5:08): You home yet?

Me (5:10): Not good, Bonnie.

Bonnie (5:10): What's wrong???

Bonnie (5:11): Where are you?

Me (5:14): Home.

Me (5:14): I have breast cancer, Bonnie.

Bonnie (5:14): What the fuck???

Bonnie (5:15): What is going on?

Bonnie (5:15): How can that be???

Me (5:16): Have to see doctor in morning. Surgery in a couple of days. I can't believe this.

Bonnie (5:17): Call me at home if you can.

Bonnie (5:19): OMG

Bonnie (5:21): Sorry if you are trying to wrap your head around it. I understand. Call me when you can. I will be thinking about you. Kim, I am so sorry.

I sent the same to Krista. She had been trying to call the house to see how my tests had gone, and I hadn't answered.

Krista (5:00): You ok?

Me (5:02): No. I can't say it.

Krista (5:03): Can I call again?

Krista (5:06): I'm on my way over okay?

Me (5:06): No. Just give me a bit and I will call you.

Krista (5:07): I need to get out and I want to see you. I won't stay long.

Krista (5:08) Okay?

Me (5:10): I have breast cancer, Krista

Krista (5:13) I am sorry, my friend. I am sorry. You are strong and you will beat this. I have no doubt.

There, I had typed it twice within minutes. Could this really be happening? Had I just put me and breast cancer in the same text? Twice?

I was supposed to meet Cliff for supper. I needed to call him, but I knew I would lose it when I heard his voice. I just needed him to come home. The clock showed that it was 5:00 p.m., and I knew he should be home any minute. The next thing I heard was the front door opening. It was Kayla, my youngest daughter.

Kayla is my worrywart child, wise way beyond her nineteen years. Not too many months ago, she went through a stage where she was afraid I was going to get sick, and many nights I lay on her bed with her, and we talked, and she expressed how scared she was that I would get sick. She told me that if anything happened to me, they would have to bury her with me because she couldn't live without me. Had she had some sixth sense that I was already sick? Now I was going to break her heart and rip her world apart; I was about to make her fears a reality.

She came upstairs, and I was sitting on the couch and could not look over at her. She said hi and then walked into the kitchen, but something stopped her, and she walked back to where I was sitting so that we were face-to-face.

"What's wrong, Mama?" she asked.

I stared at her. *How do you tell your child that you have breast cancer? Lord, I don't want to do this,* I thought. "Nothing," I choked out. "It's nothing."

"Mom? You are scaring me. What's wrong?" The panic had set in for her already, and I hadn't even said anything yet. I couldn't speak, and I couldn't look at her, and she asked again, her voice rising higher and her fear coming to the surface. "Mom, tell me. What's wrong?"

"I have breast cancer, baby," I whispered. There. I said it again. I devastated my child.

I will never forget her reaction and how helpless I felt at that moment. Her instant reaction was to cry as she dropped her purse and fell onto the couch beside me. She cried hard and kept saying, "No, Mom," Oh my God," and "No, this can't be happening" over and over.

I reached for her and pulled her into my arms while she cried and cried and cried. The lump in my throat grew bigger and bigger. I couldn't cry. I had to stay strong for her so she wouldn't think I was afraid. The pain I felt at that moment wasn't for me; it was for my child. For the first time in her life, I could not protect her from something, and the thing that was hurting her so much was me! My thoughts echoed her words: *This cannot be happening.*

The phone rang, and caller ID told me it was Cliff. He was going to wonder where I was, and I knew I had to answer.

"Honey, where are you? I thought we were meeting for supper" he said, his voice relaxed. He was still living the life I had lost an hour before. I didn't want to shatter his world. I needed him to come home. I wanted to still be in his reality, not the one I was now living.

"Honey? What's wrong?" He was starting to feel that something was not right even though I hadn't said anything. He was already putting the pieces together, but I knew that the reality was still so far away for him. I started to cry. "Come home," was all I could squeak out.

"Honey? What's wrong?" Now there was a sense of urgency in his voice, his panic clearly coming to the surface. He knew it wasn't good, but he just didn't know what the bad news was. "Kim? Tell me! What's wrong?" He never used my given name unless there was something wrong.

"I have breast cancer." There. I had said again. But it still took away my breath and caused the lump to grow bigger in my throat.

"Oh my God. No! No, honey," he said. He was heartbroken, shocked, devastated, shattered. I heard it all in his voice. "I will be home in a minute." In an instant, our phone connection was broken. *Please let him get home without having an accident*, I thought.

I turned my attention back to Kayla. She was still crying uncontrollably, and I was afraid she was going to make herself sick. I tried to comfort her while trying to keep my own panic under control. I needed to focus, I kept thinking. Focus. I tried to slow down my breathing and kept trying to swallow that lump in my throat because it felt like it was going to choke me.

Cliff arrived home, ran up the stairs, fell to his knees in front of me, and dropped his head into my lap. He cried more than I have ever seen him cry; his body shook uncontrollably. My strong husband who had made it his life's purpose to protect me and our family could not protect us from this. He was feeling helpless, and he was a mess. As Cliff knelt in front of me and Kayla sat tucked under my arm, they cried and shook for what seemed like hours. I heard myself reassuring them that everything was going to be fine, that we had caught it early, and that with surgery I would be okay. I am not sure even I believed my words at the time, but at least someone was saying something. At times I felt like I was hovering over the three of us, watching this scene unfold. I felt that I now understood what it meant to say you were having an out-of-body experience. *Surely this is a dream*, I thought. *This cannot be happening to us.*

Kelsey. Our oldest daughter, Kelsey, was leaving for a cheerleading event in LA that night. We couldn't tell her before she left, I thought. There was nothing to tell right now until we saw the doctor and the surgeon, and I knew that could be more than a week away. We all agreed that we would not tell her and ruin her trip. There would be enough time for that the following week when she returned home. We needed to protect her for as long as we could was all I was thinking. So I sent her a text to wish her a safe trip rather than calling. She would know there was something wrong if I spoke to her. It was safer to text.

Now the hard logistics of who to tell, when, and where to start had to be faced. I was supposed to be flying to Toronto the following morning, so I had to tell Brian I was not coming. I knew in my heart that I was not ready for that conversation, but I had to. Then I backed out. My brother's wife was also dealing with breast cancer. She had been diagnosed only four months previous and was in the middle of her chemotherapy at that time. That was why I was going to visit, to see how they were all doing and to spend some time with their three children. How could I tell him that his sister was also sick with the same disease? He had already faced so much in the past four months and now this.

Text. I decided to use the easy way out and text. I felt like such a coward, but the news was so fresh to me. I had already said it out loud three times. I was not ready to say it again.

My text to Brian and Pearl simply said, *Hey guys. No easy way to say this. I found out today I have breast cancer. I have to see the doctors tomorrow. Surgery next week. I cannot come tomorrow. I am so sorry. Give me a couple of hours and I will call ok?*

Brian's response immediately was, *For fuck sake! Jesus jesus fuck!* Then three minutes later, *I love u sis, fight that shit.* It was a tough day for him too. I felt so bad for bringing him more pain. I had hoped that the upcoming weekend would be a good weekend for him; we could visit and laugh. Now I couldn't even go. I asked Brian to please not say anything to anyone until I figured it all out.

Mom and Dad. They knew I was going to Toronto the next day. They would know something was not right if I canceled. My first thought was to try to protect them and tell them a lie. Perhaps I could tell them I broke my leg. Would they buy that? Probably not, I thought. I needed to call. It was already 9:30 p.m. in Newfoundland, so I knew that if I wanted to get to them tonight I had better do it now.

I took the cordless phone and went into the bedroom to make the call in private. Dad answered.

"Hey, Dad," I said, choking back the tears. I did not want to bring this hurt and worry onto my parents.

"Hey, Kim. What are you doing?" he said.

"Dad, I have some bad news." *How am I ever going to get through this?* I thought.

There was silence. Dad seemed to instinctively know that what was coming was not good. How I wished I didn't have to say the words.

"Dad, I have breast cancer." *When is that statement ever going to be easy to say?* I wondered, my heart breaking for my father.

I heard him suck in his breath as he said, "Jesus, Kim." I could almost picture him rubbing his face while holding the phone. I knew he was slumped at his desk, wondering already how he would tell Mom.

I started to talk really fast. "They caught it early. We have to see the doctor tomorrow. I should be having surgery in a week or so. It is going to be okay." I don't really remember the rest of our conversation. I just wanted to get off the phone. I didn't want to hear the hurt and pain in his voice anymore. We said goodnight and exchanged "I love yous" after I promised to keep him up-to-date on what the doctor said in the morning.

Big breath now. Big breath.

Those were tough ones, but I still had a sea of my close friends to get the word to. Already I was exhausted. I turned on the fan in the bathroom, buried my face in a towel, and let the tears flow as my chest heaved. I was so scared and felt so alone. Finally, I collected myself and walked out of the bedroom, ready to face the next challenge, or so I thought.

Kayla was in her room, so I went down to talk to her. She was scared. I wanted to let the tears flow, fall to the floor, kick and scream, throw something—anything. But I knew I couldn't. I had to keep it together for my family. They could not see me fall apart. I had to stay strong. Kayla and I talked for a while, and she said she wanted to call her friends, so I left her alone and found Cliff sitting in the living room.

He looked shaken. He was pale, and I could tell he was fighting down the panic. I crawled onto his lap, and we cried together. He held me tightly, and I wanted to tell him he was hurting me, but the pain felt good in a way. I felt safe. *This cannot be happening to us. This must be a dream,* I kept thinking. *Perhaps tomorrow they will tell us it is a mistake.* Cliff kept asking how they could tell for certain that it was cancer without a biopsy.

That question was asked by so many people in the next week that I got tired of hearing it even though I kept thinking the same thing. This had to be a mistake.

I knew I had to tell my friends, but I was exhausted. Krista and Bonnie knew already, but we had such a tight group of friends that I knew they all had to be told. I made the decision to call Tracy and ask her to make the calls for me. It was a tough call to make, but I knew I did not have the energy right then to call everyone myself. They loved me, and I knew they would all understand. I was exhausted, and Cliff was exhausted.

Poor Tracy. She held it together while I told her everything I knew and asked her if she would please let our friends know for me. Many weeks later, I found out how hard our call had been on her and how much harder yet it had been for her to be the bearer of my devastating news. To this day, I have not discussed the conversations she had with Tammy, Linda, and Simone. I still feel bad for putting that task on her shoulders, but I knew I needed help then. I asked her to let everyone know I knew they were there for me but right now we just needed to collect ourselves before we could talk. I was so scared that Kelsey would somehow find out while she was away and stressed how important it was for everyone to keep tight-lipped about it until she got home on Monday.

Within an hour, Glen and Tracy were at our door to offer us support and comfort. I didn't cry while they were there. We talked matter-of-factly about what I had been told today, and again they expressed their hope that it was a mistake, that a biopsy would prove the radiologist incorrect. While we talked, it was like we were talking about someone else. *This is not really me we are talking about,* I kept thinking. *How can we be talking about breast cancer and me in the same sentence?* It didn't seem real.

After they left, I poured myself a bath and sat in the water, stunned. How could I be crying and not make a sound? The tears were just falling from my eyes, and the lump in my throat was still there, hurting. I couldn't swallow it, and I couldn't cough it up. I hugged my knees, put my head on them, and cried and cried and cried. A headache set in, and the back of my head started to throb. How was I ever going to get through this? How was my family ever going to survive this?

As I sat there rocking in the water, I started to shiver. *How long have*

I been in here? I wondered. The water had turned cold. I got out and dried off. I stared at my breast in the mirror. It looked the same. I touched it for the first time since I had gotten the news, and I pushed where they thought the cancer was. I couldn't feel anything. Could they have been mistaken? *Please let it be a mistake.*

Cliff was waiting for me when I opened the door and once again enfolded me in his arms. He asked me again if I could have probably heard them wrong. Perhaps they hadn't said it was cancer but something suspicious.

"Maybe I did hear them wrong," I said. "Let's try to sleep and see what the doctor says in the morning."

Cliff fell into bed exhausted, and shortly after I could hear him sleeping soundly. I went to check on Kayla, and she was wide awake but appeared a little calmer. She wanted to come with us in the morning to the doctor. I gave her some Advil to help her sleep.

I finally lay on the couch, but sleep would not come. This was the worst time of the day for me. I cried softly. I didn't want to wake anyone. I got up and paced the floors, walking quietly so that no one could hear me. I stood in the doorway of our bedroom and watched Cliff sleep. He looked so peaceful while he was sleeping, but I knew as soon as he opened his eyes in the morning that the nightmare would rush back to him. I wanted to crawl in next to him and have him hold me and tell me it was going to be okay. But I knew he couldn't say that, and I didn't want to wake him up. It had been a rough day, and he needed sleep.

I crept down over the stairs and quietly opened Kayla's door. She was also sleeping now, hugging her teddy bed. Nineteen years old and she was getting comfort from a teddy bear. The sight of that brought me to my knees. I stumbled back to the stairs, sat on them, and bent over holding my stomach as the tears flowed. Oh my God, I couldn't believe this was happening to us. I worried about Kelsey. How was I going to tell her? I prayed that she didn't find out before I could get to her.

I crawled back up the stairs on my hands and knees, tears falling from my eyes onto the carpet. I had no energy left to walk.

I knew I had to start facing some of the e-mails that were coming in. My e-mail in-box was full. Everyone needed reassurances and wanted to help in some way. I sat at my desk and watched the blue screen load up, and the first message I saw was from Mom. She was as shocked as everyone. My breast issues had been no secret for years, but after three surgeries and multiple biopsies, nothing had ever shown up. Mom's written words echoed my thoughts: *how can this be cancer now?* I had no answers for her and tried my best to reassure her that they had caught this early, and it seemed like they were going to deal with it quickly. I knew my parents were scared. I was too. I was so scared. I missed the laughter in our house already. I missed the innocence of thinking I was healthy. I missed the days before the word *cancer* was ever said to me. I missed yesterday.

Next I moved on to an e-mail from my dear friend Bonnie. I knew how scared and concerned she was for me. She had been one of the first to find out that day. I just wanted to reassure her that I would be okay and to delegate the nasty task of passing on the news to our co-workers. I knew she would take care of that for me, as hard as it would be. I asked her if she would please ask everyone to say a prayer for me.

Then I took on the task of composing a mass e-mail to my sisters. These girls were more like sisters than friends, and I knew their hearts were heavy with worry. Tracy, Tammy, Simone, Linda, and Krista—my chosen sisters. Each of them had reached out to me, and I needed them to know that I felt their love. I told them I was trying to process this in my mind. I told them that this had taken me to my knees and that I was scared. I asked for their patience with me and said I needed to know that they were there for me. At that moment I adopted the Martina McBride song "I'm Gonna Love You through It." I knew at that moment that I would need all the love I could get to get through this.

The sleeping pill I took earlier started to kick in, so I turned off my computer and fell onto the couch. My sleep was broken, and the nightmares were vivid when I did sleep. I didn't remember what they were upon waking, but they had scared me. My body was tense, and the muscles in my back hurt when I woke. Cliff woke up to an empty bed around 5:00 a.m. and came looking for me and carried me back to bed with him. We lay together and cried in each other's arms. Neither of us could believe this was happening.

*When we wake up in the morning and turn our soul
toward You, You are there first.*
——Soren Kierkegaard

*Can you hear me God? I don't have words, so can you listen to my
heart? I am so scared.*

Kayla came into our room the next morning, still visibly shaken and
upset. She had not slept very well. She insisted on coming to the doctor
with us. I wanted so badly to shield her from this, but she was having no
part of it. She was coming. She had already called her boss to let him know
she would not be in.

Cliff and I decided we should call his family that morning and let
them know what was happening. I was afraid they would find out some
other way, and that would just frighten them all even more. Cliff left the
room to make the call as I got dressed. A short time later, I heard him
say something. Then I heard what sounded like the phone hitting the
floor, and I rushed out to the kitchen. He was sitting there with his face
in his hands. He couldn't speak through his tears. I took the phone and
spoke to my brother-in-law Dyrick as Cliff left the kitchen. I told him it
was going to be okay and asked him if he could let everyone know for us.
It was easier that way. How do you keep saying the same thing over and
over to everyone?

Dyrick told me that he loved me and to be strong, and we hung up
with promises to keep in touch. Now the news had been set in motion,
and I was so sad for the pain it would carry with it for all our loved ones.
They were so far away, and I knew they would all feel helpless. I prepared
myself for the onslaught of phone calls, e-mails, and texts I knew would
start coming as soon as everyone got the news.

We all got ready to head to the doctor. We took showers, but no one
could eat. We had a hard time meeting each other's gazes. *What is in store
for us today?* we all seem to be thinking. My appointment was at 9:00 a.m.,
and we were sitting in the waiting room at 8:45. No one said a word, but
we held hands. I sat in the middle with Cliff to my right and Kayla to my

left. I remember thinking that the other people waiting must have been wondering what was wrong. Why did we all look so sad and scared?

Dr. Nechifor did not keep us waiting long and called us into the room shortly after we arrived. She confirmed that yes, I had heard correctly. The radiologist had reported that there was breast cancer present in my left breast. She was very kind as she talked to us, looked directly at us when she answered our questions, and took her time with her responses, ensuring that we understood everything she was saying. I was sitting in the chair next to her, Kayla was sitting on the bed, and Cliff stood in the middle of the room the whole time with his fists clenched at his sides. He asked her how they could tell it was cancer without a biopsy. Dr. Nechifor said the radiologist would have had to have been pretty confident to make that conclusion. This was his area of expertise, and while there was always a chance he could be wrong, it was unlikely.

I looked over at Kayla, and she was sobbing quietly. She looked so scared. Her eyes were as big as saucers and red from all the crying and lack of sleep. I longed to take her in my arms and comfort her, but at that moment there was nothing I could do for her. It was taking all my energy to stay present.

Again, I felt like I was floating in the room and watching everything happening below me. The lump in my throat continued to grow, and I wondered how I was breathing around it. Swallowing was impossible.

I cannot think. Cancer? No!

Through a haze, I heard Cliff taking charge and asking what the next steps were and how fast we could get a biopsy done. She told us we would have to wait a week to ten days to have it completed in Red Deer. A week to ten days was an eternity, and that answer did not satisfy Cliff. He asked the doctor if there was anywhere we could go to have it done sooner.

"We are willing to travel. Just tell us where to go," he pleaded with the doctor, still standing in the middle of the room with his fists clenched tightly at his sides.

She left the room to check on availability anywhere else within driving distance, and as we waited for her to return, the only sound in the room was the rustling of the tissues that both Kayla and I held. I could hear her sniff, and I could hear Cliff breathing, but I was unable to look at either of them, afraid that if I caught their gazes, I would lose it. I started at the floor as we waited. The doctor returned a short time later to say that if we could go to Devon, Alberta, which was a two-hour drive from Red Deer, we could be seen today. We got the directions and forms and headed out right away.

The drive to Devon was a quiet one, and I chose to sit in the back, letting Kayla ride up front with her dad. No one talked, and Kayla took charge of sending texts to family and friends to give the update on what was happening. I was grateful that she was there to take over that task for me. I didn't have the strength to say anything to anyone at that moment and was happy she was taking charge. I remember thinking on the way that this time yesterday morning I had been sitting at my desk at work going over my to-do list for my trip to Toronto. I could not believe that when I should be heading to Calgary to catch a plane, instead I was headed in the opposite direction to have a biopsy to confirm that I had breast cancer. I shook my head as I lay back on the seat, closing my eyes in hope that sleep would find me. It didn't, but I kept my eyes closed so I would not have to speak.

We arrived at the clinic an hour early, so we headed over to the drugstore to pick up some snacks. None of us had eaten, and it was starting to catch up with us. We strolled through the drugstore like any other family and even managed to share a few laughs—a temporary relief from the insanity that was now our lives.

Once at the clinic, I was checked in, and we sat, again holding hands. Again, I sat in the middle. I looked at Cliff; he was so pale. I worried about Kelsey, about her finding out while she was away. I worried if we had made the right decision or if she would be mad at me for keeping it from her. Kayla had managed to pull herself together and was texting like crazy to her friends. She popped in her iPod earphones, trying to escape into her music, and I saw her sneaking glances at me.

When I was called into the room, they both stood and hugged me. The doctor who performed the biopsy was an Englishwoman and very kind, and I later found out that she was very well respected in her field. She asked me some questions and appeared to be very efficient; however, she did not answer any of my questions directly. I asked her if she thought the radiologist could be wrong, and she evaded my question. Her only answer was that she would probably not give the diagnosis until the biopsy was confirmed, as there was always a chance it might not be cancer. I stared at her eyes as she performed the procedure, but she gave nothing away in her expression. She had seen this many times before, probably too many times.

The biopsy was painful, but my heart hurt more. I just wanted it to be over with. As I lay on the cold table with the lights down low, a river of tears started again. I could feel them running down my cheeks and pooling around my ears, but I didn't make a sound, and when the doctor asked me if it was hurting, I said no. I just wanted it over with, I wanted to go home and be in the safety of my home.

Once we were finished, as she helped me sit up on the bed, she told me it would be a week before the reports were sent to my family doctor. After explaining what to expect after the biopsy, she left the room. My breast ached, my heart was breaking, and I felt so alone. Cliff and Kayla greeted me as I came out. Kayla took my hand, and Cliff steadied me by placing his hand on my back. We headed home.

I crawled into the backseat and once again pretended to sleep. I knew that if my eyes were closed, no one would talk to me. They would not want to disturb me. Kayla busied herself again by sending out mass texts to let everyone know what was happening, and I tipped back my seat, pulled my coat tightly around me, and listened to the quiet sound of the radio.

I must have drifted off to sleep because I was suddenly startled with the sound of a big *bang*. As I sat up with lightning speed, I realized that a rock had hit our windshield and scared us all half to death. We drove on. No one said a word. It was fitting in a way; the windshield was cracked, just like my heart.

We were almost home when I got a call from Dr. Nechifor's office to confirm that my appointment with the surgeon would be on Monday. The secretary gave me the address and time and I wrote the information on a scrap of paper before hanging up.

When we got home, the phone calls started, and Cliff and Kayla took charge and answered them all, protecting me from having to talk. Everyone wanted to know what was happening, wanted to speak to someone, wanted reassurances or to give reassurances that everything was going to be okay. No one really knew what to say other than that they loved us. Everyone felt so helpless.

Once again I retreated to the bathroom, turned on the water in the tub, sat in the corner on the floor, and buried my head in a towel. I cried and cried as I tried to catch my breath. My chest felt like it was going to explode, and I wondered how I was ever going to get through the next few days, the next few hours even. I wondered how I was going to get the strength to deal with this. How was I going to protect my family?

Was I going to die?

Kayla was in bed when I finally came out of the bathroom, and Cliff had fallen asleep in the chair. I woke him up, walked him to bed, and then went to cuddle with Kayla. We talked, and she asked me over and over if everything was going to be okay. I said it would be fine. We were all going to be okay. I stayed with her until she fell asleep. As I walked up the stairs, I felt like the weight of the world was on my back. I was so tired and so confused. I tried to rest on the couch, but sleep wouldn't come. Tears continued to run out of my eyes, and I wondered once again where they were all coming from.

I turned on my computer and counted more than twenty-five e-mails that had come in since we left that morning. Everyone expressed love, concern, and support. I was overwhelmed and turned away. I knew I could not answer any of them at that moment, and it was about that time that I promised to never e-mail when I wasn't in a good place. I knew only too well the power of words, and I didn't want to write something and then regret it after I hit send. I did not want to worry anyone. At that moment, all I was thinking was, *I don't want to say good-bye*, and I knew that was not a good time to send an e-mail to anyone.

While I felt I owed my family and friends a response, I knew it would have to wait until tomorrow. I sat back and read the messages, and the context of the e-mails surprised me. They were not full of questions to be answered but full of love and support.

Love you, Tracy wrote. *You were my only thoughts before bed and my first thought this morning. I am here for you, my friend. It is going to be okay.*

I love you more than you will ever know, Krista wrote.

Tammy sent a long e-mail full of instructions on what to do when we saw the surgeon: have someone take notes, stay off the Internet, and don't compare your diagnosis with someone else's. It was all the practical information you would expect from a nurse friend. Then she closed with, *You know we all love you, and we will be there for you even when you don't ask or want us to. Don't try to be a superstar and deal with this on your own. Love you!*

And my sweet Simone wrote, *I will be with you as you see your doctor today. I will not stop thinking about you all day. You were in my prayers last night and this morning on my drive to work. You were all I would talk about with God. I love you, and I am available for whatever you may need.*

From Linda came a quick and to-the-point message: *Gloves up, baby. Get back in the ring. Xoxo.* She had used that phrase many times with me during challenges I had faced in the past. I felt warmth in her reassurance that I was a winner and I could do this.

Blurry-eyed and tired, I was relieved. There was nothing I needed to respond to. My friends had reached out in the best way possible, sending their love but wanting nothing in return until I was ready. *I am so blessed,* I thought as I shut off the screen, pushed away from the computer, and prepared to go to bed.

I finally fell asleep wondering what tomorrow would bring for me and my family. I wished the weekend was over so we could meet with the surgeon and finally see Kelsey and talk to her. I was afraid she was going to find something out before I could talk to her. I asked God to please keep her safe and to grant me the opportunity to give her the news myself.

Friday morning, we all woke up, and Cliff decided to go to work. There was nothing he could do at home, and we both felt it was better for him to be occupied at work. Kayla was still in no shape to go to work and wanted to stick close to me, so she called in to her work to say she would be taking another day off. We headed over to Krista's for lunch and were greeted with the warmest hugs. As we sat with her and her mom and talked about everything other than what was happening, I met her mom's gaze, and her eyes told me how much she cared. No words were necessary. After lunch, Kayla and I left to go for a drive and decided to go see Cliff. It was so easy to pretend that everything was okay. We were driving around town just like any other mom and daughter. I looked healthy, and other than the pale expression on Kayla's face, so did she. I realized I hadn't cried yet that day, but that lump was still in my throat, threatening to choke me at any minute.

When we got home, I retreated to the bathroom to deal with another meltdown and hide. The fan made just enough sound to muffle my sobs as I buried my face in a towel and cried. I have since come to know that the episodes I was dealing with were panic attacks, but I did not know that at the time. I curled up in the corner of the bathroom and tried to breath into a towel while trying to slow my heart rate, which was even harder to do when I was crying uncontrollably. Many times that weekend and in the months that followed, I thought I was going to have a heart attack on the floor in the bathroom.

The weekend brought visitors who tried to cheer us up while at the same time tried to avoid the pink elephant in the room. Mark and Simone arrived with flowers, hugs, and reassurances of love and support. Simone looked deeply into my eyes as I answered her questions; she was fearful but trying hard to stay positive for me. We talked for some time about what had happened, and we cried together. It felt good to talk about it, to say how scared I was, to cry. But I didn't want it to be all about cancer. I was already finding that I needed to bring the laughter and fun back into our lives. I was not ready to crack any jokes yet, but I knew we needed to get back there again to be healthy.

Linda and Darcy, fresh home from their family trip to Jamaica, arrived all tanned and looking so healthy, and they brought along all the pictures of their holiday. As we flipped through them, I couldn't help but wonder if I would ever make it back to Jamaica. Eight of us went in 2009, and we had so much fun. Looking through those pictures brought back memories of life on the beach, drinking slushy drinks, and basking in the sun with the hardest decision of the day being if we napped at 2:00 p.m. or 4:00 p.m. Life had been so much easier then. It had been so much more fun. Life before breast cancer. Life when I was just like everyone else. I wondered if Cliff and I would ever experience those simple pleasures as husband and wife again. I envied my friends and their innocence. I envied their healthy lives. I envied that they could leave my home and go home and fall into each other's arms, relieved that they were healthy and that cancer had not knocked on their doors.

One evening, I went over to pick up Krista to come visit and stay for supper. It was so pretty out; the snow was falling gently, and we had the fireplace lit downstairs, where we had just finished renovating. It was cozy, and I was happy we had completed this major project (only three weeks before). Cliff barbequed wings, and Krista, Kayla, and I curled up and watched a movie as the snow fell gently outside. It was hard to believe that all was so wrong in my life. If someone had looked into the window that evening, everything would have looked peaceful. My mind drifted from the movie. I couldn't help but hope it was all a big mistake. Maybe I would be the lucky one and they would tell me, "The radiologist made a mistake." I quietly thought, *I promise not to even be mad! Am I really that one in nine woman who has breast cancer? This can't be happening.*

Earlier that day, Cliff and Kayla had gone for a drive. I thought they just needed to talk, but they had intended to go to the jewelry store and buy me a charm for my bracelet to cheer me up. But they came home fighting, and I didn't know why. I could just tell that they were both clearly upset. I found out later that Kayla had wanted to buy a charm supporting breast cancer, but Cliff didn't want anything to do with that. I knew his thought was that to purchase a charm in support of breast cancer would be an admission that it was indeed cancer, and his mind was not ready to go there yet.

Sunday, Tammy showed up to chat. She, Kayla, and I talked for hours, and it did us all good. Tammy helped us focus on something other than the terror in our lives in that moment and kept our minds off tomorrow's appointment. It turned out to be a good day and offered a great distraction for both Kayla and me.

Cliff was away all day working. It was good for him to keep occupied and not hover over me. He kept watching me whenever we were in the same room, and I knew he was worried. I kept telling him that there was nothing different now than there had been last weekend, and last weekend I had shoveled snow, so he had to give up hovering. But we both knew everything was different now. Every time I moved, he jumped up ahead of me to do whatever I was going to do and kept asking me over and over if I was okay.

After Tammy left, I headed out to the grocery store, but I had something else in mind. I had to see my friend Bonnie and give her a hug. I texted her when I pulled up outside her house and asked her to come outside. I greeted her on the sidewalk with a big hug. No words were spoken; no words were needed. I just needed a hug from her. We parted as I told her I would see her on Tuesday, and I watched her go back inside before I drove away. I knew that the events of the past week had changed her, and I also knew I had been made stronger because she was there for me.

I avoided the computer most of the weekend other than e-mailing Mom and Dad. Mom was full of questions, and I could only imagine how tough this was on them being so far away. Her biggest question was how they could be confident this was a cancer diagnosis without a biopsy. Unfortunately, I didn't have the answer to her question, but I tried my best to keep being positive, saying I would get them up-to-date as soon as I knew anything. It was the best that I could do.

I haven't been where you are. I haven't walked in your shoes.
But I'd like to walk beside you and help whenever I can.
  —Juanita Dwyer

Chapter 2
Dealing With Reality

Can it really be Monday? I thought as I woke up the next day. So much had changed in such a short amount of time. It was going to be a long day, as Cliff and Kayla had both returned to work and I was home alone. I spent the day cleaning the house and trying to keep my mind occupied on anything other than my appointment that afternoon. The wait was tough on our family in Newfoundland, and we all knew that with the three and a half hour time difference, it would be well into the evening before they got any news. The waiting, the fear of the unknown, was always the worst.

Cliff picked me up at 3:00 p.m., and we headed to the surgeon's office. As we drove, I wanted to jump out of the car and run away. I knew I could not do that, that we had to face this together. As we were sitting in the waiting room, a young woman came in. She was clearly a cancer patient. She had no hair and a hat pulled down over her head. I admired the strength she seemed to have. She appeared to be very confident. But I was afraid as I thought to myself, *Is that going to be me? Am I going to lose my hair?* I could feel Cliff's eyes on me as he watched me watching her. I was scared, and I couldn't look at him because I didn't want him to see the fear I knew was written all over my face. I cast my gaze down to my lap and watched as my hands pulled apart a tissue; I knew those hands were mine and understood why they would not stay still, but I felt disconnected from them, disconnected from my arms, my body.

As we sat there, another older couple, perhaps in their seventies, sat across from us. I kept catching their gaze and knew in my heart that they were here for the same reason as us. The older lady looked as scared as

I felt, and her husband looked like he wanted to be anywhere but where he was at that moment. They were called into the doctor's office, and I watched them walk down the hall, their shoulders slumped forward, his hand on the small of her back. She looked so frail and scared as she clutched her handbag in front of her. It was almost an hour before they exited his office, and they were both clearly shaken. The older gentlemen watched me as he walked down the hall, and when he sat back down as his wife dealt with the appointment desk, he gestured to his chest and then glanced at his wife. Breast cancer? I was afraid to ask. I didn't want to know, and I looked away until they walked toward the elevators. I wondered what the conversation in their vehicle would be as they drove home.

Dr. Hardy was running late, and when we finally got in, he apologized for having us wait. We thanked him for seeing us and then immediately asked how the radiologist could make the cancer diagnosis without the biopsy results. We jumped right in, not interested in small talk. His response hit both of us in the gut. He said they would have to be pretty confident that it was cancer to say that. Then he reviewed the radiologist's report with us and went through all the scenarios.

"Nothing is for sure yet until we get the report," he said, but he reviewed the different situations. He expressed his confidence that it had been caught early and that my prognosis was good.

As he spoke, I held Cliff's hand tightly and watched Dr. Hardy write out the information as he spoke. I closed my eyes for a minute and could hear him speaking, but my mind left the room and went to a quieter place, a place where the words cancer, tumor, surgery, chemotherapy, and radiation had never been uttered. It was nice and peaceful there, but I knew I had to come back.

When I opened my eyes again, he was telling us that five weeks of radiation would be standard in my situation and that he would also recommend a lumpectomy, and he explained why. Of course everything would be determined based on the biopsy report once it was received. He asked me if I was prepared for surgery on March 28, exactly two weeks from the day I had found out. I was grateful that we had a preliminary treatment plan in place, but I was scared at the same time. This was all happening so fast. We left his office with a surgery date, instructions for the surgery, and several possible outcomes, again all dependent on the biopsy report.

I called Dad from the parking lot to give him the news, and when I hung up, Cliff reached over, pulled me to his chest, hugged me tight, and we both started to cry. I was so scared and held on to Cliff, hoping that if we blended our strength together it would help us through the next few months. We were both thinking, *How could this be happening to us?* It was like a nightmare that would never end.

And what will the end be? I wondered. *Am I going to die? Did they catch it in time? Am I going to die? How did we go from healthy and happy with not a care in the world to this in a week?*

We were now very anxious to talk to Kelsey. It had been five days since we had found out, and we had not told her anything. She was flying home that night, so I knew I needed to talk to her first thing in the morning.

It was Mackenzie's birthday, so we headed over to Glen and Tracy's to see her and share in some birthday cake. Conversation was kept very polite, and we briefly went through what the doctor had told us. They had other company, which was a good distraction, and we stayed for a short time before returning home.

Once we arrived home, Tammy and Madison came over for a quick visit and brought me over a locket Tammy had made for me. It was just beautiful, and that locket accompanied me to every treatment months later; it was a reminder I wore around my neck of the love that surrounded me every day, and it helped ease the pain.

I watched the clock all evening, anticipating Kelsey's arrival back in Alberta. I was getting very anxious to talk to her now but knew it would have to wait until tomorrow. I tried to occupy myself by returning e-mails to my friends and family. I didn't feel strong enough to talk on the phone; that felt too personal, and my voice was still too shaky to talk to anyone. I knew they would be able to tell I was not doing as well as I pretended if they heard my voice, and I wasn't ready yet to give up that facade. It was easier to stick to e-mails and texts, and I prayed everyone would understand.

My brother's wife was also struggling with her own breast cancer diagnosis; she had found out four months before and was currently undergoing chemotherapy while raising three small children. I wondered how she was doing it. How was she so positive, and why wasn't she as scared as me? Or was she? I was afraid to ask. She proved to be a good source of information to me during those early days, sending me e-mails and texts and helping me remain calm.

Every time I sat at my computer, my in-box was flooded with e-mails. The amount was almost overwhelming, but I read every single word of every single e-mail. Everyone was so kind, and I could feel the love from every written word. I had such a wonderful support group wrapped around me, but I hadn't realized just how many people cared until the e-mails started to come in, not only from close friends and family but also from people who were just acquaintances, people I had worked with in the past, and friends of friends I had met just briefly. Everyone cared. Everyone wanted to reach out and in some little way let me know he or she cared. I will spend a lifetime repaying their kindness.

I had to make one more phone call that I had been putting off for days, knowing how much this one would hurt. It was to my cousins Todd and Sharon. I did not want them to hear this from anyone else and felt I owed them a phone call, not an e-mail. Sharon answered, and we greeted each other, but she quickly realized something was wrong. I spoke quietly as I sat curled up on the couch, my body shaking. She was not expecting this, and I could hear the pain in her voice. Our conversation was whispered, almost like it was easier to receive the news like that. I asked her if she could please tell Todd for me. I didn't have the energy to go through it again. I hated to deliver the news to yet another person I loved. I knew how much it was hurting everyone, and I was sorry to be the person delivering the pain. I was exhausted as I hung up the phone. Sharon sounded sad, and I could just imagine the scene at her home at that moment as she told Todd what I had just said. Todd, who was like a brother to me. More pain. When would I stop causing all this pain, I wondered.

I prepared myself to return to work in the morning. It would be my first day back at the office since we found out, and I had to face everyone. As I readied myself for work, making lunches and ironing clothes, my thoughts once again went to Kelsey. I would have to see her the next day to break the news. I wondered how I was going to tell her I had breast cancer and how she would react. At that moment, I would have given anything not to have to cause her that pain. I hated having to keep saying it over and over.

There was little sleep for me again that night, and as I lay in bed listening to Cliff sleep, I watched the shadows dancing on the ceiling. I touched my face. I could feel tears running down my cheeks, but until I touched them, I hadn't even known I was crying. *Where is the river of water coming from? When will the tears stop? My reserves must be dried up by now.* I worried about how I would handle myself at the office tomorrow. I felt that I had to stay calm and happy, that was what they were used to. But would I cry? Would I be expected to cry? How would everyone react to me? I wanted it to be the same as it had been before, but I knew it wouldn't be.

In the morning, I found myself at my desk, opening up a mammoth load of e-mails from co-workers expressing their concern and support. My boss Spencer had sent out an e-mail to the district, letting everyone know my situation, and the e-mails poured in. It warmed my heart. We had our Monday morning meeting, and Spencer welcomed me back to the office and asked me if there was anything I wanted to share. I was thankful to him for the opportunity. I thanked them all for their kindness and gave a brief background on what we knew so far, asked that they treat me as they always had, said that I was still me. There were a few questions, and then we all headed back to work. It felt good to be back with my team and just be me, even if it all seemed superficial to me at the time.

Shortly after the meeting, my cell phone rang. It was my doctor.

She simply said, "Kimberley, the biopsy reports are back. The breast cancer has been confirmed."

I have breast cancer. Me! Breast cancer? Me?

All my hope flew out the door, but surprisingly enough I didn't react. I just felt empty. I simply thanked her for calling. We confirmed my surgery date, and she said she would leave me in the hands of my surgeon and the cancer clinic now. I immediately called Cliff to tell him what she had said. He was very quiet, and then finally he said he had not been expecting that. He had been hoping for news that it had all been a mistake. Now that hope was gone, and we had to face the new reality. Breast cancer. I hadn't even asked the type, stage, grade—all the things I had been reading and keeping notes on. I didn't even ask. I was numb.

I went to the washroom to splash water on my face, and as I looked at myself in the mirror, I could see the agony in my eyes. When I returned to my desk, Bonnie had left me a card and a journal at my desk; her words simply said to write it all down, that it would help. I made a promise to do that and then left the office to go find my daughter and give her the news.

As I sat in the parking lot, I sent out a mass text to everyone to get the biopsy results out there. I felt it was so cold to deliver the news that way, but I was emotionally drained and could not face everyone with a phone call or text. I prayed they would understand and be patient with me while we processed this news and figured out the next steps.

I called Kelsey and told her I needed to see her. I asked if she could meet me outside her apartment building. She didn't ask any questions and just said she would be waiting for me.

She was waiting outside as I pulled up, and as she jumped in the car, I could tell she knew something was wrong.

"Mom, are you okay?" she asked as she looked over at me.

I wanted this over. I didn't want to say it.

I told her as quickly as I could, the words just falling out, the script I had made up in my mind forgotten as I tried to reassure her that it would all be okay. My heart broke into a million pieces as she put her arms in the air, reaching out to me; it reminded me of when she was a little girl and she hurt herself and would come running and throw herself into my arms for comfort.

We held each other and cried, not saying a word. We sat there and rocked back and forth crying. I felt bad for causing her so much pain, and I wanted to tell her it would all be okay. I said the words, but I wanted to believe it myself. *How much longer will I be able to hold my children? What is in store for me? Will the pain ever stop, the tears?* I missed the joy and laughter in my life.

I want my life back! I screamed inside. *Enough! I want to wake up now.*

34

Finally, I let her go. Kelsey was tired, jet-lagged from her trip and exhausted from the days of competition. I told her to go back inside and relax and that I would keep her up-to-date and call her later that evening. We exchanged "I love yous," and I watched her walk back into her apartment. I could see that she was still crying. I cried heavily as I pulled away from the curb. Everything was blurry from the tears that flooded my eyes.

I was relieved that Kelsey now knew, and I felt like I was starting to get some control over my situation now that my family all knew. Cliff, Kelsey, Kayla—how I wished I could have protected them from what was happening. Causing them so much pain was breaking my heart. The anguish was a physical pain that I could not heal. Unable to face my friends at work, I headed home and spent a few hours staring at the walls and crying. I was so sad and felt scared and alone. It was my time for a real pity party, and I let it all out. I cried as I paced up and down the hall, wondering what was going to happen. Was I going to die? Was I going to live? I let it all out before I reigned in the terror and tried to get a grip on my new reality.

There were still so many people I needed to let know; you don't know how big your network is until something like this happens. I pulled myself together and headed down to the office building of my old co-workers to let them know the news. As I pulled open their office door, I knew I would be greeted once again with love and support, but I was tired of being on the receiving end. I wanted to be the comforter, not the one being comforted! I spent a few hours there, going over everything, and we even managed to get in a few laughs. For a short time I was able to relax, and even though I couldn't pretend that everything was okay, I could still share some laughs, and it felt good. Those girls were there for me, and I knew they would not let me feel sorry for myself and that they expected more than that from me.

When I arrived home, there was a package at my door from Sharon, Todd, and Finn. It was a four leaf clover charm for my bracelet. I could read the panic in Sharon's written note; she was scared and concerned for me, and I immediately sat at my computer to send her a note of thanks and reassurance. The love … the love was just bursting at the seams. I also gave her the update on the biopsy report I had received from my doctor that morning, that it was not a false positive.

As I opened the e-mails coming in, I was again touched with the love and support I was getting. I had always seen the beauty in these people and had always known I was blessed with such beautiful and caring friends, but since my breast cancer diagnosis I can say that I have seen heaven on earth. I have seen angels working, felt the warmth of their embrace, and many times floated on their wings.

From my friend, Janice, one of the girls I had just visited that afternoon, I received the following message: *You are such an inspirational woman, with so many who love you. I know you will find the strength to get through this. Please take advantage of your friends in your time of need, as we all know that you are always one who is banging down doors to help others.* How could I not feel a glimmer of hope when reading something like that?

I received an e-mail from my friend Lana, who was traveling in New Zealand for a month. I knew she would want to know what was happening, but I debated about sending her the news until she returned. Lana had provided me such comfort over the years, helping me over humps and bumps at difficult times in my life, and we had both gone through the loss of a close friend and co-worker to cancer a few years before. I needed for her know what was happening. She had always been my analytical friend, one to sit outside the box and tell it as it was. I needed that insight, and her reply e-mail came almost immediately and was full of practical advice and her confidence in me to handle this as best I could. She even made me smile a few times, and I was happy to hear from her.

Sleep that night came a little easier for me; however, I still had that lump in my throat that would not go down or come up. Kelsey called several times throughout the evening to make sure I was okay. Kayla went out with her friends for some much needed girl time, and I was happy to see her starting to adjust to what was happening. Things were starting to settle into a new normal for us, and I tried to focus on getting through the next few days before surgery next week and preparing ourselves for the outcome of the results of the surgery.

The following morning found me sitting back at my desk at the office, feeling somewhat refreshed and ready to face the day. Everyone was so kind, and I got lots of hugs and heard myself laughing out loud often. It felt good to be back to a routine even though I knew it was not going to last long. As the news set in, it got easier to pretend everything was okay. My in-box was once again full of e-mails, but I forwarded them all to my home address. I felt it was better to deal with that at home; while at work, I wanted to concentrate on work. For me it was so much easier to do it that way and have a separation of the two.

One e-mail in particular caught my eye and caused tears to gather. It was from my co-worker Linda, who I had always felt such a kinship with. She wrote, *I am thinking about you, and I have asked my angels to watch over you during this time, Kim … I have good angels. Your positive attitude will get you through anything, my dear."* Thank you for lending me your angels, Linda. They helped me a lot!

Cliff called me several times that morning to see how I was dealing with everything, and I wondered how I ever got so lucky to have such a wonderful man in my life. It was many months later before he told me how panicked he was, how it hurt to breath, and how every time he thought about me and cancer in the same sentence it felt like someone was kicking him in the stomach. He was living in his own nightmare, but he tried his best to keep it together for me. All women should be as lucky to have someone to love and protect them like I had.

During this time, I tried my best to keep up contact with my brother by text. He was worried and living his own nightmare as he dealt with his wife's illness, but he was such a wonderful source of information for me. I often wished we lived closer together, not provinces apart. It would have been nice to have family close, nice to have a family member close enough to hold me, to wipe away the tears, to laugh with. I knew the friends I had would step up to the plate for me as fast as any family would, but I longed for my own family, for my parents, my brother.

It was exhausting keeping everyone up-to-date and reassured. I felt I owed them all that much, but it was hard, and I found it easier to do up an e-mail and then cut and paste it to each person. When I did that, I felt like I was cheating, but it was the only way I could deal with the overwhelming amount of e-mails at that time, and I felt it would have to do. I knew if it was someone else I would understand and just be happy to get a response, so I let it go at that.

I got through the week, some days on a wing and a prayer, but I did find that getting up for work helped me more than even I could have thought. One afternoon, Bonnie sent me an e-mail to ask how I was doing. Sometimes it was easier for us to e-mail even though our desks were steps away. My response to her was, *I can't believe this is happening.* As I hit send, I bolted for the bathroom; tears erupted, and my stomach shook. I hid in the bathroom for some time, not wanting anyone to see me crying. I was afraid if they saw me crying, they would tell me to go home and that I didn't belong there. I was afraid they would not understand that right now work was what was keeping me sane, keeping me stable.

When I came out, Bonnie was waiting for me with a big hug and a reassuring rub on the back.

"It is going to be okay, Kim," she said, but her eyes told me she was worried and that she was thinking exactly what I didn't want her to think: that I needed to go home. She tried to convince me to go home, but I told her I needed to work, and she must have heard something in my voice because she let it drop. We went back to our desks and our work. I was so happy to have her friendship.

As the day went by, I found the panic starting to set in again, and I called my doctor to see if I could get in to see her. Already I had lost my anonymity, the receptionist recognized my name immediately. I was probably my doctor's most recently diagnosed cancer patient. I spent the day writing questions for her on the back of an envelope at my desk.

As I waited in the reception area of the doctor's office, I looked around and wondered how this could be my life. Just last week I had been carefree with no worries. Life was good. Now I had breast cancer. Was this some sick joke?

Dr. Nechifor called me in, and we entered her office. As she started to go over my report, I started to cry, and finally I asked her the question I had been afraid to say out loud since I first found out the news.

As tears rolled down my face, I looked at her and asked, "Am I going to die?" I looked into her eyes and sobbed, trying hard to be strong, but I was so scared. "Am I going to die?"

How could you prepare yourself to ask that question?

She wheeled her chair close to me and touched my leg. *Did I really ask that question?* I wondered. Is that what I was afraid of and had been afraid to ask? She gently told me we needed to get the results from the surgery. Then we would know for sure what we were dealing with. She talked about early detection and how lucky I was that we had found it. We talked for thirty minutes, went over everything, but the one thing that screamed in my mind was that she never once said, "No, you are not going to die." She didn't say it because at that moment she didn't know what my fate would be.

I thanked her repeatedly for sending me for the mammogram. We both knew that decision may have saved my life. We discussed me working and agreed that I should stop until after the surgery and see how I was feeling then. She also offered me something to help with my nerves, and to this day I wonder why I turned down that offer of help. I did not disclose the panic attacks, seeing them as a weakness. I wish I had just told her then, told anyone, and gotten the help I needed rather than waiting for months and suffering through those times when I was alone and scared on the my bathroom floor. Knowing now what I didn't know then, I would have gladly accepted the medication to help me through those rough times.

I returned home exhausted, now with only one day left to work. Again my computer screen was full of e-mails and my phone full of texts.

I talked with Tammy during the evening, and she told me that she and our friend Angela were working on a carpooling schedule to bring me back and forth for radiation treatments when the time came. At that time I understood that I would have to travel to Calgary five days a week for five weeks, and they knew how hard that was going to be, so they were arranging a schedule with my friends. I collapsed into tears. Everyone was so kind and loving. I was surrounded by such beauty even though my life seemed so dark right then. I kept thinking of how blessed I was, and how ironic that was. My friends rallied around me and folded me in love, and I was more thankful than I would ever be able to express.

At a time in my life when I needed it most, people were just coming out of the woodwork, and I felt like I was floating on love. The battery on my phone only lasted half a day; the texts coming in just drained it. The support was unreal. Tammy told me that they had about twenty volunteers already to drive me to my treatments. It was amazing. When I told Cliff, he had to leave the room, he was overwhelmed. When he returned, I could tell he had been crying, and we just held each other. We were so thankful.

Kayla left to housesit for Tracy for two weeks, and she was only gone an hour when she texted to say she wanted to come home. I knew the separation would do her good. She needed to get away from me for a while and be a normal teenager. I didn't tell her to come home, and she didn't ask again. She would be fine; I knew it. Later in the evening, she called to say she had just had a nice hot bath in the jet tub and was crawling into bed. I prayed she would get a good night's sleep and that the thoughts that kept her up at night would stay away.

I worked on some e-mails throughout the night, as sleep and me were not been getting along again. I paid particular attention to the e-mails going to Mom and Dad, as well as to other family members. I knew how important it was for them to get firsthand information and how hard it was for them to be so far away. I knew everyone was feeling the stress of my surgery next week, and we all wished it was over. Mom and Dad were planning on coming out to stay with me for a few weeks after the surgery and when I had the treatment plan. I looked forward to seeing them and knew it would be very emotional for all of us.

The worst at that point was not knowing what we were facing. Would it just be surgery and radiation? Would one surgery be enough, or would I need more? Would I lose my breast? Chemotherapy? Lose my hair? Be off work for how long? The unknowns were limitless. The fear of the unknown kept me up.

I looked outside, and the snow was softly falling. Cliff had lit the fireplace for me before he went to bed, and the wood crackling offered me some comfort and warmth. I grabbed a blanket, curled up on the couch, and stared into the fire. My mind started to race again, and I reached for a sleeping pill. I must have finally been exhausted enough because the next thing I knew Cliff was gently shaking me awake. It was time for my last day at work for a while.

I spent my last day at work cleaning up my work space and getting everything ready for the temps that would be covering for me while I was away. My co-workers brought in lunch, and we visited in the boardroom as we ate together. It felt good to be with everyone. We all avoided the topic of my pending surgery next week, but I knew it weighed on everyone's mind. The atmosphere all day was almost festive, and some of the girls went out in the afternoon and brought in the fixings for orange floats, which we shared at coffee break. As the end of the day neared and people left, they stopped by my desk and gave me hugs and told me to get well and get back to work as soon as possible. It was too hard to say good-bye, so I said, "See you soon." I loved my job so much, I loved the people with whom I worked, and I knew I would miss that place. Before I left the office, I sent out a note to thank everyone for his and her kindness over the past week and said that while I was scared, I was determined to give this 100 percent and be fully recovered and back in my game as soon as possible.

Cliff had dropped me off at work that morning and was waiting for me at quitting time. As I crawled into the car, I started to cry, and he reached for my hand and told me it would only be for a short time and not to worry. I would be back to work before I knew it, he said. I hoped he was right. It seemed so unfair, but I knew I could not bargain with this one; it was out of my hands. And I knew my workplace would be waiting for me when I was well enough to return. We pulled out of the parking lot as I watched the building in my rearview mirror and wondered if I would ever be well enough to return.

That night I felt a little lighter knowing that all I had to do now was concentrate on getting my strength up for my surgery and trying to get some rest. I spent hours going through e-mails, so many beautiful messages full of inspiration, hope, and support.

My co-worker Marg wrote, *Believe in the power of all of your friends and family wishing and praying you well ... and the huge success rate of conquering this form of cancer. Until we hear from you again.*

My boss Sharon wrote, *I am thinking of you and praying for you, and I know with your great attitude and outlook on life, you are going to be okay.*

Just take one step at a time and know there are so many people who care about you.

My friend David in Newfoundland wrote, *With your positive attitude and the love you and Cliff have for each other, this will be beat.*

On Saturday, Kelsey and Kayla decided to make it a date day, and we headed out for lunch and to do a little shopping. I was exhausted, and we didn't make it very far. As we sat at lunch, Kelsey was watching my plate and kept encouraging me to eat more, but my appetite was not that great, and I just picked at my food. I was just happy that we were together. As we sat eating lunch, we tried to decide what to get their dad for his birthday, which was only two days away. We finally decided on a personalized license plate for his Mopar—to read *obnoxious*—and spent the remainder of the lunch date trying to come up with a seven-letter spelling of it to fit on the license plate. We howled with laughter at some of the ways we spelled it and laughed even louder when we asked the waitress if she could tell what we had spelled. I think she thought we were playing a trick on her, which made us laugh even louder.

After lunch, we headed to the motor vehicle registry and ordered the plate, and we were all excited. We knew Cliff would love this gift, and since it was from his daughters, it would mean so much more. As we headed home after our day, I soaked in the fun with my daughters. What a great day to have them together and have some fun, share some laughter, and just forget about what was happening in our lives right then.

I started thinking about the logistics of my surgery date and how we were going to get the word out to everyone once Cliff saw the surgeon postsurgery. I knew he needed help to get the word out after the surgery, and I knew he didn't want to make all those calls himself. We had to be at the hospital at 6:00 a.m. for a bunch of tests, and I knew that by the time the surgery was over he was going to be exhausted. I talked with Tracy and Krista and asked for their help, which they offered unconditionally. We broke up the list of people to notify between the two of them, and I forwarded e-mail addresses and phone numbers for everyone. Who would have ever thought it would be such a production just to get out word on how the surgery went?

Working this all out was exhausting. I finally put away my lists, turned off my computer, and headed out for a drive. I just needed some time to myself. I drove out to the country and turned off my phone as I parked on a hill that overlooked the fields. I sat there for an hour, just looking over the snow-covered fields and watching the cattle move about. I could see the sun slowly making its decent in the horizon and marveled at the beauty of the outdoors. I wondered how many more sunsets I would see. Would God spare me and let me live to see a lifetime of them? I sat there and cried, taking advantage of being alone, letting the sobs take over, letting it cleanse my body. It felt so healing to sit there and cry with no one around to hear me. As the sun finally fell below the horizon, I turned around and headed back into town.

Later that evening, I ran into my friend Angela. It was the first time we had seen each other in person since the news. I told her how much her carpooling idea meant to me, and we held hands while fighting back tears. Angela had lost her dad not that long ago to cancer as well and every time I saw her, I could see her pain. I knew how much it hurt her to see me as well, plus it brought up all the hurt and pain of missing her dad again. Her beautiful blue eyes were a sea of tears as we embraced, reassuring each other that I would kick this.

Monday arrived, and it was Cliff's forty-sixth birthday. The fact that my surgery was only two days away put a damper on the celebrations, and I wished I could give him the gift of good health for his birthday.

Krista and I went for lunch, and she gave me a beautiful charm and a card. We hardly discussed my health or upcoming surgery and had lots of fun teasing our waitress and enjoying our meal. We laughed lots, and it felt good to forget for a while what was happening.

While we were eating lunch, Cliff called to tell me he bought a new truck. Every person deals with stress in his or her own way, I guess, and Cliff's way of dealing with it was a little pricier. We had been discussing a new purchase for a while, but I was not expecting it that day, and any guilty thoughts I had about not getting him anything for his birthday quickly exited my mind. Krista and I shared a laugh about that.

The day before surgery was set to be a busy day, so I tried to concentrate on getting back to my e-mails and cleaning out my in-box. So much support flowed through continually, and I was not sure when I would be able to respond, so I wanted to get as many emails answered now as possible.

That evening Cliff and I finally talked about the truck purchase, and he asked why I was feeling so nervous about it.

"What if I am not here to help pay for the truck?" I said.

Cliff became angry. He stood up and said, "Fuck off, and don't ever say that again." He was so mad that I said that. He left the room as I sat there trying to process his reaction.

He was afraid.

He was afraid to face what I had just said. He didn't even want his mind to go there.

We were both quiet as we prepared for bed, both of us lost in our thoughts and fears. I had expressed mine, but I knew Cliff would never verbalize his. We were very different that way, and that was his way of protecting me and himself from what the future might hold for us and our family.

> *If the only prayer you said in your whole life was "thank you," that would suffice.*
> —Meister Eckhart

Chapter 3
Surgery

The day before surgery, I was scheduled to go to the hospital for a range of tests, including blood work, an ECG, and a chest X-ray. I told Cliff I wanted to do this on my own and passed on the same message to friends who offered to accompany me. I felt the need to take this step into the unknown on my own, somehow thinking it would make me stronger.

As soon as I stepped into the hospital lobby and the doors closed behind me, I wished I was not alone. I was not brave, and I needed someone with me, but it was too late. As I raced from department to department, getting my tests done, I calmed myself by replying to my friends' texts and checking my e-mails on my phone. Several times I almost gave in and asked someone to come be with me, but before I could reach out for help, I dropped my phone back into my purse and busied myself reading the three-year-old magazines lying around the waiting rooms. Looking back, I still wonder why I took a stand that day. What did I think I would accomplish by doing this alone?

I tried to avoid the gaze of anyone and everyone, wondering if people could tell from looking at me that my life had been turned upside down, wondering if they could tell that I had breast cancer. *Has it really only been two weeks?* I thought. *How is that possible?*

Finally, my tests were completed, and I was escorted to meet with the preadmission nurse. As we went through the forms and went over what I could expect the next day, I felt the panic starting to rise, and as much as I tried to beat it down, the break had started. Before I knew it I was crying in my chair as she pushed a box of tissues my way. I heard her talking to me about a sermon she heard in church last Sunday, and I wondered if she thought I was going to die. Was that why she was talking to me about church and God? At that point I was sorry I had told Cliff I could do this on my own. I needed him with me. I needed to hold his hand and lay my head on his chest. I needed him to stop this woman from talking like I was going to die.

She then went over a test I was to have done before my surgery in the morning—a sentinel lymph node biopsy. This was the first time I had heard this would be performed, and I was scared. It sounded painful and frightening. I asked her for the material on the procedure so I could review it when I got home. I knew I would never remember the name or what she told me, so I took the material she offered, crumpled it up, and dropped it into my purse.

We were finally finished, and I rushed outside the hospital and gulped in the fresh air. Snow crunched under my feet as I made my way to the car. I couldn't wait to close my front door and let my home engulf in me its comfort, letting me hide away from everyone.

I spent the afternoon with my open overnight bag on the bed, staring back at me, empty. *What do I pack?* I wondered repeatedly. I was only scheduled to be in the hospital for one night, and every time I thought about it, I got scared. Finally I threw in a change of clothes to come home in and some toiletries, knowing Cliff and the girls could bring me anything I forgot.

I suddenly remembered the information on the sentinel lymph node biopsy. I dug it out of my purse and headed to my computer to see what it was all about. As I was waiting for my computer to load, I sent my sister-in-law a text and asked her if she'd had it done and if it was painful. Her answer to both questions was simply yes. As I researched the procedure, I was not reassured and suddenly found myself more scared of that biopsy than the surgery itself. At least for the surgery I would be asleep; with the biopsy I would remain awake. I was scared.

We spent our evening quietly. I napped in the tub and woke up with a start. The water had cooled off, and I was shivering. Reality came flooding back fast, and I started to cry again. Cliff gently knocked on the door and asked me if I was all right. He had heard some movement and wanted to check on me. I said I was fine and that I would be out in a moment. Then I ran the hot water to warm me up again and drown out the sound of my cries. I tried to talk with God, but I didn't know what to say. I still couldn't believe this was happening and wondered if it would ever sink in or if I would always have this feeling of disbelief.

I suddenly realized that I hadn't really even thought about what would happen tomorrow, the outcome. Would I be cancer free after tomorrow? What if the cancer had moved? What if it was somewhere other than in my breast? What if they had to remove my breast? So many questions and I didn't have an answer to even one. I decided to take it minute by minute. It was my body and mind's way of protecting me from what might be. I tried again and asked God to please watch over me and my family, but I wondered if he was even listening. Had God abandoned me in my time of need, or had I abandoned him? And if God loved me, how could he let this happen to me?

Surgery day arrived after a restless night.

Fear not … God is with you. I read this passage before I get out of bed. Maybe he was listening. I needed him to be listening. I needed all the help I could get.

I tried to pray. I tried so hard.

The alarm was set for 6:00 a.m., and it was still dark as we crawled out of bed and got ready, both of us feeling weary from the restless night we had spent pretending to be asleep so as not to disturb each other. I showered as Cliff made a coffee, and we did our best to avoid talking. We were both in survival mode and needed to keep things light so we could get through the morning. This was not the time to say how scared we were or even how much we loved each other. Either admission had the potential to take us to our knees again, so we kept our distance and tried to keep our emotional baggage at bay just for a little while, just to get us through the next few hours.

I crept downstairs to see Kayla before we headed out the door. She was still sleeping as I bent to kiss her forehead. She opened her eyes and reached up to hug me, and I could smell the warm smell of sleep on her. I wanted to hold her forever.

"Good luck, Mama," she whispered in my ear and then let go and lay back down on her pillow with her eyes closed.

I choked back the tears as I backed out of her room. She had already fallen back to sleep. Cliff waited for me at the top of the stairs with my overnight bag slung over his shoulder. I wondered how it was staying up there; he was hunched over so far. He had the weight of the world on his shoulders. My big strong bear of a man looked so vulnerable, his eyes so sad.

As we headed out to the car, I tried to calm myself as I took Cliff's hand. We drove to the hospital in silence, both trying to make peace with the day. I looked into the windows of people's homes as we drove by. Some windows were still dark while some people were waking up and getting ready to start their days, lights on and cars warming up in the driveways, the exhaust fumes rising into the sky like broken ghosts. I wondered what their stories were and wished I was like them again, wished we could go back to that place more than two weeks ago.

As we got out of the car in the hospital parking lot, Cliff took me in his arms and hugged me close and told me it was going to be okay. He looked sad, like he wanted to pick me up and run as far away from the place we stood as possible. I wished he would.

We were greeted by the nurse on the ward, who got right down to work and prepared me for the sentinel lymph node biopsy and then escorted me downstairs to have it completed. We were shown into a room where the biopsy would be performed, and everyone was very kind. They let Cliff stay with me, and I was happy he was there. They told him to take a seat at the end of the room, and it was comforting to have him with me in the room even though I had to twist my head very far to see him because he was sitting behind me. I felt better for him that he was there too because as long as he could see me, he knew everything was okay.

The procedure was performed, and I was pleasantly surprised that it did not hurt as much as I anticipated. Four injections of radioactive dye were injected into my breast, and then I had to lie there for about half an hour so a machine could trace the dye as it moved toward the lymph node. Cliff later told me how fascinating he had found it as he watched the dye move on the screen.

Next they moved me to another room to insert a wire into the tumor in my breast so that the surgeon would know exactly where to go. This was done by ultrasound, and once the wire was in place, I was sent back upstairs to wait for my surgery.

Cliff and I sat and talked quietly and even managed to share a few laughs. The nurse finally came and told me it was time to go. I rushed to the washroom. Nerves were taking over once again. Then I took Cliff's hand as we walked to the elevator. He was allowed to come as far as the OR doors with me, and we held each other's hands tightly as we rode down in the elevator, both of us looking straight forward, not saying a word. Once we reached the doors, Cliff reached down and took me in his arms, and we hugged. I tried hard not to cry, and I worried that he was going to break my back, he held me so tightly. Finally the nurse told us it was time, and he let go. We kissed and said good-bye.

When the OR doors opened, a friend who was also a nurse was waiting on the other side with her arms wide open, waiting for me to walk into them. I was relieved to see her and knew I had Tammy to thank for giving her co-workers the heads-up that I was coming. Cindy sat with me after she wrapped me in a warm blanket, and we talked quietly as we waited for Dr. Hardy to come see me. It was comforting to have a friendly face at my bedside as I waited for surgery, and I will always remember Cindy for her kindness and compassion that day.

As I was wheeled into the OR, I found myself starting to shake, and I had to go to the washroom again, but I knew it was too late. It was cold in the OR theater, and all the people were looking down at me, their faces covered by masks. As they tied my arms to the extensions on the bed, I tried to look into people's eyes, but they were busy doing what they needed to do. I wanted someone to hug me and tell me it was going to be okay, but I knew they had a job to do, and hugging me while preparing me for surgery was not it. I could feel tears running down my face as someone asked me my name and date of birth.

The next thing I knew I was waking up in my room. Cliff was sitting beside me, looking tired, and he jumped up as soon as my eyes opened, kissed my forehead, and leaned in for a hug, careful of my bandages. He told me he had talked with the doctor, and they had gotten the entire tumor and taken three lymph nodes, and one of those looked swelled. *What does that mean?* we wondered. We both knew that if cancer was found in the lymph node, it would mean I needed chemotherapy as well. At that time that was what we considered the worst case scenario.

I called Dad and reassured him that I was okay; I only remember I made that call because Cliff told me later that I had. I was exhausted and drifted off to sleep, and Cliff fell asleep sitting up in the chair beside me. He was tired and mentally exhausted. I tried to get him to go home, but he would not leave.

Linda showed up with a big bouquet of chocolate strawberries from my girlfriends, and flowers were delivered from my co-workers. I was so tired but tried to visit for a bit and watched Cliff out of the corner of my eye. He was fading fast, and Linda noticed and tried to convince him to go home as she said good-bye, but he insisted that he wanted to stay for a little while longer. Tracy and Tammy stopped by for a quick visit but didn't stick around long. They knew it had been a long day and that I needed to rest.

Dr. Hardy poked his head around the curtain to say hi and to speak to us again. I asked him that if he were to make a guess, would he think there was cancer in the swollen lymph node. I knew I was asking more than he was prepared to answer, but I had to ask. He said he wouldn't be surprised if there was and wouldn't be surprised if there wasn't. He was not committing to anything until the results came back, and I respected that he didn't give me any false hope.

Finally, my children arrived with arms full of flowers and supper for me. It was so good to see them. They look so healthy to me, their cheeks red from the cold air outside and out of breath from rushing through the halls. I watched and listened to them as they both sat on the end of my bed, talking a mile a minute, asking questions, offering assurances that all would be okay. Their eyes darted back and forth from me to their father, looking for any signs that things had not gone as well as we said they had. They asked how I was feeling, and I saw the concern in their faces. But they both looked relieved. I think I must have looked better than I felt! After about an hour, I finally convinced everyone to go home. It had been a long day, and I was tired.

Cliff bent over to kiss me goodnight, and I told him to get a good sleep as I loaded the children up with the flowers. I was going home in the morning, so I figured it was best to get them home now while we had lots of help.

Finally, I was alone. Swollen nymph node, clear margins, radiation, chemotherapy, biopsy reports—so much new terminology in my vocabulary. I tried to process all that had happened in the last two weeks, but I was tired and soon found myself falling to sleep only to be woken by a kiss.

Cliff had returned.

He had left the hospital and gone to the jewelry store to buy the cancer charm Kayla had wanted to buy last week. He laid it on my bed, kissed me goodnight, and left again, this time to return home and sleep. Shortly after he left, Kayla also returned, bringing me some snacks. My family was worried about me, and I know they hated to see me in that hospital bed. They were as scared as I was.

My night was restless, and I tossed and turned all night. My blood pressure was very low, and the nurses were concerned and kept coming in to check it. I was worried and scared and was afraid to close my eyes, afraid I wouldn't open them again.

I kept checking my phone and started texting Mom and Dad at 3:30 a.m. The time difference meant it was already morning on the East Coast, and they were up. We texted back and forth for a while, and I drew some comfort from those exchanges. I also felt good that I was letting them know I was fine. Finally I fell to sleep, but nightmares kept waking me up, sweating. I couldn't wait to go home.

Cliff arrived at 8:30 a.m. to pick me up, and he looked refreshed and rested. We waited for the nurse to go over all the patient care and change my bandages while giving instructions on how to care for the incision site at home. I was too nervous to look, but Cliff was all business, asking the nurse lots of questions about how to care for it. He told me it didn't look bad. He seemed pleased. He was so much more relaxed, and I knew it offered him lots of strength to know the surgery was over and it was one less thing we had to go through. We still didn't know what was going to happen, but for now we were over one hurdle. We smiled at each other as the nurse bundled me up into the wheelchair for the ride to the front door. Cliff left to bring the car around, and I chatted with the nurse. She was busy and kept apologizing to me for having to rush me out, but I was so relieved to be going home that I didn't care.

Cliff arrived back. When he kicked the wheelchair brake off and said, "Let's go home, honey," it was music to my ears. As he wheeled me out of the hospital, we bantered back and forth, and he asked if I wanted him to pop a wheelie with my wheelchair. He was happy to be leaving the hospital. He hated the smell of it, hated everything about it and was almost skipping as we got closer to the door. But before we made it to the door, he made a quick detour to buy a dream home lottery ticket ... Because, as he said, "You never know."

We arrived back to the safety of our home, and it felt good to be back in my own environment. Cliff took my overnight bag as I walked gingerly up the stairs and looked around.

Home, my heart sang.

The way I felt, you would have thought I had been away from home for a month. It was time to crawl into my nest and try to sleep, and I thought it was funny how that five-minute car ride had tired me out.

I retreated to my bed, but sleep wouldn't come. As I lay there listening to the phone ring, I tried to listen to what Cliff was saying, but all I could hear was a murmur. The phone continued to ring, and I felt sorry that he had to deal with those calls, but I was not ready to talk. *How many times have I thought that this really can't be happening?* I wondered. I fought down tears as I touched the bandages on my chest. Had they gotten it all, or was the news going to be bad? I wanted this over. I wanted this to have never happened. As I tried to find a more comfortable position in bed, I found my pillow was wet. Tears were flowing from my eyes. *Will I ever stop crying?*

I must have fallen asleep because when I opened my eyes again my husband was leaning in to give me a kiss. "Sleep well?" he asked softly. I knew he would feel so much better to see me up and around, and as I moved I was surprised with how good I felt. Other than some tugging at the surgery site, I felt little discomfort, so I got up and suddenly found myself full of energy.

As soon as I had received my surgery date, I had started cooking and freezing meals, so we looked into freezer to decide what to bring out for supper. I knew we could all use a good meal. As supper heated in the oven, I started to organize the cupboards in the kitchen, finding a renewed energy I hadn't had in a while. The sounds must have been comforting to Cliff because the next time I looked, he was asleep in the living room. I watched him sleep and once again wished I had never brought him this kind of pain. But I also knew that there was no one I would rather have had by my side. He had always had my back, and I knew he would always be my biggest supporter and would stand by me through whatever I had to face.

Cliff and I met on the playground in my neighborhood when I was eleven years old. I think I loved him from the first time I met him and knew I would marry him someday. At forty-four, I had already been with him for three quarters of my life and didn't remember my life when he wasn't a part of it. I always thought ours was the consummate love story. We grew up together, married when I was twenty-one, and then had our daughters. We were babies having babies, and we loved it. Our family was always full of love, and Cliff was always our protector. We never had to worry about anything when he was around, and I knew this was breaking his heart. For the first time in his adult life, he could not protect us or make it better, and it was making him feel helpless. I saw it in his eyes every time he looked at me. I felt it in his strong embrace every time he hugged me tightly. As I watched him sleep that day, I fell in love with him even more.

I walked quietly into the den and started to respond to the e-mails that had come in over the past few days. Once again I was overwhelmed with the love I read on the screen. Surrounded by love and feeling so blessed, I started at the top and worked my way down.

Dearest girl, my cousin Sharon e-mailed. *Know that you are in our thoughts and on our lips every day. If you get stir crazy, just say the word and we will come.* No pressure. Just letting me know she was available at any moment.

I sent an e-mail to my friend Bonnie at work and asked her to thank everyone for the beautiful flowers that had been delivered to my hospital room, and I immediately got a reply from one of my crazy co-workers saying that he thought the attached picture (of the flowers) was of my surgery scar. Thanks for the smile, Wietse! As I felt the smile spread over my face, it felt good. It was one of the first real smiles I'd had in a while.

Several e-mails brought forth encouraging words and thoughts. No questions. I appreciated those so much, as they contained no pressure to respond right away. Offers of food, cleaning services, chauffeuring, company, hugs—it was all there. From both sides of the country, family, friends, co-workers, acquaintances—it was all there, and how loved I felt.

I composed a message and then once again cheated by cutting and pasting the body of it and then crafting my response to each individual. I knew everyone would understand, and I felt it was so important to respond to everyone individually, as each person had taken the time out of his or her day to think of me and send me e-mails.

Cliff came in to check on me, and I started to read some of the e-mails to him. "People are beautiful," I said, to which he replied, "So are you. It is because you are who you are that people are like that." At first I wanted to argue, but then I thought of the old saying, "You surround yourself with people just like yourself." Many times I had spoken those words, but I finally heard them.

Len and I are sending you all the positive energy in the world, one friend named Cindy wrote. *You deserve the best. Your positive attitude is inspirational! With that kind of attitude you can face anything and win.*

Positive? Inspirational? I was feeling anything but that, but I was somewhat proud of myself that I was putting that side outward despite the nightmare I felt I had playing on the inside. Perhaps if that was what people were seeing, maybe I would start to feel it more, I thought. After reading that e-mail from Cindy, I made a promise to myself to start focusing on the positive. Positive energy, positive thoughts, positive steps forward. While I broke that promise many times in the coming months, it was a start for me. I renewed that promise as many times as I broke it.

As I moved down the list of e-mails, my best friend in Newfoundland made me laugh out loud with her description of teaching her sixteen-year-old son how to drive and how they were going to get arrested for driving up and down the same cul-de-sac at 7:30 in the morning every day. Either that, she said, or she was going to lie down and let him run over her and get it over with. It made me happy to know that there was still some normalcy in the world. Life really does continue on for everyone, and it was a good wake-up call for me that day.

I took a lot of comfort from an e-mail from my friend Chris, a cancer survivor himself. He offered himself to me if I ever needed to talk while reminding me that he had beat the "Big C" and I would too. Chris had always been a big inspiration to me as I watched his struggle from afar, and I always marveled at the smile on his face no matter how he was feeling. I responded back to him to let him know I was now using him as my role model of how to be positive and how to get through this time in my life.

Cancer or no cancer, Chris was one of the happiest men I had ever met.

Chris responded back with some wise words that helped me so much that day and continue to resonate with me to this day. *I am cancer free,* he wrote. *I think the key to dealing with cancer is not dwelling on it. Sit your family down and tell them you don't want a pity party. Tell your friends the same thing. Always stay positive. Never ever believe anything but that you will beat it. Kim, you will beat this. No doubt about it.* Thank you, Chris, for your words. You helped change the course of my future.

I managed to eat some supper on my first night home, and the home-cooked meal was comforting. Shawn and Tammy arrived for a visit and to see how I was holding up, and I kept wishing that things were like they had been before. I didn't want them to be visiting their "sick" friend. We kept the conversation light, and Shawn kept us laughing with his antics. It felt good to laugh and pretend everything was okay, but every now and again I would see Cliff watching me, and I knew he was remembering it all. I heard him comment to Shawn that he could forget what was happening, but then it rushed back and kicked him in the stomach.

My living room was overflowing with flowers. Cliff's employer had sent a beautiful bouquet, and I received beautiful roses from Cliff's sister and her family. Along with the flowers I had received from work and my daughters, there were now five arrangements in my living room, and when my company left I busied myself moving them around the house. The smell was starting to remind me of a funeral home. As beautiful as they were, to me they were a symbol of my cancer. I plucked out a yellow rose and held it to my nose, wanting to enjoy the beautiful aroma, wanting to remember the joy a rose could bring.

Cliff decided that tomorrow he would return to work, and I was happy. I needed some time alone to process my thoughts and to just "be". As we settled in bed that night, he took me in his arms, careful not to disturb my bandages, and I felt comfort in his body heat. I was happy to be back in bed with my husband, safe in his arms, and as I watched the shadows dancing again on the ceiling of our bedroom, I drifted off to sleep.

Once Cliff left for work the next morning, I crawled out of bed, stood before the mirror, and wondered who that woman staring back at me was. I had to get ready to go to the hospital to have the drain removed from my breast, and Krista had offered to take me. I didn't want Cliff to take any more time off. We didn't know how much time he would need in the future for my treatments, and we wanted to save his time off for that.

It took me almost an hour to dress, and I was waiting for Krista when she arrived. We headed to the hospital, not really talking, and I thanked her for coming with me.

The removal of the drain was a breeze; however, the discussion after was very emotional. The girls at the breast health clinic had been so good with me since this all started, but I had avoided picking up the information they provided to all newly diagnosed cancer patients. My nurse knew that and had it on hand for me. As she went through the material, I could feel the blood rushing through my ears again. I was not able to believe that she was talking about me and cancer in the same sentence. I just wanted her to go through it as fast as she could so I could escape the little examining room that was threatening to swallow me up.

As we left the hospital, I tried to hold the briefcase of material given to me with the cancer logo hidden from sight, not wanting anyone to know my secret. I had cancer. I reached for Krista's hand. "Thank you," I said through my tears, and she nodded and held my hand tightly, unable to speak through her own tears. It seemed like I had a million opportunities a day to say thank you.

Once I was home and settled, I tried to get some sleep, but I finally gave up and once again sat at my computer. I found a lot of comfort being busy responding to e-mails and catching up on Facebook. Some days I could find myself lost on the computer for hours, and it helped keep my mind busy, and sometimes I even managed to forget what was happening for a short time.

I felt bad for my parents. They were so far away, and I was trying to do my best to keep them informed several times a day.

I wrote to Mom and said,

Still working on the emotional part of all of this. Having a really hard time processing that it is me they are calling a cancer patient. I still can't believe it. Most days I am doing okay, but every day I have a few moments by myself where I allow it to flood me, and I get in a good cry. I have been doing lots of reading, and the one thing that keeps being said is that the survival rate for breast cancer is so much greater when people are positive. So that is what I keep thinking when I find myself slipping into the darkness of fear.

Some days it feels like I am having an out-of-body experience and this is really not me. And my heart breaks when I look at Cliff. He is so worried, and I see the fear in his face when he sees me lying down, even though he knows I need to rest. I know we will both feel so much better on Thursday when we see the doctor and find out the results of the lymph node biopsy. At least if I know one way or the other, we can get a game plan and start to deal with it. Cliff is my biggest cheerleader, and he keeps telling me we will beat this. He never says "you" It is always "us." I cannot imagine women who have to go through this who do not have husbands who shower them with as much love as he has showered me with.

Everyone keeps telling me how strong I am, and I laugh inside because I think if they could only read my mind. But after reading one of the books my doctor recommended, that is normal as well. You can still be strong while being scared. Bell's palsy was a walk in the park compared to the overwhelming emotions of this. It is so much easier when you can forget that this is happening, which we do for short periods of time. But then it hits again, and it is like every bit of wind is sucked out of me. Early mornings are probably the worst, when I wake up and just for a minute, I start to think about work and what I need to do today. Then it all comes flooding back. I watch Cliff's face change every morning as well, when the reality rushes in for him. Some mornings we don't even look at each other. It is easier that way. Nighttime is bad too … When everyone is asleep. Then there is too much time to think, and I have a hard time getting to sleep.

I knew they were scared, and I hoped that by letting them know a little part of what was happening, it might help them rest better until they could visit and see for themselves that I was okay.

My friend Christine brought us supper, and we had a good brief visit. I had always considered her my moral compass on this earth, one of my earthly angels, and she brought me such love and joy. That evening she did not disappoint as she unwrapped her homemade meatloaf and garlic mashed potatoes, all the while hugging me, giving me love, and reassuring me that I was in God's hands and he would take care of me. I wondered how she could be so sure of that but trusted that she would keep talking to God for me when I wasn't able to.

It was boy's poker night and Cliff's turn to host. While he had discussed canceling, I knew he needed the break, and it would do everyone good. Tracy arrived to pick me up and take me to the bookstore. I was in search of some good books. I needed a positive story to read about cancer survival and took some time to peruse the health and biography aisles. I picked up three books and keep putting one back. It was titled *Living Well Beyond Breast Cancer*. Tracy saw my confusion and asked me what was wrong. I told her I worried that it was too premature to buy it. She grabbed it out of my hand and headed to the checkout counter. Once we got to the vehicle, she gave it to me and said, "Read it when you are ready."

I was not ready to go home, so we picked up a coffee and drove around the city for hours. That was something Tracy and I had done for years. When one of us was feeling overwhelmed with life or needed to talk, we drove and chatted. In and out of neighborhoods, we drove about twenty kilometers an hour to the countryside and back. She let me talk and ramble on and on. Everyone should have a friend like that. She offered advice, words of wisdom, and a loving ear and then brought me home when she knew I was done.

I felt renewed once she dropped me off at the curb, and as I entered the house, it was full of men laughing and having a good time. As I lay on my bed, reading one of my new books, I could hear praise like "Good luck" and calls of "All in" yelled repeatedly, the sound of poker chips being thrown to the table, and glasses clinking. It felt good to be home. Before I fell asleep, I asked God, "Can you feel what is in my heart?" That was all I could say. While I wanted to talk to him, I didn't know what else to say.

The weekend passed in a blur. We were invited to Linda and Darcy's for supper on Saturday night, a night she had labeled "Time to Regroup." As I prepared to go, I found myself breaking down in the bathroom, crying once again. My heart was breaking. Cliff opened the door, and when I looked up, he was looking at me. He didn't have to say a word. It was all written on his face. I saw the pain in his face every time I looked at him. I told him I would only be another minute and turned away.

Food was plentiful, as were the drinks, but the men were all still recovering from the poker night antics the night before and were a little more subdued than normal. It felt good to be around everyone and just enjoy the company, but I found myself and Cliff exchanging glances throughout the evening, each of us wanting to be reassured that the other was okay. *Do I look as sad as he does?* I thought. I caught Simone looking at me. She looked concerned and offered me a tender smile when our eyes locked. *Do I look as sad as she does?* I again thought.

Sunday, April 1. April Fools. *How I wish this were all a bad joke,* I thought as I noticed the date. I crawled into bed with Kayla, and we had a nice long talk. She was still scared and confused but had been doing very well with getting back into the swing of her social life, and I was happy for her. We snuggled and talked about her night, and the next thing I knew, Cliff was crawling in on the other side of me. The three of us lay on the bed for an hour and laughed and chatted. It was times like that when I wished Kelsey still lived at home. I missed her so much. Finally Kayla had enough. We did a group hug, and we all got on with our days.

My friend Angela arrived in the afternoon for a visit, and we sat in front of the fireplace and had a good chat while the fire roared. Angela talked about her dad's passing from cancer. She was still raw with emotion, and I saw the hurt in her beautiful blue eyes. She talked about her dad's journey and some of the challenges he had to face and offered her support to me in whatever form I needed it. She also told me she understood my need for space, having seen the same need in her dad, and I was comforted by her understanding. As she walked down my walkway, I watched her leave from the window and hoped my girls didn't have to experience her kind pain anytime soon. At Angela's age, the loss of a parent was painful. How would my girls even deal with it at their ages? As she pulled away from the curb, I sent up a little prayer to her dad, George, in heaven and asked him to watch over his little girl.

Alone once again. Everyone had started back into his or her routine again, and I knew I had to get into one of my own. I got a shower for the first time and removed some of the bandages. I had been told not to get the incision site wet and took lots of care in doing exactly as I had been told. By the time I was showered and dried off, I was soaking with sweat again. I almost laughed out loud at how long it took me to do everything those days. Me, with my type A personality, who could have four things going at one time, now had to take an hour to get showered and dressed. I was looking forward to the day when my energy was back and the bandages were gone. As I busied myself with some light housework, I found that minutes would go by without a thought of cancer. *Is this the beginning of the healing?* I wondered. I sure hoped so. Thursday was our appointment back with the surgeon to get the biopsy reports, and I knew that in order to get through the week I would need to adopt some coping skills so that I was not consumed with what was going to happen.

I kept busy and met Bonnie for lunch one day. She caught me up on all the gossip at work. I had a telephone chat with another friend Ruby, who had just gone through breast cancer last year. I'd had several conversations with Ruby over the last year about her experience, and we talked very candidly about what I could expect in respect to radiation. She had not required chemotherapy but was happy to share her radiation experiences with me. It was so good to talk to someone who had been where I was right now. We talked about everything from breast reconstruction to the fear that it might come back. She told me to keep my chin up and stay positive and that it would all be okay. She told me radiation would be a breeze, how wonderful the staff at the cancer clinic in Calgary were, and to not be afraid. Thank you, Ruby, for your compassion and outreach in what you knew was my time of need. It was just another example of those endless acts of kindness.

Tammy and Tracy dropped by several times for a chat. Simone, Linda, and Krista called. They all did their best to keep me close while Thursday loomed closer and closer. E-mails poured in by the dozens along with offers of soup, sandwiches, and wine and offers to sweep my floor and clean my closets.

I had four of my old co-workers come for lunch one day and served them spaghetti and Caesar salad. They arrived armed wine and gifts but most importantly warm hugs. We shared a ton of laughs, and it felt nice to just be one of the girls, even if it was just for an hour. As they left, they told me to stay positive, that my results would be just fine, and that if I needed anything, they were there for me at a moment's notice. They left after extracting the promise from me to keep them informed on Thursday's results as soon as I was able. After we exchanged "I love yous," they walked out the door. I so wished I was going back to the office with them. I had spent more than ten years working with those girls, and it warmed my heart to know that our friendship extended far beyond the reach of our office cubicles. I felt blessed to be surrounded by such beautiful people in my life and was thankful for those relationships and deep friendships.

> *Kindness in words creates confidence. Kindness in thinking creates profoundness. Kindness in giving creates love.*
> —Lao Tzu

As the week progressed, I found I became more relaxed as the doctor appointment got closer. I wondered if that was a sign of denial or if it was just easier for it to be that way. While I worried about the results of the biopsy taken during my surgery, I had a sense that everything would be okay.

Things with Cliff became more relaxed as well. Our kisses were tender and affectionate, and we both remarked that we were enjoying our kisses and embraces more than we had for a while. He was always so gentle with me, and we seemed to take more time saying hello at the door. It was a renewed tenderness that had somehow been lost over the years in the hustle and bustle of living a busy life and raising a family.

When we hugged, I loved the feeling of being swallowed in his arms, protected and safe. We listened to each other breathe and just enjoyed the moment. I loved the smell of him. I loved how good it felt to be in his arms.

"You know you are my everything," he whispered in my hair.

I continued to thank God every day for the simple things, for my family, and for the love I was showered with.

My friend Debbie sent me an e-mail on the eve of my return appointment and wrote,

Hi, Miss Kim. I just wanted to let you know that I am thinking of you. While hearing about others who have had the same surgery as you won't make everything better, just remember that you can beat this and lead a long, long life. So, Miss Kim, you can be scared, angry, and even a little depressed but never defeated because you will be the winner in this battle.

What a difference a few simple strokes on a keyboard can make to a person's day.

The night before my appointment, I sat down at the computer to work through the flood of e-mails coming in to wish me good luck tomorrow. I was amazed at the number of people who remembered the day, and I wondered if they had put a reminder in their calendars. How did they remember these things with their busy lives?

I sent a long message to Mom and Dad to reassure them that we would contact them to let them know as soon as we were done. The time difference of three and a half hours continued to be even harder in times like those. My appointment was at 4:00 p.m., which meant it would be late in the evening their time before they heard anything. I knew it was hard on them as well as Cliff's family. It would be a long day for everyone.

I busied myself all day, trying to keep my mind occupied. My friend Shawn came to see me and let me know he was with me in spirit as we went to see the doctor. As we hugged, he said, "Love you, sis. We will get through this. We are family." He had always been like a brother to me, and I knew he would make it right if he could.

> *Let us not become weary in doing good, for at the proper*
> *time we will reap a harvest if we do not give up.*
> —Galatians 6:9

Chapter 4
My Treatment Plan

Cliff worked away in his garage, and I went about my day, neither of us wanting to talk about what today would bring. We were each lost in our thoughts. I hoped the news was good and prayed that Dr. Hardy would not have to tell me the cancer had spread or that it was in the nymph nodes. We figured our best case scenario was no spread and no chemotherapy. Our worst case scenario—well, I couldn't even go there.

We arrived at the doctor's office and sat quietly, holding hands. As I looked around the room I couldn't help but think how life had changed for us. As my name was called, we stood up and walked down the hall, hoping for the best and nowhere near prepared for the worst.

Dr. Hardy was so kind, and I knew as soon as he started to review the report it was not going to be good. He said there were no surprises and that they did get clear margins on the tumor in my breast, which was good news. However, cancer was found in the first lymph node; that was the bad news. That would mean six months of treatments – radiation and chemotherapy. There it was. I felt like I had been punched in the stomach, and I bit down on my lip to try to stop the tears, but they came anyway. Cliff reached for my hand and held it tightly as we sat close together and listened. Cliff asked lots of questions while I sat there stunned.

Chemotherapy. My first thought went to Cliff's mom, Jane.

The only experience I had with chemotherapy was watching Jane endure it years ago. I remembered how sick she had been after her sessions. She had suffered so much, throwing up constantly and wasting away to a shell of herself. During it all she had never once complained, and I used to marvel at her attitude and composure. Many times I told her that I could never handle it if I were ever faced with it with the same grace that she did. She had always smiled and responded, "You will do what you have to do." She battled cancer for three years, always with a smile on her face, and she never complained, such a beautiful woman facing her fears head-on with strength and courage. She had always looked to shield us from her health issues. Little had I known during the time that I had been learning from her how I would someday handle my own journey. Jane was such an inspiration for me, and even after she lost her battle with cancer, she continued to be my role model of how to deal with adversity. I had reached a day when I started to look back and draw on her courage, strength, and lessons in order to get through my own trials.

I was scared to be sick. I didn't want to suffer, and I didn't want my family to watch me suffer. I wondered if I could be as strong as Jane, and I doubted my ability.

Dr. Hardy left the room after giving me instructions to undress and lie on the examining table so he could take a look at my incision to make sure all was well and remove the final bandages. Cliff helped me undress. Then he leaned over me as I lay down and kissed me on the forehead. "It will be okay, honey," he said. He was still processing the information as well and was doing his best to reassure me. We were both scared, and I knew his thoughts had gone to his mom's fight as well. His eyes looked sad, and if it was true what they said about eyes being the windows to the soul, his soul was sad as well.

We finished up with the doctor and then headed to the parking lot. Once the doors of our vehicle were closed, we fell into each other's arms and cried. Even now, after all that has happened, I still look at the parking lot with sadness every time I pass it, remembering all the tears we cried every time we were parked there. Cliff looked into my eyes as he held me and said, "You are my hero, you know," which made me cry harder. I didn't feel like a hero, and I felt like such a fake to be called a hero. *I have cancer. What is heroic about that?* I thought.

I called Dad as promised to give him the news and then sent out a quick mass text with the bare information and a promise that I would send more details later. I called Kelsey and Kayla and talked to each of them, letting them know what was happening and reassuring them that I would be okay.

Cliff and I looked at each other and wondered what to do. Where did we go? How should we process this information we had just been given? We both felt like our world had fallen apart, and we didn't know how to deal with it. We were lost. We were scared.

Wow, I thought. *Really?*

I reached for my phone to text Tammy. *Can we come over?* I asked.

Yes, was her immediate reply.

We were greeted with hugs and tears. So much had happened, and we needed to be with our friends. Cliff left to go get Kayla, and when they returned, we all sat and talked. Tammy, being a nurse, had the ability to separate her emotions from the analytical way of looking at things, and I was counting on that to get us through the evening. While it had driven me crazy at times in the past when she looked at things from a systematic viewpoint, I knew it would help us now. We needed to separate the emotions from the reality and needed someone to help guide us down that course. We talked for hours and even managed to share some laughs when Shawn, who shaved his head, suddenly realized that we would be twins with our bald heads. As we bid them goodnight at the door, I thanked them both for being there for us in our time of need and providing everything we needed to get through the night. Once again, my chosen family had come through for me and helped me breathe slowly once again.

As we drove home, all I could think was wow. *Wow, is this really happening? Wow, how can this be happening? Wow*, I thought as I shook my head, watching the lights of the cars passing us, glad Cliff was driving because I couldn't see past the tears that were silently gliding down my face, hidden under the darkness of the evening.

At home we all went our separate ways, lost in our thoughts. I went to the bathroom and closed the door as tears flooded my eyes. As I looked in the mirror, I pulled my hair tightly back. Already I was not looking forward to losing my hair. I crumpled to the floor once again, grabbed for a towel, and let the tears come. *How can this be happening?* I wondered for the millionth time.

It was time to send out an e-mail. I knew friends and family were waiting, and I needed to get the news out there, if for no other reason than to reassure everyone it was going to be okay. It took me about an hour, but I finally hit send.

Hi, everyone.

Just wanted to send out an e-mail to give you an update. Please forgive me for sending out a mass e-mail, but it is easier right now.

Cliff and I saw Dr. Hardy today, and unfortunately the news was not what we wanted, but when explained to us, it is not as bad as it would first seem.

The facts are that cancer was found in one of three lymph nodes that were removed … the first one … Because there was cancer present in one, the normal course of action because of my age is to attack this as aggressively as possible. There is a very, very slight chance that there may be a cancer cell or two that slipped past the lymph nodes, and because of that they will treat me with chemo as well as radiation. It looks like I will also have to take Tamoxifen for five years. The purpose of the chemo is to make sure that if there are any stray cancer cells anywhere in my body, they will be found with the treatment and destroyed. Dr. Hardy did advise us that the type of cancer I have responds very well to treatment, and there is no indication that it has moved anywhere else whatsoever.

The more we think about it and discuss it and the more time that passes, the more comfortable we are about the chemo … It just reassures us that they are doing everything possible to assure that I will live a long healthy life cancer free. I can't say I am looking forward to the next six months, and while I know it is going to be a tough road, I will come out on the other side knowing that everything possible has been done to ensure that we have kicked this out of my body for good.

So the plan right now is that I will be returning to work a week from

Monday, April 16, and will work until my treatments start. The doctor said it is best to get back into a normal routine, and I am looking forward to getting back to a familiar environment and feeling useful once again. We will have to meet with the oncologist to get the schedule of treatments and go from there. As of now we don't know if it will be chemo and then radiation or both together or radiation first. That is up to the cancer clinic to decide. Treatments will not be started for at least a month, if not more. I have to be completely recovered from surgery before they will do that.

So, that's that. It is what it is! We will face it head-on, and with your prayers, love, and support, we will come out on the other end stronger than ever.

I am calling it a night now. It sure has been a long day.

Love, Me

I wanted to sound stronger than I was feeling, and as I reread it several times, I knew I did. As I hit send, I reached for a sleeping pill, crawled into bed with my husband, who was already sleeping, and started to think about how I needed to refocus. Everything I had read to that point said that survival rates were directly related to a person's attitude. I needed to start feeling what I was trying project out there, and maybe that would help. As my pill took effect, I felt the darkness taking over, and I welcomed it.

The next morning, my in-box was once again full of e-mails.

Kim, if there is any one person who can do anything, my money is on you. We are all with you, my brother-in-law Norman wrote.

Nothing you can't handle, Janice wrote.

The devil we know we can face and fight … the unknown is a tougher battle, wrote Ingrid.

Then a message from Tammy made me cry and laugh at the same time:

Feeling vulnerable or questioning "Why me?" or being scared … that is not a measure of your strength. That's being human.

Your strength is the way you love your family and friends and the way they return that love to you. Your strength is your integrity, modesty, and kindness. Your strength is your gratitude and your humor. You are strong! You are very strong, Kimmie, but what you are going through or have yet to go through requires more strength than any one person should have to handle. And that is where we come in … your family and friends … We will be the added strength you need. We will do whatever we can to make you stronger and keep you strong.

But I have one concern … you wrote this at 4:30 in the morning! You have a turkey supper to cook for us tonight. You need your energy and sleep to make this delicious dinner. Jeez Kimmie … priorities

And Chris once again came through, speaking like the true cancer survivor he is: *The key is to always keep your perspective. Try to compartmentalize it, try to never let it overwhelm you, and don't dwell on it. What you said below is exactly what worked for me … So, that's that. It is what it is! I will face it head-on, and I WILL BEAT IT.*

Good Friday woke us up with the sun shining, and it was a beautiful day. Easter was a time for renewal, and we tried hard to face the day positively. Mark and Simone came over for a visit, and we laughed and visited, not focusing on what had happened but rather enjoying the day and the company. They seemed to sense it was a time to be in the present, in that moment, and that I didn't want to talk about cancer. I think we all enjoyed the little vacation away from the problem, and after they left, Kayla said it sounded good to hear Simone and I laugh our obnoxious laughs.

We met up with Shawn and Tammy for supper, but our festive mood from the afternoon had dimmed. Everyone tried to make idle chitchat, but our minds were somewhere else. We were all happy when the bills were delivered and we could go home. It had been a long week, and everyone—my family and friends—were feeling it.

The tears had dried up, and I wondered why. *Are there no more? Where have the tears gone?* It had been almost a day since I had last cried, a record for me since March 14. Why?

Over the long Easter weekend, I started to focus on the logistics of what was going to happen over the next several months and tried to make a plan. I knew I needed to deal with the loss of my hair and was already planning to shave my head before it started to fall out. I did some reading, and everything said to take control and do it myself. I hadn't figured it out but knew I needed a plan before my treatments started. Every time I walked by a mirror, I wondered how I would look with no hair. I tied a scarf around my head and then pulled it off, frustrated. I did not want to lose my hair. I was scared to lose my hair. Once I lost my hair, I knew everyone who saw me would know I had cancer. I did not want that to happen.

Kelsey arrived, and we had a nice visit, but I noticed her questions were very guarded. She wanted information but was not sure how much information she actually wanted. I let her guide the conversation and followed her lead, keeping in mind that this was all scary for her. While I didn't want her to be afraid, I wanted her to be informed.

Kelsey had moved out several years before and had been making it on her own ever since. I had always been so proud of her fierce independence, though some days I wished she needed me more. She was very much like her father in the way she handled situations, very privately, and she liked to keep her thoughts and emotions to herself. Since she found out about the cancer, she had asked very little other than to call daily to see how I was doing. Some days I wondered if she was just avoiding the topic, but I came to understand that it was exactly the opposite; this was how she was facing it. As we visited that day, she was happy with the little information she asked for, and then the conversation veered off to her work, cheerleading, and school. It felt good to just visit with her, play board games, and be Mom, not the mom who was sick. I took her lead and followed her.

My soul finds rest in God alone ... He alone is my rock and my salvation: he is my fortress, I will never be shaken.
—Psalm 62 1:2

This was the first Easter since Cliff and I were married that I didn't have a crowd sitting at my table for Easter Sunday dinner. I was not feeling up to cooking for a crowd, and Cliff and I agreed that we would spend a quiet Easter Sunday at home. While I worried about our decision, it turned into a wonderful day full of relaxation and no stress. The cancer was making changes to our lives in every facet, but this change we just rolled with. It felt good to be quiet for a day and not get caught up the hustle and bustle of the Easter Bunny commercialization of Easter.

Our twenty-third wedding anniversary also fell on Easter Sunday. It was hard to believe that we had been married for twenty-three years already, and when I thought back to our wedding day it seemed like a lifetime ago.

Several times throughout the day, I felt that familiar rush of panic surfacing, and I started the internal dialogue to calm myself down. I wondered if I would be doing this for the rest of my life and how long the rest of my life would be. The panic was exhausting. Cliff and I decided to drive to Olds and visit my cousin and family to get our minds off what was happening and to get a change of scenery. As we drove, we talked about everything that had happened in the past month, and Cliff told me he had been scared too. He confided that he was having chest pains, and he knew it was from the stress. We both reflected on how this time a month ago everything had been so much easier, and neither of us could believe this was happening to us or that this was our life now. We both wanted to go back to where we had been before we got the news. If only we had a magic wand.

As we were driving home, I received an e-mail from Sharon, who we had just visited. She was worried that she offended me when we were discussing my hair and how it would grow back. I was sad that she was worried I would be offended and was once again reminded how this was changing how everyone around me responded to me, even when they tried so hard not to let it. I reassured her that she had not offended me and told her to please continue to treat me like always. It made me sad that we even had to have the conversation; it made me sad that people second-guessed what they said to me; it made me sad to think that my loved ones were unsure of me anymore.

When we arrived home, I once again headed for the bathroom to hide. On the drive home, I could feel my anxiety level creeping up to the point that I felt my head was going to explode. As I sat and rocked on the floor behind the locked door with a towel pressed to my face, I was terrified. Tears silently rolled down my cheeks and soaked the towel, my heart raced, and the lump in my throat grew and grew. I could see snapshots of Cliff and my daughters playing behind my closed eyelids. I could see Kelsey and Kayla on their wedding days, looking so beautiful but sad I was not there. I could see Cliff with another woman and watched her remove my pictures from the shelves in my home. I could see the three of them standing under big tall trees, holding flowers, crying at my final resting place. I knew I need to get a grip on this thought process or I was going to go crazy, but it seemed like those thoughts just took over, and I had no control.

As I sat and rocked back and forth on the bathroom floor, I kept repeating, "I am not going to die. I am not going to die."

> *Though I walk the valley of the shadow of death, I will fear*
> *no evil, for You are with me; Your rod and Your staff, they*
> *will comfort me.*
> ——Psalms 23:4

I found some comfort in the Psalms passage, as it spoke directly to me that night, and I felt it was not about dying but about surviving. Being afraid of what misfortune the future may hold can keep you stuck in the darkness of depression and anxiety, right where I had been since this all started. I knew I needed to start to deal with the anxiety before it became a major problem in itself. I knew there was a direct link between attitude and recovery, and I knew that to increase my recovery odds I needed to work on the mental part of my well-being as well.

I decided to start my week off on a positive note. I took Kelsey and Kayla to lunch, and we had a nice visit, although I noticed that Kelsey appeared to be stressed and uptight. I asked her what was happening, but she didn't want to share too much. I felt bad that I was adding to the stress in her already busy life and wished there was some way I could spare her this worry.

My promise to myself to stay positive seemed to work for the short term, as I didn't experience any panic attacks for a while and managed to deal with the emotions on an individual level as they crept in. As Cliff and I walked around the neighborhood for our nightly walk, I watched the people working in their yards; they seemed so carefree and alive, while we dragged the weight of our troubles behind us. How I wished my life was as simple as everyone else's appeared to be at that moment.

Even while thinking this, I knew it not to be true. Everyone had issues, just as we'd had ours before this happened. But looking back, I would have loved to have the opportunity to trade for what we had been going through with our old problems; they seemed so immaterial and unimportant compared to what our problems were now. It is true when they say if you don't have your health, you don't have anything. I was learning just how very true that statement was.

I came across a passage in my reading that goes, "Prayer is simply inviting God to play an active role in your life." I thought I had always done that but wondered if I really had. *Do I really pray like Jesus, or do I just go through the motions?* I wondered. Had God recognized that and was now telling me something?

Juanita told me she wanted to come and so did Cliff's sister, Peggy, and her husband, Dyrick. I spent hours trying to coordinate their visits with Mom and Dad, who were coming in June. I was excited about them all visiting and was happy to have someone from home here with us, especially during treatments. I knew Cliff could use the visit from Dyrick as an opportunity to unwind and just relax. I could see the pressure building up in him daily. Some days he returned home from work and he was fine; other days he looked sad.

I hated knowing that I was the cause of all his anxiety and wished every day that I could take it away from him. When we walked at night, he talked a little about it but not much. I knew there was so much more going on inside his mind that he wouldn't share. He said he had no doubt I was going to beat this, but he was worried about the chemotherapy and did not want to see me sick. We were both scared of the unknown and just as scared to share our fears with each other.

On Monday, I got a call from the cancer clinic to advise me that an abdominal X-ray and bone scan had been ordered for me for the following week. I was unaware that I had to have those tests done, and I felt the panic starting to set in again as I asked myself why they were doing them. Did they think it had spread? Was there any indication that it had spread and no one had told me? I decided not to tell Cliff about the tests, thinking it would only worry him more, and I wanted to try to shield him from any more unnecessary worry. I called my friend Krista, and as I told her about the tests, I broke down and started to cry. Just hearing me say the words caused me so much worry. I told her that I would go to have those tests on my own and then tell Cliff about it afterward. I couldn't bring more worry on him. Krista gently told me that she thought I was wrong to hide it from Cliff and that he would want to be there for me. I told her I would think about what she said, knowing even before I hung up that she was right. It was unfair for me to make that decision for Cliff.

Peggy called one evening, and we firmed up her dates of arrival. She had been waiting until Mom and Dad booked their tickets so that there was no overlap of visitors. Peggy was anxious to arrive and see me for herself, and I knew it just killed her that she was so far away and unable to do anything to help. As we talked, I told her I didn't want her to see me sick and that I wished she was coming under different circumstances, but I knew she would take care of everything while she was here; she would take care of me. She told me I would be okay, that everything would be okay because I had an angel watching over me, and we both knew without saying that she was referring to her mom, Jane.

Since Cliff's mom had passed away, Peggy had kind of taken over that role for her brothers and their families. She was always the one I turned to for help of any kind, and I knew she was there for us no matter what. As tough as this was on her, all she showed me was a brave face and a supportive ear. I couldn't wait for her and Dyrick to arrive.

The e-mails flooded in all week from friends and family.

Krista wrote, *Whatever you need—me there, me not there, me listen over e-mail, me listen over text, me listen over phone, me listen and look into your eyes, me not hear you talk about it ... WHATEVER you need, I'm here. Always and forever. I love you, my sister.*

I came across an article in which Beverly Thomson from CTV had been interviewed. She was a breast cancer survivor. I found it comforting when I read her words and how she dealt with her diagnosis and the panic and fear she first felt during the initial stages. *She is just like me*, I thought. I loved how she said that she would "focus on living life—enjoying it and making a contribution." It had been ten years since she was diagnosed, and she was living life to the fullest and enjoying every day. I knew there was a lesson to learn from knowing her story.

After a walk one evening, I noticed that my bra was wet, and when I looked, there was a clear liquid draining out of my incision. If I moved my breast at all, the liquid just poured out. I rolled up some bandages and taped them over the incision and tried to forget about it, but within half an hour, I was back in the bathroom to look again. The bandages were soaking through, and I started to get worried. Was this a sign of infection I wondered as Cliff hovered behind me. I called the provincial health link number and talked with a nurse. She assured me that this was normal for that kind of incision, that the fluid should be draining out rather than staying inside, and that I had nothing to worry about as long as I was not running a fever. I ran out of bandages, so I made a makeshift one out of a facecloth and got up throughout the night to change it and put a fresh one in its place.

I spent some time with Kelsey one evening. We went shopping, and she helped me with my purchases. Time with her was precious, and I tried to see her when I was having a good day. That way I thought she wouldn't worry as much about me. We enjoyed each other's company, and it was good to spend time together. I missed her and wished we had more time together.

As the week progressed, my energy level got better, and I was able to move around the house and get some housework done. It felt good to get back into my groove, and by Thursday I felt well enough to head out and visit my work and co-workers. It felt good to walk through the door and be greeted with such warmth. I spent some time with my boss Spencer going over a plan of filling my position while I was away doing treatments, and we talked about me returning to work until my treatments started. I couldn't wait to get back. They treated me the same as they always had, and it felt good not to have people shy away from me. A co-worker named

Doug said, "So, Kim, you are on the right side of the sod. That's good." I burst out laughing and as he joined me in my laughter, we high-fived.

I had gotten really good at returning all my e-mails and Facebook messages on a daily basis. It was important for me to respond to every one of them. I was touched that people took the time out of their days to reach out to me and felt that the least I could do was acknowledge their messages and thank them. I am not sure if people will ever know how much their words have meant to me.

Joanne wrote, *Love you and praying for you. I'm very thankful that you are who you are, 'cause you can kick this in the ass!*

Linda wrote, *Well done, brave lady! xxoo!*

And my dear squirt Pauline wrote, *Sending lots of love your way. Praying for strength for you and your beautiful family.*

I had reached out to my friends over the years, and now they were reaching back out to me at a time I was in my greatest need. You can live on that kind of love!

Friday found me making excuses to get out of a movie with Tammy, coffee with Colleen, and a visit from Sharon and Finn. The week had caught up with me, and I was feeling the need to hibernate once again and not have the pressure of pretending I was okay. As I canceled plans, I worried that people would just give up on me if I keep doing that.

I stayed in bed until noon and ignored the phone as it rang and buzzed with texts coming in. Cliff was feeling the stress of the week as well; his mood got more somber as the days went by. We had taken to watching TV in different rooms at night when he was home, neither of us knowing what to say to the other. I was afraid this was pulling us so far apart at the time, but I didn't know what to do to fix it. He sounded sad on the phone when I called him at work, and then when he came home, he often didn't want to talk. Some days I felt so close to him; other days I felt like I was living with a stranger.

Some minutes I felt I needed to just start screaming to get out all the feelings I was suffering inside. I wondered, *If I started screaming, would I ever stop?* Other minutes I was mad, mad that everyone else was going on with his or her life while mine had stopped. I felt bitterness and envy, two things I had never felt in my life, and it was tearing me up inside. How could I feel bitterness and envy toward the very people who loved me? I worried that if I told anyone they would think I was a horrible person and stop loving me. So I kept it all inside, and it made me crazy some days.

I dreamed of my life before this all happened and wanted to be back there. I remembered the little things that had bothered me then and wondered how that could have ever been such a big deal to me. I missed the innocence of my life, our life.

Friday night, Cliff and I went out for supper and had a good talk. Despite the feeling of drifting apart, there was a newfound tenderness between us since this had all happened, and we both felt it and talked about it during supper. Physically we felt closer than ever before, which seemed so strange when we felt like we were in different worlds some days. Our embraces were tenderer, and our kisses were unlike any we had ever shared. We had been together for so long that neither of us could remember life without each other, and we were both scared that it could be taken away from us. We were both scared about what the future held for us and our family.

You are responsible for the energy you bring.
——Oprah Winfrey

The weekend marked the one month anniversary of our life changing. As I lay in bed that morning, I reflected back on the past month, and it seemed like a dream. I had a hard time remembering the chain of events as it happened, and I was still stuck on disbelief. I wondered how we had gotten through it to date and where we would get the strength to get through the next month.

I tried to focus on Tammy on Saturday, as she was putting her dog to sleep. The dog had been sick for a while, and the time had come. I spent the day texting her to make sure she was okay, knowing firsthand how painful that decision had been for her to make. It was a tough day for her family and a gentle reminder to me to get off my soapbox because everyone else had pain and troubles as well. I was not the only one suffering, and the world was not going to stop because of what was happening to me.

I was troubled with negative thoughts all weekend and had a hard time focusing on anything or being positive. I worried constantly that I was going to die, not be around for my children, and not see my grandchildren. I could almost picture Cliff marrying again, going on with his life without me. I couldn't shake those images and thoughts, and they prevented me from sleeping or eating. As I lay on the couch, I cried long after everyone else had gone to bed and allowed myself to have the pity party that had been coming for a while. I felt that the cancer had taken away the security I had always felt when thinking about the future, and I wondered if my thoughts would always be consumed with the thought of cancer. Would I become one of those people who worried that every ache and pain was a sign of the cancer returning? I didn't want to be that person.

Monday arrived bright and sunny. It was my first day back to work since my surgery, and I was excited to get back. My incision was healing nicely, and it felt good to get back to dressing up and get out of the yoga pants I had been wearing for weeks on end. Everyone was so kind and concerned, and after some quick questions about how I was feeling, I fell right back into the groove, just one of the guys.

On the morning of my tests, we arrived fifteen minutes early, and Cliff and I sat in the waiting room, wringing our hands and taking deep breaths. As I watched Cliff, I wondered if he would ever get a good night's sleep again. He looked tired and hadn't slept well the night before either. Every time I moved, he woke up. Even when he was asleep he was worried, and his mind was never resting. I wanted to sleep in the guest bedroom, but he didn't want me to, saying he slept better with me by his side.

I was shown into the room where the ultrasound on my abdomen would be performed, and I had déjà vu from the month before. As the technician glided the wand around my stomach, I stared at her face, but she was busy completing her task. I looked at the screen, and it was all grey, black, and white; nothing looked familiar to me. Once it was completed, she asked me to stay where I was and then returned within minutes with the radiologist.

He simply said, "It's all clear. Nothing to worry about there."

I started to cry as I jumped off the examining table to quickly dress and went to tell Cliff. When I entered the waiting room, Cliff was watching the hallway and saw me as soon as I turned the corner. He met me halfway.

I took his hand and guided him to the stairwell, where I broke down and told him the test was clear. We hugged and cried. *One down, one to go,* we thought as we pulled ourselves together and prepared for the next test.

We went downstairs for the bone scan and were shown into another room. As I was prepped for this test, the technician could see how shaken we both were, and she sat with us and shared that she was a nine-year cancer survivor. When I asked her how old she had been when she was diagnosed, she had to stop and count the years. As she was counting, I wondered if I would ever get there, to a point where every date was not burned in my mind. She shared a little bit of her journey with us, and I was grateful as I listened to her, a total stranger, giving us hope that I could get to where she was someday. She looked so healthy, beautiful, and happy. I wanted to be healthy, beautiful, and happy again.

When the scan was complete, she told us "unofficially" that everything looked good. I buried my face in my hands and wept. When I looked over at Cliff, he was quietly crying, holding a tissue to his face with one hand and his glasses in the other.

It had been an exhausting day, and as Cliff helped me off the table, my feet didn't touch the floor as he held me tightly in his arms. I could feel the wet of his tears on his cheeks. We were so relieved. We thanked our technician repeatedly, and I reached out to hug her, telling her that she would never know how much her kindness had helped us today and that we would remember it forever.

As we walked out of the building and raised our faces to the sun, I sent up a prayer of thanks. We were over another hurdle, and the clean scans gave us an added boost to keep moving forward. All my scans had come back clean, meaning there were no other masses anywhere in my body, and we took so much comfort from that information. I suddenly felt like I could take on anything now that I knew there was nothing else growing in my body. If there were any stray cancer cells floating around, the chemo would zero in on them and destroy them before they could grow; that was my added insurance.

Cliff and I hugged in the parking lot, kissing each other's faces, standing so close together it was difficult to see where one body stopped and the other started, all while reassuring each other that we were going to be okay. Cliff looked so relieved and even had a smile on his face. I knew he had been prepared for the worst that day and was thankful we had gotten the news that we did. As he walked to the car, he had a spring in his step that I hadn't seen in a while, and it made me smile. In that moment, for now, everything had been righted in our world.

That evening I had an appointment to have my hair cut, and my hairdresser, Kim, and I talked about wigs and when I should get one. She had done some research on them and had information for me on where to go and what to look for. She was very kind to me and cut quite a bit of the length from my hair, hoping to make it easier to manage until I shaved it off. As I watched her work and watched my hair fall, I knew this would be one of the last times for a long time that I would be sitting in her chair, and it made me sad.

When I tried to pay her, she refused to take my money, saying, "No. This is my way to help. Please let me do this." As she hugged me, she said, "Please don't cry, because you will make me cry." She sent me on my way, and I was once again overwhelmed with the kindness shown and how a person, with a simple gesture, could turn something so hard into a wonderful memory full of love.

Losing my hair was something I kept pushing to the back of my mind. When alone, I kept standing in front of the mirror and pulling my hair back as tightly as I could, wrapping scarves around it to see how I would look. For as long as I could remember my hair had always been my security blanket, and I had always prided myself on my thick hair. The image looking back at me was foreign with the short hair, and even with my hair pulled tightly to my head I still could not imagine what I would look like bald. I worried about how Cliff would react. I worried if he would still be attracted to me with no hair. Would my friends look at me differently? Would strangers stare? Right then I could still blend in with everyone else; the cancer had no outward signs that anyone could recognize. But I knew that once my hair was gone, there would be no hiding my condition. I would no longer be able to hide.

When I got home, I started researching wigs, and it all became overwhelming. There were so many kinds and styles. My only experience to date with wigs was the fake ones people wore on Halloween, and even those I never liked. I was worried about how I would look in a wig. Would everyone know it was a wig? Would it fall off? Would it itch or scratch? As I was looking, Cliff walked into the den and looked over my shoulder to see what I was doing.

"It will only be for a while, honey," he said quietly. "It is a small price to pay."

Small price to pay, I thought. *You are not the one losing your hair, so that is easy to say.* But I didn't say the words out loud. He didn't deserve to be hurt like that, so I swallowed my words and anger and nodded. "I know," I said sadly as he left the room.

I received confirmation that Juanita would be coming from Newfoundland next month for two weeks, and I marked her arrival on my calendar with shaking hands. Already I was eagerly anticipating her arrival and knew she would bring lots of laughter and fun into our house, a much needed distraction from what was now our reality.

While getting ready for work the next morning, I checked my e-mail, and it was once again flooded with e-mails from friends and family expressing their joy that my scans had come back clean. Tammy called me "amazing," Peggy said I was an "inspiration," and Simone said I was "so strong." Those words echoed in my mind all day, so much so that I had a hard time concentrating on my work, and when Cliff picked me up in the evening to go home, I started to cry. "I feel like such a farce because I am not any of those things," I cried to Cliff. "What if people really knew how I felt? They would be so disappointed in me." I felt like such a fake and was afraid that everyone would find out that I was not amazing, inspirational, or strong. The truth was I felt weak, scared, alone, and terrified.

Cliff told me it was okay to be all those things but that I had to remember the positive too. He said that when I kept it together, it helped everyone else kept it together, and that was inspirational; that to get out of bed every day and face whatever was thrown my way was being strong; and that he always thought I was amazing, no matter what. He told me how proud he was of me in how I was handling everything, that I was his hero, and that it was okay to have moments where I fell apart. That was normal, he said. I cried all the way home, and it felt good to let it out, to let Cliff see me in that vulnerable place, and to let him take care of me and make it better. I suddenly didn't feel so helpless anymore, and it felt good to pass some of my fears onto Cliff and let him hold them for a while. I was so tired, and I needed him to be strong for me at that moment, and as he always did, he came through for me and helped chase away some of my fears.

> *Christ accepted you, so you should accept each other, which*
> *will bring Glory to God.*
> —Romans 15:7

Being honest, authentic, and accepting in your love, even with people who misunderstand or reject you, helps them see what God is like. *Could the biblical passage above be speaking directly to me?* I wondered about my inability to accept what people were saying about my strength and courage? If I believed what they were saying about me, would it help me become more like it, and would I start to believe it myself?

By the week's end, Mom and Dad and Peggy and Dyrick also had their travel plans confirmed to come visit. It was looking like I would have company for the full month of June, and I couldn't wait. Work was so busy, and while I was there, each day it was easier to blend in with everyone else and forget my troubles. Bonnie kept a tight watch on me, making sure I was eating and not getting too overwhelmed with my workload, but other than that my co-workers kept treating me as they always had, which was good for me.

I found it was easier to stay in touch with my friends through e-mail, and avoiding phone calls and invitations to visit once again became more common than not. I knew I had to work on that. I felt it was safer for me to communicate through e-mail or texting, that way they did not have to hear my voice, and I didn't have to pretend to be upbeat, which was exhausting. I didn't want every conversation to be about me; I wanted it to be the way it always had been. I wanted to make people laugh, not cry. I didn't want pity. I wanted my old life back.

On the weekend, I had some good internal conversations with myself about pulling up my socks and getting on with my life. I didn't want the cancer to consume my every thought, and I didn't want to become one of those people who focused on every ache and pain, running to the doctor for every little thing, worried that the cancer had moved somewhere else. I knew I had to take back my life and start living it like I had before my diagnosis or else I would lose myself and the life I had and loved so much. I spent a full day focusing on me, all the good in my life and all that I had to be thankful for. I knew it was time to start being strong, inspirational, and amazing, not just faking it. I pledged to start looking for one thing to be thankful for that had nothing to do with cancer every day and build on that. I knew there would still be days I would wallow in self-pity and sadness for what was, but I vowed that it would not take over my life. Already I had given it a month to consume me, and I knew it was time to take control of my life and get back to living it, not just going through the motions.

That day, my first offer of thanks was for Cliff. I was so thankful to have him in my life and to have him walk this journey with me. He loved me unconditionally, had seen me at my worst, and had listened to my hateful words with a calmness that only he had. He had dried my tears as his own rolled down his cheeks, held me tightly when I wanted to run away, watched me sleep, and held me when the nightmares caused me to cry out in fear. More importantly, he made me laugh, said things that made me buckle over and lose my breath with laughter, told me I was beautiful over and over again, and believed in my strength long before I recognized it myself. He sat in countless waiting rooms with me and held my hand tightly while talking with the teams of doctors, taking notes in his head, and his facts were always clear and precise. He let me nap but always woke me when he felt I was wallowing and got me moving again, even if it was for a short walk around the block. And he took all those phone calls and repeated our story over and over while his heart broke, just so that I would not have to do it. He proved to be my biggest cheerleader even when he was falling apart himself, and he always managed to make me feel safe, no matter how big and empty the room was, how scary the news, or how dark the night. How could I not be thankful for such a beautiful life partner? I am so blessed to be married to this man. I didn't remember my life without him. I didn't want him to know a life without me.

I set a date to meet with the wife of a co-worker of Cliff's. Diane was a breast cancer survivor and had reached out to me through her husband when she found out I had been diagnosed. I finally called her, and we made a date to get together. It was one of the best things I had done to help me move forward. I was so nervous about meeting with Diane, wondering what to ask and hoping that hers was a positive experience I could learn from. I didn't need any negativity right now and was unsure if I could even deal with it, but from the moment Diane greeted me at her door I knew this would be nothing but a positive experience for me.

She answered all my questions with the utmost and raw honesty, never once making me feel like my feelings were silly or unfounded. As she had stated in an earlier e-mail, she knew firsthand what I was going through and was more than prepared to answer all my questions and quiet my fears.

She brought out her wig and showed me how easy it was to put on and told me some stories about wearing it. As I listened to her talk and held her wig, I no longer feared it. She talked about losing her hair and the reactions of her family when she was bald, and she was a testament to me that my hair would grow back as she sat there with her beautiful head of blond hair. We laughed together when I told her that I kept looking for all the bald women but hadn't yet seen one. She said she had done the same thing when she was going through it.

She talked about the effects the chemotherapy had on her and how important it was to take my antinausea meds on time, as they would keep me from throwing up. She told me about the one time she did get sick and how the cancer clinic had taken care of her right away.

Diane promised me that there would come a day when I wouldn't think about cancer all the time, that there would come a day when I lived my life just like I had before I heard the word *cancer*, and that there would come a day when I didn't think every ache and pain was a new cancer growing.

And finally, Diane told me it was okay to be scared but not to be afraid. Be scared of the unknown, but never be afraid, because you lose your strength to fight when you are afraid.

When I left her house that day, I was filled with hope and a renewed energy, having sat and talked with someone who had just gone through the exact thing I was going through and survived. She was back to work and living and loving life, and the cancer had not taken that from her. She was alive. She was beautiful. She was a survivor.

It is okay to be scared, but not to be afraid.
——Diane Laramee

As I drove home, I detoured to the ball field where Cliff and my friends were practicing for the upcoming first ball game of the season. I tried to participate by getting out there and throwing the ball around, but it pulled on my incision site, and Simone saw I was struggling and made me sit. While I was grateful for the concern, I was resentful. I was feeling resentment that I could not participate and have fun with them, and I was bitter that they could all get out on the field and run around and I had to sit, not able to join in. Before cancer I would have been on the field, heckling the batter and probably doing cartwheels and not paying close attention to the game, cracking jokes, and throwing rocks at the girls. Now I had to sit on the sidelines and watch the rest of them play and hear their laughter, no longer part of their jokes, which I couldn't even hear. I felt lonely and headed to my car without saying good-bye. The wind carried their laughter to me even as I reached the car.

At home I sat on my deck and said to myself, "I have to stop this. I want to be strong. I want to be inspirational in my fight. I will not shut myself off from my life anymore."

My one thing to be thankful for that day was my children. I remembered the days they were born and how much fun we had as a family while they were growing up. I remembered their tiny little fat feet, baking cookies with them while it snowed outside, and cuddling on the couch while watching Disney movies. I had always been so thankful for my daughters, for all the beautiful memories we had made, and for all the beautiful memories we would make in the future. I was so thankful that I was blessed with these two perfect creations of God, and I prayed that I still had a lifetime to experience their lives with them. I wanted to be at their sides as they took their husbands, be there to hold their children, buy a housewarming gift for their first houses. I wanted—I needed—to be there. I was their mother; they were my life.

My goal to stay in a good, positive frame of mind was lost on me as the work week rolled along. I struggled to get through the days and hit my low midweek, feeling so depressed and fighting back tears as I tried to wrap my mind around what my life had become. Sitting at my desk, it got harder and harder to smile and chat, pretending that my world had not fallen apart.

On Tuesday, I was feeling the pressure of trying to stay upbeat and knew I was losing the battle when Juanita could read through e-mails how depressed I was and kept sending me back messages of encouragement. A visit from Kayla and Krista at the office did little to lift my mood, and I watched the clock all afternoon, willing it to turn to 5:00 so I could leave and finally let the flood gate of tears open. As I drove home, I pulled onto the side of the road and started to cry, not caring who saw me. I don't know how long I sat there, but I finally pulled myself together and started home.

Cliff greeted me at the door, and I put my head on his chest and started to cry again as he asked me over and over what was wrong.

"What's wrong?" I wanted to scream. "How can you ask me what is wrong?"

I walked past him, dropped my purse and coat on the floor, retreated to my bedroom, and crawled into bed, not taking the time to change out of my skirt and blouse. I pulled up the sheets and lay there staring out the window, silent, scared, and so very sad. I could sense Cliff in the doorway of our bedroom, but I didn't turn around. I just wanted to be left alone

Sometime later I felt him crawl onto bed with me, and as his arms wrapped around me to pull me close, he started to talk about how important it was to stay positive, to eat to keep up my strength, and how we were going to beat this. I didn't say a word. I didn't know what to say, and even if I did, the lump in my throat would not have let any words out. After a while he kissed my shoulder and said, "I love you," and then left me alone.

A short time later, Kayla came in, knelt on the floor next to my bed, rested her head on her hands, and stared at me. She said, "It's okay to be sad, Ma." She reminded me that I had so many people rooting for me and that she loved me so much and would always be there for me. As I stared at her beautiful face, tears ran out of my eyes and onto my pillow. I was so sad that I had brought so much pain to my family. They didn't deserve this. I pulled the sheets up closer to my chin as I watched her watching me. She was strong at that moment, and I was so weak. She leaned in, placed a kiss on my wet cheek, and again told me how much I was loved before she quietly left the room and pulled the door closed behind her. I was left alone, and the tears came faster as my body shook uncontrollably. I wondered how I was ever going to get through this.

Cast your cares on the Lord and he will sustain you.
—Psalm 55:22

I am not sure how long I lay there, but I could hear Cliff busy in the kitchen, pots and pans clanging together, cupboard doors opening and closing, as he tried to keep busy. I crawled out of bed, went to the kitchen, walked up behind him, and hugged his back. He started to cry as he turned around and took me in his arms. "Honey, if I could take it from you, I would," he said. "It breaks my heart to see you like this." We stood together, rocking back and forth, holding each other as we cried, our hearts breaking more and more with each tear shed. I once again realized how much pain he was in. He was walking every step with me and feeling every ounce of pain and fear that I was. I loved him so much and told him so. "I will try harder to be strong," I promised through my tears. "We will be strong together," he replied as we held each other, shedding the tears we thought had all dried up by now.

We pulled on our sneakers and headed out for a walk. Walking always helped us clear our minds and made us feel a little better. We held hands and talked about our day, shared some laughs, and stole some kisses. We both knew we had just made it over another difficult hump, and I was once again so grateful to have such a wonderful, understanding partner to help guide me through these murky, scary waters of cancer.

When we returned home, there was a gift box on my bed along with a note from Kayla. The box contained a charm called "Open Your Heart," and her note simply said, *Know I'm ALWAYS behind you. Love, Kayla.* As I held the charm in my closed fist, I fell to my knees and cried.

The next morning found me with a renewed energy, a zest for life, a happiness I hadn't felt in a while. The rollercoaster of emotions was unlike anything I had ever felt in my life. One minute I could be scraping the bottom of the darkest hole of despair, and the next minute would find me laughing my head off and loving life. I knew the events of the past evening had taken a toll on us all, and I made a promise to myself that I would continue to crawl out of my depression and look forward to the future with courage and a positive attitude. I was once again grateful for my workplace and co-workers, in particular Bonnie, who had been with me every step of the way. Work continued to be my salvation, a place to go and keep my mind occupied and away from what was happening in my life. It was so easy to forget my troubles when I was busy with other things. Halfway through the day, Kayla dropped in to see me and brought me one beautiful long-stemmed rose, and she sat and talked with me for a little while, watching me to see how I was doing. I knew the events of last night had scared her, and she was relieved that I appeared to be doing much better. After a short visit, she kissed me good-bye and headed out to get on with her day.

Once she left, Bonnie sent me an e-mail. *You are very loved*, she said. I had shared with her what had happened the previous night, and she had also been watching me closely all day. *Yes, Bonnie, I am very blessed*, I replied. I smiled as I waded through the work on my desk for the rest of the afternoon, knowing that I had gotten through another challenge, knowing that it had made me a little stronger for the next one. I was smart enough to know that I would hit bottom many times again.

As the week unfolded, I found my mind at rest and laughter on my lips more than ever. It felt good to be alive, good to be loved, wonderful to begin appreciating all the beauty around me. I soaked up the words of encouragement from concerned family and friends, and I could feel myself believing their words. *I am strong, I am courageous, and I will get through this*, I repeated in my mind over and over, all the while wondering why I had doubted it in the beginning.

My boss Spencer sent me a note: *Our workplace always picks up whenever you are around. Your smile and laugh are infectious.*

A co-worker, Jackie, wrote, *I am so thankful I met you! You are such an amazing person, Kim!*

My dear friend Juanita sent me an e-mail after hearing about my mini breakdown and wrote, *Yes, my friend, we will get through it together ... Reaching out is always the hardest thing to do because it makes everything more real, but once you reach out you will wonder why you did not do it sooner ... Yes, tomorrow will be a better day ... We are all allowed down days, but thankfully there are more upbeat days than down ones ... Love ya, chick ...*

Then another from her read,

Reality sucks for you right now I am sure, but it is all temporary, my trout, and you will look back on this, and it will be a story ... a story of how and when you found out, surgery, treatment. It is all part of a journey that won't be pretty at times I am sure. For sure May 1 will be another reality, but it will give you answers and direction and help with some of the uncertainty. Every day I pray for you, and I know you will be okay, and on your darkest of days you will feel the love and support of family and friends.

And my mom sent an e-mail saying, *You are going to have to try your best to keep strong both mentally and physically before treatments start. I know, easy to say, but you will need all the strength you can get, as it will make things much easier. Just look at the number of people who have gone through it and are now back to work and have it all behind them. You can do it also.*

> *Don't anticipate trouble, or worry about what may never happen. Keep in the sunlight.*
> —Benjamin Franklin

Friday night, Mark and Simone hosted a get-together with our friends. It was kind of like a pretreatment party for me, and it was good to visit with everyone and share laughter. We had such a good time, and it was so good to blend in with everyone and enjoy the camaraderie that only close friends can have. As I visited, I could hear Cliff's laughter from across the room, and it felt good to hear him laugh out loud again. I watched him, and I was happy to see him relaxed and having a good time. I settled in and enjoyed myself as well. It turned out to be one of the best nights since this whole ordeal had begun for us, and we both managed to forget our troubles and have a good time. The one thing I kept thinking about all night was losing my hair.

I had been thinking about losing my hair since this all happened. Actually, I had been trying not to think about it, but it kept coming up. I had known if I required chemo, I would lose my hair. Bald. I was going to be bald! *How am I ever going to deal with that?* I wondered every time I thought about it. But I did know one thing and that was if I was going to lose my hair, I would do it on my terms and not wait for it to come out in clumps. I knew I was not strong enough to handle that.

My friend Jennifer's son, Zachery, had just joined a fund-raiser at his school to raise money for cancer research. The kids were going to shave their heads after receiving pledges. When I heard about it, I decided that if I was going to lose my hair, I might as well make some money for cancer research, and I decided I would join Zachery and his team. I talked to Jen that night about what I was thinking of doing, and she thought it would be a great idea. We held hands as we discussed it and shed a few tears, and I felt much better knowing that I would have some support when that day came.

My friends are such a wonderful bunch of people. Even though we all knew my appointment with the oncologist was looming and treatments were just around the corner, no one talked about it, and everyone let me be me for the night. I loved to blend in with everyone, and the night was about fun and love and catching up with everyone, sharing funny stores, and laughing until our sides hurt.

That night set the tone for the weekend, which was spent relaxing and doing yard work, just being a normal family. Simone dropped in on Sunday for a visit, and we had a good long chat, dug deep into our issues, and shed some tears as well as lots of laughs. Our laughter rang throughout my home. It felt good to have a one-on-one visit and not be distracted. Our friendship went deep. Having raised daughters who were the same age, we had often offered support to each other through the challenges and celebrated the good times as well. When I was dealing with Bell's palsy, she had brought me over a big vase filled with M&M's. The note accompanying them read, *Each M&M represents how many moments you have warmed our hearts by simply being you. There were about a thousand more that spilled over the top, so I had to eat them.* I still have the note and the vase; the M&M's are long gone. We shared a special bond, Simone and I, sometimes just knowing from a glance or one word what the other was feeling and always being there for each other without having to ask.

That weekend, I came to understand that we all faced challenges, but it was how we dealt with those challenges that made us who we are. I also started to understand what a person meant when he or she would say to me, "I could never be strong like you if it was me." It reminded me of something I had read about Christopher Reeve and his journey through his accident and resulting paralysis. He was quoted as saying, "Before a catastrophe, we can't imagine coping with the burdens that might confront us in a dire moment. Then when that moment arrives, we suddenly find that we have resources inside us that we knew nothing about." That was exactly where I was, and I was doing the best I could with the resources I had right then to deal with my cancer diagnosis.

I suddenly started to take pride in *me* and how I was getting through this. I suddenly knew I could do this. There would be days when I would be tired, sad, or mad, but that was okay. I knew those emotions were a normal part of the process. I had to grieve for what I had lost, but I also had to start celebrating what I had—a great life; a wonderful, loving husband; beautiful, healthy daughters; and a life full of friends and family who loved me unconditionally. I was going to be okay. I just knew I was going to be okay.

My appointment with the oncologist loomed, and I started to get my questions written down and prepare myself for the report. I knew I needed chemo and radiation, and I was prepared for that, but I just needed to hear the doctor say they had gotten it all and there was no need for more surgery.

The day of my appointment Cliff and I arrived at the hospital and parked. We had both gone to work in the morning to take our minds off what was happening that day, and as we sat in the parking lot, we kissed. Our stomachs rolled. We were both anxious and just wanted this appointment to be over, to get a treatment plan set, and to get started on my road to a healthy life once again. We held hands as we walked toward the hospital, both of us lost in our own thoughts and preparing mentally for what was about to happen. As we walked under the sign that said *Cancer Clinic*, it all seemed so surreal to me. How many times had I walked past that wing of the hospital and read that sign? Now we were walking down the corridor. I could feel my phone vibrating in my purse from the texts coming in, all my friends and family offering their support to us, knowing what an important day this was, and hoping for the best.

Tammy texted, *You are beautiful. You are amazing. You are loved. xo*

We were shown into a treatment room, and we sat side by side, holding hands, not speaking, but drawing strength from each other. The doctor came in, and the first thing I noticed was his eyes. Such beautiful big brown eyes, kind eyes, and I wondered if he would give me good news or bad news. I prayed for good news as I stared at him. He thumbed through my file before he looked up at me.

The news was good. He said the surgery was my cure. The surgery was my cure! Both Cliff and I let out a big sigh but braced ourselves because we knew there was more coming. The chemotherapy was required as added insurance because there had been cancer found in the lymph node. Because cancer was present in the lymph node, the standard procedure was to administer chemotherapy, which would attack any cancer cells that might have escaped into other parts of my body through the lymph node. This would then be followed by radiation, which would kill any cancer cells that may have been missed around the lymph node and breast during surgery. He kept reassuring us that this was standard procedure and that he was very confident in my prognosis.

As we talked about the chemotherapy, the doctor went over the side effects and told me that I would lose my hair. While I had tried to prepare myself for that, to hear it out loud made me sad, and I felt tears run down my cheeks. I looked at Cliff. He squeezed my hand and said, "It doesn't matter, honey." But we both knew it did. Even now, long after the hair has grown back, I can still remember how I felt that day. How lost I felt. I can still hear my heartbeat pounding behind my eardrums, and I can still feel the panic that rose in my throat.

My husband was once again trying to stay strong for me as I watched the color in his face fade to grey. He was watching me to see how I was going to react, and I knew he was willing me not to fall apart. His hand tightly held mine, never letting go. I reached down into the bottom of my soul, pulled up as much strength as I could, pulled my shoulders back, and tried to swallow the lump that had formed once again in my throat. "The surgery was your cure," he had said, and I kept repeating that in my mind as the panic threatened to take over again. I tried to get a grip on my emotions. *The surgery was your cure. The surgery was your cure*, I keep repeating in my mind. *The surgery was your cure.*

Chemotherapy was scheduled to start on May 14, exactly two months from the day I had found out I had breast cancer. It is amazing how your life can change in two short months. I learned that day why it is so important to make sure you have someone with you for all those meetings. So much information is thrown your way. It is all overwhelming, and when there are at least two people present, you have a better chance of remembering most of what is said.

Cliff and I headed out to the car and once again regrouped. We compared notes and were both relieved that we finally had a game plan. Chemotherapy was to start in two weeks, followed by radiation, and as we counted the months, we realized it would be all over by Christmas. Christmas! We could start off the new year fresh and hopefully have this all behind us by then. I looked forward to the day this was all over, but I also knew there was no escaping what had to be done in the meantime. There was no changing our reality now, so we just had to face it with as much grace and courage as we could.

We can do this, I thought. *I can do this. I know I can.*

As Cliff drove me back to work, I responded to all the texts that had come in and sent out a mass text to let everyone know what was happening and that I would follow it up with e-mails and phone calls later. As I walked through my office doors, I was once again thankful to have somewhere to go and lose myself for a few hours each day. I gave the report to anyone who asked but busied myself with my work. For right then, I was like everyone else and had a job to do. I knew I only had a few days left to get my work space in order, so I busied myself with that and tried to forget about oncologist reports, chemotherapy, blood counts, radiation, and everything else that made me different.

Then it suddenly hit me full force. I was going to lose my hair! We had both heard the doctor tell me that, I had even cried in his office, but suddenly it hit me that this was real and was going to happen. I knew I needed to get a game plan together. I could not sit back and wait for it to start falling out. The doctor told me that sometime in the second week after my first treatment it would start to fall out. I had known this already because I had read so much about it in other women's testimonies of how they dealt with it. I knew it would be hard, but I also knew it could be easier if I dealt with it in the right way. And for me that was to take control of when it happened.

How did I go from a full head of thick hair to being bald? How would I get the courage up to bring a razor to my head and intentionally shave off my hair without losing my mind? Where was this strength going to come from, I wondered repeatedly. Could I pull off being bald? I knew I didn't have any choice, and again I found myself pulling my hair back every time I stood in front of the mirror and trying to imagine what I would look like with no hair. Every time I did it made me feel sad.

Now that we had a plan of treatment, we were also required to attend a chemo information session at the cancer clinic, which was something everyone undergoing chemo had to attend before treatments could start. As we walked into the room the next morning, I quickly scanned the faces of the people who were there, and it registered that we were the youngest. I quickly dropped my eyes as I made my way to one of the empty seats, not wanting to meet anyone's gaze. We settled in at the back of the room, and I opened my bag and pulled out my notebook to take notes as Cliff took the seat beside me. I could hear him moving around, trying to get comfortable.

The nurse gave us all the information we needed to know about the chemo, expected side effects, and how to deal with them. Some of it sounded pretty frightening, and some of it did not. I kept my eyes glued to the projector screen or my notebook, and I found my mind wandering, wondering how we had ended up in this small room with four other couples, all dealing with cancer. We should both be back at our offices, busy with everyday things, calling each other, and making plans for dinner, not taking notes on side effects of chemotherapy and which over-the-counter medicines were best for constipation. How had this happened? Cliff and I were the first out of the room when the session wrapped up, so happy to get back outside and into the fresh air.

Angels can fly because they take themselves lightly.
—G.K. Chesterton

That evening, Kelsey and Kayla wanted to go for supper with me. It was a great evening. We ordered breakfast for supper and got to catch up on all that was happening in each other's lives.

After supper, we decided to stop by the ball field where Cliff was playing softball with our friends. The rec league was having their first game, and I was still feeling the sting about not being able to play. As we headed toward the ball field, I told the girls I would rather just go home because it was too cold to go and watch, but they insisted that we go, even just for a while.

We pulled up our chairs, huddled under blankets, watched the game, and cheered on the team. It felt good to be part of the cheering section, but the competitive part of me wanted so badly to be out on the field, jumping up and down and heckling the other team. That was where I was supposed to be, not huddled up in a chair on the sidelines with a blanket pulled up over me! I watched my friends with envy, wishing so badly to be like them again.

As we watched the game, my girlfriends' daughters all came to stand in front of me. Madison, Mackenzie, Lauren, Jordan, Cassidy, and Shelby stood in a line and said they had something for me. I thought they were going to do a skit or something silly they had made up. The next thing I knew, they pulled off their coats, and they all had on personalized T-shirts they had made in support of me. Each one had something different written on her shirt.

I was overwhelmed, shocked, touched, and blessed. I felt it all, amazed that these children would do that for me. It was unbelievable. I asked them to take a picture of each of them so that I would always remember what they had written. I was not sure when it would register with each of them what that meant to me but I knew I had just witnessed a moment that I would carry with me for the rest of my life. It was a very powerful moment for me.

Mackenzie's shirt read, *Kim R. is my star. I love you. Hope.*

Cassidy's shirt read, *Kim Rideout, I will walk with you. Stand strong. Hope.*

Madison's shirt read, *I have hope for Kim.*

Jordan's shirt read, *Hope. Kim R. gives me hope.*

Lauren's shirt read, *Hope. Kim R. is my inspiration.*

Shelby's shirt read, *Kim R. is my hero.*

That night as I sat and reflected back on the evening, I kept seeing the word *hope*, a word that most of the girls had written in glitter on their T-shirts. Hope. What did hope mean to them, I wondered. Hope for a cure for cancer? Hope that I didn't die? And what did hope mean to me? The more I thought about it, the more I realized that the same questions applied to me: hope for a cure for cancer and hope I didn't die from it. I came to the conclusion that it didn't matter what the reason was for hope as long as there was hope.

I also decided that I would join the head shaving fund-raiser at Zac's school. It was time to make a commitment. I had the date for my first chemotherapy treatment, and I knew I had to decide on what to do about my hair by then. I could not imagine waking up each morning to find my hair on my pillow or to have it come out in clumps as I brushed it. I knew that would be too hard for me.

I talked with Cliff, and he was behind me 100 percent in whatever I wanted to do, so I decided to commit to the fund-raiser before I changed my mind. That night I joined the team online, noting that the fund-raising goal for the team was $5,000. After much internal debate, I decided to set my goal at $1,500.

I wrote and rewrote an e-mail until I finally got it right and hit the send button at 10:54 p.m. Now I was committed, and I knew there was no turning back.

Hello, everyone.

My chemo treatments start on May 14, and I have decided that while I don't have a lot of control over what happens to me over the next six months, I can control how and when I will lose my hair.

After lots of thought, I have decided to join my friend's son, Zac, in his school's fund-raiser. The event is called Shave Your Head for Cancer and is taking place at his school, St. Francis, on May 28. If I am going to lose my hair, I might as well make some money for the Canadian Cancer Society while doing it! So I will join all these brave young children and shave my head with them.

I am asking you for your support in helping me reach my goal and perhaps turning what could be a solemn occasion into one of celebration.

Love, Me

P.S. Below is a picture of some very special beautiful young girls who surprised me tonight with their show of support. How very blessed I am!

After I sent the e-mail, I sat back in my chair and pulled my sweater tightly around me, wondering, *What in the name of God have I done?* But I knew it was the right thing for me, and I just hoped I would meet my goal and my friends and family would support me in my decision to shave my head in a public forum. I wanted to show people it wasn't something to be ashamed or scared of and that we as cancer patients could take some control and not be at the mercy of the disease. And I wanted to take control. I was scared, but I was not going to let that control or rule my life. I was ready to take back my life. As I crawled into bed, I once again wondered what I had just done, but I knew in my heart it was the right thing for me. I curled into Cliff's back and let sleep take over.

As the following day progressed, I was obsessed with watching the ticker on my pledge page go up. At lunch I had almost $1,500, so I increased my goal to $2,000. At suppertime, that goal was reached, so I increased it to $2,500. The support was overwhelming (how many times would I use that word?), and I could not believe how generous people were. There were pledges coming in from friends of friends, people I didn't even know, and it was an amazing feeling for me. The e-mails coming into my in-box were building up as well, and I tried to keep up with answering them all. I needed to let them all know just how much their concern meant to me and how it lifted me up.

I updated my donation page with the following blurb in order to give people a little glimpse of my story:

On March 14, 2012, I received the news that I had breast cancer. So many questions ran through my mind … How could that happen? How was I the one in nine women who got breast cancer? Was I going to die? The initial reaction was disbelief, and it took me to my knees. It devastated me, my family, and my friends. Those four little words, "You have breast cancer," changed my life as I knew it forever. But I still have lots of life to live, and live it I will. In six weeks, I have had surgery, been assigned an oncology team, and have gotten use to the label of "cancer patient." In less than two weeks, I will begin six months of chemotherapy and radiation. Like so many who have taken this journey before me, I will survive, and I will replace that label of "cancer patient" with "cancer survivor," and I will do it with courage, faith, and hope. Please join me in my efforts to support research so that maybe one day our daughters or granddaughters will not have to deal with this horrible disease.

The following day, I was scheduled for a routine colonoscopy. Four years ago I'd had this test done, and I had a polyp removed, and as a result I had to have it done again. *Nothing like adding insult to injury,* I kept thinking as I struggled to drink the presolution and spent most of my evening in the bathroom, assaulted by cramps. On the morning of my test, I woke up mad. I was so mad I had to have this done, and I was just mad at the world. I was uncomfortable, I was tired, I was cranky, and I was just plain mad.

With Cliff once again at my side, we set off for the hospital before the sun came up and made our way to the proper department to be assessed and prepared. I didn't talk to Cliff all the way and shook off his attempts to hold my hand as we walked across the parking lot in the crisp cool morning air, the snow crunching under our feet. I could tell he was struggling with my attitude that morning, and I wanted desperately to stop, but I couldn't. I was mad and bitter. As my name was called, I stood up to leave the waiting room, and Cliff jumped up, grabbed my arm, and pulled me into his embrace. "Please don't take it out on me," he whispered in my ear as he hugged me tightly. Then he let me go and sat back down. Once I was settled inside the room, I asked the nurse if Cliff could come in, and when he came into the room, we hugged and cried together. He was hurting so much, and I was hurting so much. How had we gotten here, we both wondered.

After I woke from the colonoscopy, I was advised by the nurses that the procedure had not gone well. While under the sedation, I fought the doctor, and he was unsuccessful in completing the procedure. I was advised that this was normal when someone was dealing with a stressful event like I was and that I was going to have to return once my treatments were over to have the test completed again. If I thought I was mad when I woke up that morning, I was really mad after hearing that. All the discomfort I had gone through in the past twenty-four hours had been for nothing, I kept thinking. I crawled into bed when I got home and slept, hoping that once I woke up I would be in a better place again.

I spent that evening replying to my e-mails once again and letting the love and support from the words I read lift me up. Each message brought a smile to my face and helped lift that black cloud just a little farther from my face.

My co-worker Lea wrote to me and said, *I admire your spirit and your very positive attitude, and I know this will help you to get through these tough times!*

My friend Alana wrote, *I love you, Kim, and I am praying for you! You're the greatest image of joy that I have ever known, my friend, and the laughter you share with this world can beat anything! xoxoxoxoxox*

Laura and Mike wrote, *Hair is such an overrated aspect of our identities … Like the saying goes, it's what's on the inside, not the outside, that counts. Needless to say, you have nothing to worry about. Do you realize how many* times you make people smile and/or laugh because of just who you are and your perspectives?

And Leanne said, *Hey, Kim. You have such an awe-inspiring spirit, and you're going to look amazing with no hair! We have been and will continue to think about you going through so much to beat this! Lots of love to you and Cliff and your family.*

Gerald and Linette, co-workers of Cliff, wrote, *We hope that soon our friends and their families will not have to battle so hard just to live a happy life. Live strong, Kim.*

Every single e-mail I received I printed off and saved in a binder. I absorbed every single word into my being and drew strength to keep moving and stay positive. I wanted to truly feel like that positive, strong, amazing person everyone thought I was. I wanted to be that person and not feel like I was fooling anyone by pretending to be stronger than I was. What a daily struggle that proved to be.

The support came in many different forms over those days. A former boss of mine, who continues to be a dear friend, sent me an e-mail to say that her firm was sponsoring a diva table donation at a local breast cancer golf tournament in my name. Amazing.

Saturday arrived all sunny and with a spring warmth in the air. This was the day I had scheduled to go pick out my wig. A few friends offered to come along with me, but I felt I needed to do this on my own. Cliff was nervous for me and watched me closely all morning as I prepared to go. I honestly had no idea how I would feel once I arrived, but everything I had read indicated that I should complete this step before I lost my hair.

I arrived at the location and entered the front door. The wig shop was set up in a private residence, and as the owner welcomed me, I felt my heart pounding in my chest and the blood rushing behind my ears. As she guided me into her room full of wigs, I was overcome with anxiety, and tears flooded my eyes as I looked around at all the mannequin heads covered in fake and human hair, truly not believing that I was going to have to wear one of these in the upcoming months. *Oh my God,* I kept repeating in my head. *Is this really happening?* I tried to collect myself before I fell apart completely, knowing that if I did, I would not have the strength to get myself together again.

I got settled into the chair facing a mirror and watched as she pulled my hair back into a head cap to prepare me for the fittings. All I could see behind me in the mirror were the shelves and shelves of mannequin heads, each topped with a wig, their vacant eyes staring back at me. Surreal, unreal, unbelievable. As she placed each wig on my head, I could not help but feel like I had a dead cat on my scalp. It felt so unnatural to me, and I could not believe there was anyone who would not know it was a wig.

We tried on wig after wig after wig. Nothing looked right, nothing felt right, and I was getting more and more discouraged as the minutes ticked by. Just as I was getting ready to give up and call it a day, my cell phone rang, and I was relieved to hear my friend Tracy's voice on the other end. She was nearby and wanted to drop in to offer moral support. I quickly gave her the address, and within minutes she arrived and lifted my mood. She managed to extract some smiles from me in the middle of that creepy room and even tried on a few wigs herself.

Within an hour, we decided on two wigs, one very much like my own hair and another one Tracy felt would be fun—a long blond wig I knew even then I would never wear. With my purchases packed up into a neat little box, we left to return home, and I was so thankful for my friend and her presence with me that day.

When I arrived home, Kayla came into my room and asked me to try on the wigs for her. I could not get them on properly and became very frustrated; it looked unnatural and felt uncomfortable. Cliff opened the door to our bedroom, and I quickly pulled the wig off, not wanting him to see me in it, and I saw a look of pain cross Kayla's face as she watched me. This all hurt so much. Cliff sat on the bed, and I fell into his arms, weeping as he held me tightly and told me it would be all okay, it was only for a short time, and my hair would grow back. When I left the room, he took everything and threw it in the closet, thinking that hiding it from me would help, but we both knew what was behind the door, and it made us all so very sad.

Thank God once again for my angel friends who gathered around me that night. Linda, Tracy, and Tammy arrived after supper and all crawled onto my bed, and we visited, shared some laughs, and oohed and aahed over my wigs, helping to lighten the load a little. I still could not imagine ever wearing either of them, but it helped to get the approval of my friends and to once again know that they would accept me with or without hair, wig or wigless.

I spent the rest of my weekend getting ready for my final week at work until after my treatments were over. I knew it was going to be an emotional week for me, and that did not help my mood swings at all. There was so much building up in my mind—upcoming treatments, losing my hair, finishing up work—it was all very overwhelming and heartbreaking. As much as I tried not to, I found myself retreating more and more into myself, hiding away from my family and friends, trying to make some sense out of what was happening in my life. I knew I needed to get back to a good place and that it was the only way I was going to fight this, but it was so hard to do when I felt I was on the edge of a mountaintop, ready to fall.

Monday arrived, and I immersed myself at work, wrapping everything up as best I could and preparing my desk for the person they had hired to fill in for me while I was gone. I worried that they were going to like her more than me and that she would do a better job than I did. So silly and trivial in light of all that was going on in my life, but there was no rational to my thought process at the time.

Guilt was my feeling for the day as well. Kayla texted me and asked if I wanted her to stay at Kelsey's for a few days. She felt that she was annoying me, picking up on my sour mood from the day before. I felt guilty as I tried to reassure her that it was not her but me and begged her not to leave. I promised her I would try harder to be positive while at the same time quietly wishing she understood better what I was going through. But I knew she was living her own hell as well. We all were. It was an emotional rollercoaster.

I also felt guilty about pulling back from some of my friends, but I was tired of going over and over the same issues. I knew everyone was concerned and acting out of love, everyone wanting to let me know I was in his or her thoughts and prayers. I sat down and composed some e-mails to close friends, begging for their understanding and asking them to be patient with me. I needed their support so much but was unable to deal with them in person. It was hard to put on a happy face.

Cliff and I went for a nice long walk, and I vented the whole way while he held my hand and said very little, just letting me ramble on and on. I talked about how happy I was that Pearl had just completed her last chemotherapy session that day, and while she was very happy that stage was over, she was now dealing with other side effects that were scary to hear. "I hate this disease," I kept saying. "I hate this disease."

The following day was rough—my last official day at work. I fought back tears all day as I went about my work and interacted with my co-workers, who were so kind to me. I went to my boss's office, and we chatted, and he reassured me that my job would be waiting for me when I was ready and healthy enough to return. We ordered in lunch, and everyone sat in the boardroom to eat and visit during the noon hour. As I looked around the table and listened to the conversations, I knew how much I would miss this part of my daily life. Since taking the job a little over a year before, I had always found myself jumping out of bed, ready to get to the office and interact with everyone and our customers. It was the kind of office environment I had waited my whole life for, filled with fun, laughter, and a culture I had never seen before, and I loved it. Before I left I was already missing it and the people I worked with. Again I felt cheated, forced to leave, and it was beyond my control. As I packed up my desk and put my personal items in a box, I fought back tears and kept saying to myself, "It is only for a short time."

Cliff was in a funk that evening, and some days I wondered if I was talking to him too much. What a cross he was carrying, trying to stay strong when I knew he was wrestling with his own demons as well. He had to stay positive for me and be there to lift me up when I got down. How hard that must have been for him. I knew he was dreading my first chemo treatment as much as I was, but he couldn't say that for fear of making me more afraid. I caught him staring off sometimes, and I wanted to ask him what was on his mind, but I didn't because I was afraid of the answer.

Cancer affects so many areas of a person's life. Here I was, just two short months after receiving my diagnosis, and already I'd had to walk away from my job, losing that independence, and it had sent a tidal wave of fear, pain, and uncertainty into my home life. I was facing the reality that I would lose my hair soon, and I was not sure how sick I was going to be with the treatments, how my body was going to react, how I was going to look, if I was going to be strong enough. So many questions and I didn't have any answers. I was scared.

I checked the website, and my fund-raiser had now topped $4,000. I was excited to see the number, again very humbled by the support people were giving me, but as the number crept up, so did my anxiety. There was no backing down now. I was committed like never before. I also started to worry that my hair would start falling out before the day of the shave. What would I do then? I knew everyone would understand, and I knew it was silly to even worry about that happening. *It is what it is!* Then I laughed at the irony of even having the thought!

I kept myself busy by packing up to go to the staff retreat I was attending the next day. I was excited to have a change of scenery and also excited to leave my family in peace for a few days without having to dance around me and my moods. I knew it would do us all good for me to be gone for a little while.

We arrived at the lodge in the foothills of the Rockies around noon, and as I pulled up the winding road and admired the breathtaking view, I couldn't help but remember last year's retreat and how healthy I had been then. The next two days proved to be a ton of fun, and I took part in all the activities and found myself forgetting my worries for a short time. My co-worker Linda and I curled up in her room that first evening, and she read my tarot cards. While I never thought I was a believer, after that session, which left us both in tears, I now think I am. So many of the messages on the cards directly paralleled the challenges I was facing, and we were both left feeling a little stunned after it was over. The message of one of the tarot cards—"To gain maximum power, take responsibility for everything that happens in your universe by reclaiming power"—spoke directly to me. It gave me hope, hope that I would be strong enough to set out on the next step of my journey through breast cancer.

The days were filled with fun and laughter, and the evening was full of games and visiting with everyone, trying to say good-bye to all who worked in the other offices and who I knew probably wouldn't see again for some time. Bonnie and I shared a room and stayed up late into the evening, chatting about everything and nothing. It was a bittersweet time for me and a much needed distraction. Everyone was full of support and encouragement and kindness as I prepared to leave a day early in order to get home and get everything done before Monday. As I made my way back home, I received a text from both Bonnie and my boss Spencer wishing me well and bidding me a safe drive home. I was sad to be leaving them in my rearview mirror.

As Monday approached, I filled up my time as much as I could so I didn't have to think about it. I had lunch with Linda and Simone, and we visited and laughed, sharing stories over a drink. Lana came over in the evening to visit, and I spent the evening holding my sides, laughing at her stories about her recent trip to Australia.

That's the thing about my friends, something I had always admired and will always admire—their ability to laugh and make someone laugh. To me that is so important and something that filled my days, both before and after my diagnosis—laughter! I have always been one to say that it is easier to laugh than to frown and that if you greet someone with a smile, you will get one back, but if you greet someone with a frown, they will most likely frown back. How good it is to laugh. How good it makes you feel. I could have listened to Lana tell her stories for hours, and she never disappointed and left me with tears running down my face in laughter.

From day one of hearing that I had breast cancer, even through the difficult moments, my friends and I laughed. While I cried rivers of tears in fear and apprehension, when I was with my friends, we laughed. Sure, we talked about my fears and their fears as well, but laughter was always part of our conversations. We could always make jokes about it, and while the tears were cleansing, the laughter was healing.

I also took the time during that weekend to try to organize my thoughts about the upcoming treatments and how I felt about them. While I was scared about what was to happen, I was also relieved in a way that I had to undergo these treatments. In my mind, it was added security that if there were any cancer cells left floating around in my body, the chemotherapy would find and destroy them before they had time to do any more damage. I was scared, I was terrified, but I was also relieved.

One of my biggest fears was that it would make me really sick, and I wondered if I had the strength, both mentally and physically, to get through the process. Again, I questioned if I was really as strong as everyone said I was. Was that just the persona I put out there and really, deep inside, I was weak? I was afraid that I would disappoint everyone if I wasn't able to handle the poison they were going to pump into my body.

The Internet is a wonderful tool to have if you use it right. What I learned was never Google in general. If you Google breast cancer, you will get more than three hundred million results. Three hundred million! And not every site will give you the information you need, or even want, to read. In the early days, some of the sites I visited just scared me, and some of the chat rooms were downright depressing. I learned the hard way to only visit sites that were recommended by the cancer clinic and to stay away from the others. When I visited the recommended sites, I got useful, clinical information that I could use to educate myself on what was happening. I also joined an online support group for women who were going through the same things. And I came to realize that just because some of those women experienced the most horrific side effects of chemo, were burned badly during radiation, lost their hair and it never came back, or had their husbands leave them, that didn't mean I was going to experience all those things, or even any of them. Each situation was individual, and while thousands have walked this road before, my journey was going to be mine and mine alone. I used the information I read to be informed and to educate myself, but I also knew that every person was different and not to own someone else's experiences as my own.

During the final weekend before my chemotherapy started, we attended a breast cancer fund-raiser called Perky in Pink. We had attended this function for several years in a row, and as I walked through the doors that evening I thought how different it was from years before when I had attended merely to support the cause. Little did I know then that I would be attending in 2012 as a breast cancer patient myself, someone who would benefit from the fund-raising performed that night. Everywhere I looked, I saw pink. There were pink shirts, pink hats, and pink tablecloths.

I was in awe of the organizers and all they did to fund-raise to help people like me.

We had a table of ten, and I spent the evening with my friends, having a great time and forgetting about the upcoming week. I was the designated driver for the evening, and everyone took advantage of the opportunity to share the rum and Jell-O shooters that were so plentiful at our table. At one point, I looked around and saw everyone laughing and having a great time, cracking lobster shells and cutting into steaks. I envied their freedom. I envied their health. I wanted to be one of them again, but I also knew, as I had realized countless times in the past two months, that I was forever changed. At that point I sent a little prayer to God, praying that next year I would be healthy and able to come back to this event as a survivor, once again healthy and strong.

As we laughed and danced the night away, it was easy to forget my reality. I left the dance floor and returned to the table after midnight to check my cell phone to see if I had any messages, and a reminder popped up on my phone: *First treatment on Monday.* Like I needed a reminder! Reality smacked me in the face once again. I turned my phone toward Linda so she could read it, and she took me in her arms for a hug.

"Put your gloves on," she said over the music. "It's time to fight."

May 13 was Mother's Day, the day before chemo started. I had been a mom for more than twenty-one years. I thanked God that morning for giving me the last twenty-one years, and I begged for more. I even bargained with an age I thought in my own mind was acceptable to live to, and I picked seventy-five! Seventy-five seemed like a nice round number, and I wondered if that was too much to ask. I knew that by today's standards seventy-five wasn't old, but it would give me thirty more years. Thirty! That sounded like a lifetime to me.

I wanted to be around for my girls, wanted to see them married, and wanted to hold my grandchildren in my arms. I was even greedy enough to want to see my grandchildren married. I could not let my mind go to the place where Kelsey and Kayla were having life experiences and I wasn't there. I wanted to be there for everything, and I knew they needed me. Even though they were getting older, I knew they needed me for so much and would need me even more as they got older. Thinking of them walking down the aisle and me not being there and thinking of them holding their children and wishing I was there broke my heart. I tried not to allow myself to have those thoughts. I hoped God was in a bargaining mood, because I sure was. I kept thinking of the old saying, "Heaven helps those who can't help themselves," and I was hoping that heaven would help me because I didn't think I could help myself at that moment.

As our daughters cooked and served brunch to Cliff and me in the gazebo that day, I realized how lucky and blessed I was. We sat and ate, laughing and visiting. My own little family under the gazebo on that beautiful sunny day, and I let the love engulf me. I have always been so proud of my family and the love we have for each other, and I was just as proud on that Mother's Day.

The day was filled with visitors. Mark, Simone, and Tammy came for coffee in the morning and wished me luck for tomorrow, and Angela and her daughters came by in the afternoon to bring me a beautiful candle that said, *Miracles happen to those who believe.* I was touched by everyone's love and concern, and I knew that Cliff and I would be riding on that love in the upcoming months.

> *First principle: never to let one's self be beaten down by persons or by events.*
> ——Marie Curie

My family - Thanksgiving 2011
5 months before my diagnosis

My little Relay for Life Angels - Jordan, Cassidy,
Mackenzie, Shelby, Lauren and Madison.

With my girlfriends the night my hair started to fall out.
Juanita, Tammy, Angela, Me, Linda and Angela.

Showing their mama some love.

Zac and I after shaving our heads

Krista and I

Out to celebrate after shaving my hair at the school. Juanita, Me and Tracy

My brother-in-law, Dyrick, and sister-in-law,
Peggy, with Cliff during their visit

July, 2012 – Marking the ½ way mark of my
treatments. Photograph by www.tracykuhl.com

Simone and I during our last camp out before
my final chemotherapy treatment

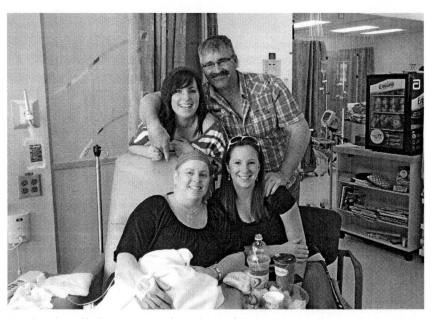

My family pulled tight for my last chemotherapy treatment. September 2012

My family at the CIBC Run for the Cure

Farm Credit Canada's CIBC Run for the Cure team - Kim's Breast Friends

CIBC Run for the Cure team - Kim's Udder Breast Friends

My poker club girls

My family on the 1st anniversay of my breast cancer
diagnosis. We made it!! March 2013

Chapter 5

One Down, Five to Go

Monday came just like any other Monday, only it was so different for me. This was the Monday I started my chemotherapy, exactly two months to the day I had first found out I had breast cancer. Two months from the day my life changed forever. As I opened my eyes that morning, I still could not believe this was real; I could not believe this was happening. My appointment was at 11:30, so I busied myself, took a bath, and checked my e-mail in-box. It was full of good wishes, prayers, and positive energy being sent my way. I wondered why none of that made me feel any lighter that morning, but I was full of anxiety and nervousness, having no idea what was in store for me.

I dressed in comfortable, loose clothes and placed the locket on my neck that Tammy had given me weeks ago. It contained pictures of Cliff, Kelsey, and Kayla. I vowed to wear the locket for every treatment and then put it away, never to wear it again, and that was exactly what happened.

When I opened the front door to leave for the hospital, on the step were two packages.

The first package I opened was from my friend Juanita in Newfoundland. It contained an opaque quartz bloodstone. The gemstone lore behind it was to offer vital life and to stimulate courage. She also sent me a long handwritten letter saying that she wanted to be with me for all my treatments and because she couldn't I now had the stone to hold, representing her. She wrote, *Be strong today, but it is okay to be scared and nervous. Remember, you are part of a team, a team that is rooting and praying for you every day. Hold tight to the stone, and I hope you will feel my love and courage being passed on to you.* As with the locket, that stone was with me for every treatment.

The second package was from a co-worker, Dana, and it contained a beautiful quilt made by the wonderful women at the organization Victoria's Quilts Canada. They make quilts for women going through cancer with the hopes that the quilts will keep them warm through the trials of chemo. The inscription sewn into the quilt said,

> *Be strong and of good courage, do not be Afraid, nor*
> *dismayed, for the Lord your God is with you wherever you go.*
> —Joshua 1:9

That quilt offered me much warmth and comfort over the upcoming months—yet another demonstration of the kindness of others in a time of need.

As we drove to the hospital, Cliff reached for my hand, and I wondered who was sweating more, me or him. We held hands tightly and did not speak, both of us lost in our thoughts. I glanced over at him, and he was pale, his jaw tight. He looked scared, but I knew he was trying to be brave for me and was giving me as much strength as he could muster. As he got our parking pass, I sat in the Jeep and took a few deep breaths, trying to calm my nerves and slow my heart, which was beating so hard that I could feel the blood pulsing through my neck. Five dollars for parking. Nothing is free.

We approached the reception area, and the secretary looked up and smiled her greeting. She said, "What are we doing for you today?"

"I am here for my chemotherapy treatment," I whispered. *Really? Did I really just say that?* I thought. We were shown into the treatment room, and my knees almost gave out from under me. This was my first time seeing this room, and I was overwhelmed. The nurse told me I had my choice of a bed or a recliner and could sit or lay down wherever I chose. We walked toward a recliner that faced a window, but the view was obstructed by a big blue construction dumpster on the outside. Not much to look at, I thought, but better than looking at a wall, and at least the sun was shining in.

As I settled into the chair, Cliff pulled up a chair close to me and held my hand. I was scared. No, I was terrified. I wanted to jump up and run away. I wanted to crawl into Cliff's arms and have him tell me this was just a dream. I wanted to be anywhere but where I was. As the nurse rolled her stool in close, she explained that she would start an IV and flush my veins with saline before the chemo was started. When she reached for my arm, I wanted to cry and pull back. I fought the tears and looked at Cliff, watching him watch the nurse. The saline was started, and the nurse told me she would be back in a few minutes to start the treatment. I tried hard not to blink, knowing the tears were trapped until I did.

Kayla arrived and took a seat next to the window. She watched my face, glanced at her dad, and then looked back at me. I knew I had to stay strong for her. She didn't need to see her mom come apart, because that would only make her even more scared than she already was. She looked so young, so healthy, and so sad. I wanted to hug her and tell her it would be okay. I wanted her to leave so she would not have to see this happening. I wanted to make it all better for her. I didn't want any of this to be happening. Tammy arrived and sat next to Kayla and started to talk to her, trying to distract her. We tried to make small talk while I tried to slow my heart rate by taking deep breaths.

I saw the curtain move, and another nurse entered and took a seat on the stool. She had a syringe in her hand and told me this was the first of three medications she would be administering into my IV. She explained what it was, what it would do, and possible side effects I could have from it. I knew she was talking, but I had a hard time hearing her over the freight train that was running behind my ears.

I looked at Cliff and started to cry. I put my head on his chest. I knew I was frightening Kayla, but I had no power to control my emotions. It felt like my insides were going to shake out of my body. It is true what they say: you are scared of the unknown, and I had no idea what was going to happen. When I looked up, Linda had arrived. Both she and Tammy were comforting Kayla, who had also started to cry. Cliff was focused on me.

My nurse, so compassionate and kind, took her time and finally convinced me to take an Ativan to help with my anxiety. I had resisted all medication up to this point but finally conceded that there was no way

I could do this without some help. I placed that little white pill under my tongue, and within minutes I felt a calmness settle over me that I had not felt for months.

Once I was settled, I was given my antinausea medications and the first round of chemo was administered. I watched the nurse's face as she slowly pushed the chemo through the IV, and I wondered how many times she had done it in the past. With one hand I held hers, and with the other hand I held Cliff's. I closed my eyes and tried to picture this liquid going through my bloodstream and attacking any cancer cells that were there, destroying them. I could feel the pressure of the IV on my wrist and thought it was strange that I could not feel the liquid entering my body. Something that strong I should feel, I thought. I waited to get sick. I waited to feel lightheaded or for that possible reaction to start, but I felt nothing. My body was tight, my neck and back hurt from being so tense, and my neck was wet from sweat. Finally she announced she was done, pushed away from me, and said she would be back in moment. Cliff pulled his chair closer to mine, and we leaned into each other, touched our foreheads together, and closed our eyes to the world around us. And I cried.

When the nurse returned to administer the second injection, I had relaxed quite a bit and was by then joking with my company, and we shared a few laughs. It was good to see Kayla smiling, and Cliff looked much more relaxed than minutes before. The second injection consisted of two big red vials of chemo (I have heard it described as Red Devil) and was told that it would take about twenty minutes to administer. As she pushed these through my IV, we chatted and relaxed in the moment. It was so good to have the company, as the time when by so much faster, and it was a wonderful distraction from what was happening to me at the moment. The nurse told me this drug would turn my urine red immediately so that I would not be alarmed when I went to the washroom. A short time later when I rolled my IV pole into the washroom, I was glad she had warned me beforehand.

The third injection consisted of a small IV bag that was connected to my IV and administered by the pump. We were told this would take about twenty minutes, and once I was all set up, Linda, Tammy, and Kayla prepared to leave. We all knew the worst was over, and I was getting pretty tired and finding it hard to keep up with the conversation. Hugs were exchanged, and they all left to go about their days. As I watched their reflections leaving in the window, I longed to be able to walk with them and to be as healthy as they all were. I was thankful that they had been with us, and I felt warm in their love.

Before we knew it, I was done. We were given the prescription for the antinausea medications, instructions on how to take it, and what to expect over the next couple of days, and then they told us we were free to go. I felt surprisingly well, just a little unsteady when I stood up. As we walked back through the doors of the treatment room, it almost felt anticlimactic to me, but I could not get out of there fast enough as I sang, "Thank you," over my shoulder. Back in three weeks, I thought. Three weeks to get healthy again. I was not tired when I got home, so I did some laundry and cleaned up and checked my e-mail, which was flooded with messages from friends and family checking in to see how I had faired through the first treatment.

Kayla came home and made up a bed on the couch for me, and I lay down and slept for a few hours. I woke up when Kelsey arrived for a visit. She hadn't been able to come to the hospital because she wasn't feeling well and had a cough, so I visited with her in the gazebo for fear I would catch what she had. I wanted so desperately to hug her and feel her warmth, but I knew it was too risky for me to catch any bug, so we kept our distance. After she left I could feel the tiredness creeping in, and I walked slowly up the stairs to get back into the house. I was starting to feel like I had the worst hangover in my life, and I was very tired, but already I was feeling thankful that I was not nauseated.

My fear of being nauseated was not unfounded. My only close experience with cancer up to this point in my life had been watching Cliff's mom, Jane, fight her own battle with cancer years ago. Her story had not ended the way we wanted it to, and we had lost her far too young.

We had watched her battle through chemotherapy, and at the time the antinausea drugs we had now were not available. We had watched her suffer through the rounds of chemotherapy and lose weight to the point she was a mere shadow of who she had been, unable to eat. We watched her melt away, unable to do anything but sit with her and try to make her comfortable. Again I was reminded of the lessons I had learned from her in those years that she fought so hard to live: to fight. To fight hard. She never gave up and always put her best out there for her children and grandchildren. She loved life and was a fighter; the cancer had just fought a stronger fight, and she was unable to hang on.

The Christmas before I was diagnosed, we had returned to Newfoundland to attend the wedding of Cliff's niece Jennifer. I had been asked to do a tribute to Jane at the wedding reception, and below is a portion of what I wrote. Through my words I tried to express the impact she had made on me. Little did I know that she was teaching me how I would fight my own battle against cancer years after she lost her battle.

A lot of people have stories about their horrible mother-in-laws. I do not. Bottom line is I loved her with all my heart and am a better person for having known her. She taught me the value of kindness, to be kind without expecting anything in return. She taught me to love with everything you have. She taught me that if you are going to give a hug, make it count. I always felt comfort in her embrace. Anyone who has been hugged by Cliff knows that he learned the same lesson.

My own experience with this wonderful woman was one of warmth, love, compassion, and understanding. She accepted me into the family like I was meant to be there, though begrudgingly at first I have to admit. After all, she knew my agenda was to marry Cliff, and to her that meant he was moving out! But I managed to wiggle my way into her heart, and she took over mine.

Family was her grounding. Her children and grandchildren were her life. Norman, Earl, Peggy, and Cliff and the families they created meant the world to her. She loved to be surrounded by family, friends, and laughter. She was happiest when her home was full, and she thrived on the chaos we created.

You can't remember Jane without remembering her cooking. She loved to cook, but more than that, she loved to feed us. Many times I watched her eat long after everyone else was almost done because she was so busy making sure we had enough on our plates. I believe she was not only feeding us food; she was feeding us with her love.

Some of my fondest memories of Jane are of watching her laugh. She had a laugh that, while not loud, came from the bottom of her belly. Her face crinkled up, she covered her mouth, and many times she darted to the bathroom to avoid an accident. I loved watching her laugh, and I loved to make her laugh.

Jane had a compassion that was rare. She believed that everyone was equal, didn't have a jealous bone in her body, and to this day is still one of the kindest, most beautiful women I have ever had the privilege to know and love. I can only hope to become half the woman she was. I miss her every day.

Nanny Jane called all her grandchildren her angels. Courtney and Mitchell, Jennifer and Christopher, Andrew and Bradley, Kelsey and Kayla—she loved each and every one of you to the very essence of her soul. Nothing made her prouder. When any of you came into the house, she would always say, "Here comes Nanny's angel." It didn't matter how many of her angels were already there … Here would come another angel.

Jennifer, if Nanny Jane was here, she would tell you that you were her favorite. Then when you weren't listening, she would say the exact same thing to each of your cousins. You were all her favorites. She loved each and every one of you the same—a deep, profound, fierce love from one of the greatest women I have ever had the privilege to know and love.

Each of you carry her legacy and live it every day—one of kindness and compassion, love of family, loyalty to friends, laughter and happiness, and a joy for life. I pray that you will continue to make her proud and carry her in your hearts for the rest of your lives. She deserves nothing less than that.

Having watched Jane struggle, I had always admired the resilience, grace, and strength she exhibited. As much as she suffered, she never complained, never demanded, and never looked for pity. She always wanted to talk about you and not about her. During her periods of remission from cancer, she lived each day as fully as she could, returning back to work and never talking about her cancer or her pain. That was how I wanted to make my journey, and I wanted people to talk about me in the same way I talked about her. I wanted to be as strong as she had been.

I fell asleep the first night of my treatment with thoughts of her on my mind and could feel her strength running through my body. It was a restless night, and I woke every hour or so, drinking lots of fluids to flush the chemo through my system like I had been instructed and curling into Cliff and drawing on his warmth when I did crawl back into bed. Each time I moved, he reached for me, sometimes still asleep, asking me in the darkness if I was okay and if I needed anything. I finally gave up on sleep around 5:00 a.m. and snuck out of the bedroom, closing the door softly behind me, hoping Cliff could grab a few hours of uninterrupted sleep before the sun came up. It took a few hours to go through my e-mails, and I tried to answer as many as I could before he got up. I finally decided that the best way to keep everyone informed was to do an update I could send to everyone. This was the first of six updates I sent out while going through chemotherapy.

Subject: One Down, Five to Go

Good morning, my friends:

I am one day closer to living a healthy life! Hands together please!

Just wanted to give you an update on how things are going. And to thank you all for the phone calls, e-mails, and text messages yesterday. Please forgive me for not answering most. It was a stressful day, but we felt all the love and support coming our way and are so thankful to have so many of your rooting for me.

Cliff, Kayla, and I arrived at the hospital at 11:00 and were shown into the treatment room, which is a huge room with a nurses' station in the middle, not much unlike the emergency room treatment area. (Kelsey was totally bummed. She had the day off but has a bad cold so was unable to come.) Our nurse, Taneal, came over to introduce herself to us and spent quite a bit of time explaining everything that was going to happen and the drugs that would be administered in my first "cocktail." Any romantic notions that I had of it being like a Captain Morgan cocktail were quickly squashed! The side effects of each were explained in detail, and the more that was said, the higher my anxiety level became. I would like to say I was a brave old soul; however, Tammy had arrived at that point to sit with us, so there are witnesses that I was not. I started to get quiet anxious, and the more I tried to suppress it, the more obvious it became. The nerve on the side of my neck started to throb harder than a card player holding a royal flush. It was bad. I was hooked up to the IV and administered a healthy dose of saline to flush out my veins.

Around this time, Linda arrived to visit and bring Cliff and Kayla a coffee. The staff in that ward are unbelievable. As each new arrival peeped around the curtain, she was told to come on in and pull up a chair. No questions asked.

Time came to administer the first drug of the three I would be getting, and I couldn't hold it together anymore. My nurse took her time talking to me, and finally I agreed to take an Ativan. Wow … That is a nice drug! I highly recommend it in stressful situations, or even when your kids are giving you a hard time. It takes the edge off for sure. I quickly settled down. There were lots of jokes about me becoming like Breezy and chewing the window blinds (an inside joke for those of you not familiar with Tammy's dog), and the treatment itself went off without a hitch from there on out. No reactions, no discomfort, no nothing.

We were given a nice long lesson in antinausea drugs as well as a prescription for four, two of which I will take daily and two which are an added insurance if I need them. One hundred and thirty-eight pills in total for five days (if required). I was given them before the treatment started at the hospital as well.

We arrived home, and I was feeling pretty good, so I did two loads of laundry while Cliff ran to the pharmacy and drugstore, armed with his list of things to get. I thought this would be my moment to get some stuff done while he wasn't hovering; however, while putting the clothes away, the floor started to come up to meet me, so I thought perhaps I might be overdoing it, and I made my way to the couch and decided to take it easy for the rest of the day. Kelsey came by for a quick visit, and I had to meet her in the gazebo. Because of her cough, the nurses recommended that she not come inside. When she left I could not believe how long it took me to make it back into the house. I felt like an old woman.

The side effects have not been as bad as they could be so far (knock on wood). I am quite swollen today from all the liquids administered yesterday by IV and all the water I am required to drink. I was told to drink about two liters a day for the next few days to flush the chemo drugs through my system as well as to get up throughout the night to pee so as not to let it sit in my bladder. That is all Cliff needed to hear. If I put the water bottle down at any point yesterday, he was picking it up and giving it back to me, telling me to drink. By the end of the day, I had drunk almost three liters. He also set his alarm to go off at two-hour intervals to wake me to go to the washroom.

I have not been sick (thank you, Lord); however, I felt like I was suffering the worst hangover I have ever had. My stomach was really off, and I had a headache that would not go away. Unpleasant especially when you didn't have any good, funny stories to tell about the night before that made you feel like it. But oh well!

We had a very restless night, and the alarm clock was not needed. We went to bed at 10:00, and then I was awake every hour or so. I tried not to get up much because every time I moved, Cliff woke up. I finally got up at 5:00 and told him to sleep. I hope he can get a few hours of uninterrupted sleep now. My husband is exhausted, and I love him so much.

This morning finds me feeling better than yesterday, although I have been warned that side effects could hit at any time up to seventy-two hours, so I am still a little scared. I still feel like I am suffering that dreaded hangover, and my headache lingers on, though I know that some of that is from lack of sleep. I have been managing to eat; bread is my choice of cuisine right now. My energy level is still in the basement, and already I am frustrated with that, and it has been less than twenty-four hours. I have to take it day by day because looking at being like this for six months is way too daunting.

So that is my update for today. Thank you again for your love, prayers, and support. I count my lucky stars every day for each and every special person in my life. Despite all, I am so blessed.

Love, Me

After Cliff got up, I crawled back into bed, feeling like my chemo hangover was getting worse and hoping that some sleep would get rid of the headache that was lingering. It was good to have Cliff home. He kept placing a bottle of water in my hand with instructions to drink, checking up on me every half hour or so as I slept.

That night I experienced my first "chemo flush," and it was frightening until I found out what it was. My face and neck started to feel flushed, and the top of my head got really warm. At first I didn't know what was happening and took my temperature, but it was normal. Cliff was worried and kept touching my face and asking if I was okay. I decided to look online to see if I could find out what it was and discovered that it was a common side effect of the steroids, and we both relaxed a little.

Wanting some fresh air, I went to the deck, lay back in the chair, and relaxed, listening to the birds singing and feeling the warm breeze blow through the gazebo as the bumble bees buzzed in the lilac trees in my yard. It was so peaceful, and with my eyes closed, I could go to a place where I was not sick, back to my life before March 14 when I heard those words. I wished I wasn't sick. I wished for my old life back, but I knew as much as I didn't want this to be happening, it was and I had to be as strong as I could be to get through it. And I knew that I would get through it. I would be okay.

Make your smile change the world, but don't let the world change your smile.
　　　——Author Unknown

My smile was not going to change, I promised myself.

My yard offered me a sanctuary right then, one of peacefulness, quiet, safety, and nature. As I sat there listening to the life going on around me, I could hear the children down the street jumping on their trampoline, giggling as their mom told them to be careful. I could hear the neighbors working in their yard, starting up the lawnmower and then running over rocks that flicked out and hit our adjoining fence. I could hear Cliff and Kayla in the kitchen, unloading the dishwasher, banging dishes, and I wondered why nothing was getting broken and made a mental note to ask them to be easier on my dishes!

Life goes on, I thought. I sat, too weak right then to make it back up the stairs I had run up countless times in the past. But with a small smile on my face, I thought, *Life goes on.*

My third day posttreatment found me having a really good day. While it was strange for me to get up so early, I was up and starting my day at 5:30 a.m. I checked my e-mail, my heart growing bigger with each e-mail I read. Most were responding to my update, and I was thrilled that it had been so well received.

Thank you for the update. As I read with tears in my eyes, I feel so proud of you and can't help but think how your thoughts, feelings, and experience are so beautifully written. You are an amazing woman surrounded by amazing people. You are in my prayers, wrote Lori.

I love your letter; you are so funny … Have you ever considered writing for a living? … I think you will do amazingly well, Kim. Thinking of you tons. In love and light …, wrote my co-worker Linda.

Thanks for the idea, Linda!

Thank you so much for the update! It was great. I think you are a trooper despite your anxiety—which I think would be normal for anyone. Before you know it this will all be behind you, and you will once again be back to healthy you again. Take care of yourself and stay positive. Hugs, hugs, hugs, wrote Donna Marie.

Chicklet wrote,

I think it is so awesome that you are sending these updates. It is journaling therapy, which will help you through this. I have to say my heart is breaking for you and your family. It is one thing to hear about "someone" who has cancer and imagine in your mind that it must be horrible, but it is quite another to actually have someone you know and love experience it! I am grateful that you have the amazing family and support system that you do, and I admire you for being able to be grateful and appreciative even in the midst of this whole experience. You are amazing! Sending my love and hug.

I keep you in my prayers every night and know that you'll get through this. I know that you have a strong network of people helping you, but should you ever need anything that I can do for you, please let me know, Maureen said.

Kimmy, you are one of the strongest people I know. You are a blessing to Simone and I, a true friend, and an all-around wonderful person. I am very grateful to have you in my life. We were thinking of you all day yesterday. If you need anything or need us or me to do anything, you let me know; I/we can be there in seconds. Love you so much, big hugs! my handsome Mark wrote.

My dear friend Skipper wrote,

Just read your e-mail, and now I have tears in my eyes crying for you. I am sure things will work out. There is a saying that I refer to often after Anna passed away: God will not bring you to something without bringing you through it. I have said prayers for you at every Friday mass I go to, Kim. Don't worry about the hangover, etc. There are better days ahead, and I am sure your courage and Cliff's help will bring you through this all. Love you, Newfie, and think of you often.

As I read through the e-mails, my heart swelled, but I once again felt like a fake. People thought I was so strong, so courageous, and here I was cowering, having panic attacks, and questioning my faith at times. But then I recognized and told myself again for the millionth time that it was okay to be sad and scared. It didn't mean I was weak or less deserving of the encouragement I was receiving from people in my life. I could accept their words and breathe them in, drawing strength from the support and letting those very words help me grow strong and courageous. Maybe that was what it meant to be strong and courageous, that you didn't need to be a pillar of strength all the time but that you could be okay with the moments of sadness and fear and recognize them as a stepping stone for healing rather than a weakness. I thought about those people sitting at their computers, fingers flying over the keyboard as they sent their messages to me, and I sent out a silent thank you to each and every one of them, wondering if they knew how I would soak their words into my soul.

When Kayla got up, she had a fever and a sore throat. With her history of strep throat, I sent her off to the doctor to get checked out. Then she was banned to the basement until the results came back. We thought it was funny; she was like a gnome living under the bridge. So worried that she would be carrying some bug, we sanitized everything and had hand sanitizer at every corner of the house, knowing that if I were to come down with strep throat at this point, it could mean a hospital stay for me. Cliff was also not feeling well, but we chalked that up to him not getting enough sleep and the stress catching with him. Both Cliff and Kayla spent the day sleeping, and I realized once again as they slept that the cancer was not just my cross to bear; it was hurting everyone.

While my house was quiet and everyone was sleeping, I caught up with friends on the phone and was pleased to receive a call from Mrs. Thody, my friend's mother. She was a three-time cancer survivor, and it was so good to speak to her, knowing she had beaten it and would soon celebrate her seventieth birthday. Talk about inspirational! It was stories like those that helped those of us fighting right now, knowing there were so many people out there who did survive and for whom the diagnosis of breast cancer was not a death sentence. Mrs. Thody had lived to see all three of her children grown, married, and starting their own families. She was a grandmother and enjoying her golden years. I wanted to grow up to be just like her!

I was happy with how good I was feeling at that point, though I was moving pretty slowly and feeling worn out. Cliff had a ball game, and as he prepared to leave, I started to feel sorry for myself that I couldn't go. I felt left out and wished nothing more than to be able to pull on my sneakers, grab my glove, and hit the field with all my friends and share a beer after the game. But the fatigue prevented me from even getting dressed to go.

Worry never robs tomorrow of its sorrow, it only saps today of its joy.
—Leo Buscaglia

One of the support programs that was (and still is) offered to cancer patients was the Look Good, Feel Good program. I had signed up for it a month before I had my chemotherapy schedule, and it fell the same week as my treatments. That morning I was feeling well, so I decided to go. I met up with Krista for lunch and then headed to the hospital, where the program was being held. As I entered back through the cancer clinic doors, I was once again hit with the disbelief that this was my life. Was I really going to a workshop to show me how to draw on eyebrows and camouflage that I had no eyelashes because chemotherapy had caused them to fall out. Really?

As I settled in, I looked around the room. I noticed there were more volunteers than patients; there were only three of us. One lady was older than I was. The other appeared much younger, and she was wearing a scarf on her head. I stole glances at her across the table. I wondered how long she had been in treatment and had so many questions I wanted to ask her, but I was afraid to ask. I didn't want to intrude. After a little while, she shared with the group that she had proceeded to shave her head the week before because she didn't want to worry about it falling out. She asked if we would like to see, and as our heads bobbed up and down, she pulled off her scarf, and I sucked in my breath; she looked so beautiful. I told her that, and she smiled as she cast her eyes downward and fumbled with her scarf, covering her head once again. I was amazed at how very shy she was but that she had so much courage to show us her naked head so soon after she had shaved it. I was thankful she shared her story with us. I drew strength from this beautiful stranger.

The workshop provided each attendee with a box full of cosmetics and lotions, all intended to help us in our journeys through cancer treatments with the hopes that if we looked pretty on the outside, we would feel pretty on the inside. I already doubted the power of the makeup and knew that once my hair was gone and the dark circles appeared under my eyes, I would struggle with feeling pretty again. I hoped the chemicals they injected into my body would not be too hard on me over time, and while I was resigned to losing my hair, with less than two weeks to the date I would be shaving my head, I wondered if perhaps I would be one of the lucky ones and keep my eyelashes and eyebrows. I felt that was such a small thing to ask.

As I started the car, I had an e-mail come through on my phone. It was from Krista and it read,

My dear friend/my sister: I want you to know how proud that I am of you ... of your strength, of your courage, and of your ability to maintain your wonderful/twisted/warped and somewhat fucked up sense of humor. I know that you have probably had MANY people tell you how they are proud of you, and I know that YOU KNOW that I am ... But I also wanted you to read it. I am here for you in whatever capacity you need me. I know that you know that, and that is reassuring to me—that I don't need to always tell you and you just simply know, just like I would with you ... Love you fiercely.

As I read her message, I wept. Sometimes I felt so alone even though I had an army of support. I had almost a constant need to be reassured that people remembered me, were rooting for me, and loved me. I knew that need was unfounded and silly, but in my darkest moments, those e-mails and texts from people just reaching out to say they were thinking of me helped me take another breath, another step and helped to remind me that I was loved and would be okay.

The following weekend was the big kick-off for camping—the May long weekend. Cliff and I hadn't missed camping this weekend for as many years as I could remember, and I was very sad that we would not be heading out to the woods with all our friends. As everyone prepared to leave, I sent out a message full of cheer and best wishes while my heart was full of sadness. We wanted to go so badly, and I allowed this to drag me down emotionally. I turned off my phone and pledged to keep it powered off until everyone returned on Monday, not wanting to get those texts from my friends saying they missed me and inquiring how I was feeling. I was jealous that they were able to go and I wasn't. I didn't like that feeling at all; in fact, I detested it, but there was no denying how I felt, and I struggled to turn those emotions around.

The blues just got worse as the weekend went on and were amplified when I received an e-mail from Dad telling me that they had canceled their trip out to see me because Mom was not feeling well enough to travel. This news sent me spiraling downward. I started to feel sorry for myself and mad. I tried my best to keep busy, trying not to think about all the camping fun I was missing and about my parents' canceled trip. I tried so hard to keep upbeat so that I didn't drag Cliff down into that gutter with me, but it was hard.

Kayla was also having a hard time that weekend, thinking about my first chemotherapy session. I crawled onto her bed with her, and we chatted. Then she started to cry, telling me how scared she had gotten when she walked underneath the cancer clinic sign at the end of the hall in the hospital and how her knees had almost buckled as she walked down the hall. I remembered how I had felt the first time I walked underneath that sign and felt so much pain for her, sad that she had to have those feelings of fear as well and not at all surprised that her reaction had been so similar to mine. Up until now we had lived a charmed life, secure in knowing that all was okay. Now our lives had been turned upside down, and we were forced to deal with issues that were, for us, story lines for a TV show.

As we talked and cuddled, I knew she was looking for reassurances that I would be okay and would continue to feel as well as I had been so far. I reassured her as best as I could while silently praying that I would be okay and that nothing would happen to prove me wrong. As we cuddled, I wondered how Kelsey was doing, if she needed the same comfort from me but was unable to get it because she no longer lived with me. I hoped she was okay and that she would reach out if she needed me.

Just when I thought I was at my lowest, I received an e-mail from my friend Blair, aka Bubba, that read,

You and your wonderful family are in our prayers every day. You will triumph over this as a family, and you have an unimaginable number of friends who love and support you all. Lori and I are here anytime for anything you need. We mean this sincerely. You simply have to ask, as we may not know when and how to help. Remember that you are amazing, and God is awesome. You are in great hands.

As I read this message, tears poured down my cheeks, and it gave me the strength to pull up my socks and keep moving for another little while.

That first treatment was also my introduction to constipation like I had never had before, and it was something I would struggle with for my first three treatments. I quickly learned that this was one of the side effects you deal with before it becomes an issue. My advice to any newly diagnosed patient requiring chemotherapy would be to stock up on all the over-the-counter products recommended and begin taking them before it becomes a problem. It took me a couple of treatments to get a handle on that problem, and I suffered the bloating, cramps, and headaches that go hand in hand with constipation.

That week, I also experienced my first cravings for something that, once eaten, made me physically ill. Having grown up in Newfoundland, fish had always been a staple in my diet, and I was always a lover of any kind fish. I craved our Friday fish fry. This was something Cliff and I had been doing for a long time: coming home from work on a Friday, cooking up a bunch of different kinds of fish (salmon, cod, shrimp, scallops), and heading to the couch to watch the news while we ate. Well, it is true when they say some smells you loved before will turn you off after chemo. The smell of the fish made me ill, and I spent hours afterward boiling nutmeg on the stove, opening all the windows, and lighting every candle in the house to get rid of the smell. It was months before I could even think of fish without feeling ill and even longer before I could eat it again.

As the weekend passed, it took my energy with it, and a fatigue like I have never felt before moved into my body and settled into my bones. I felt like someone had drilled a hole in each of my shoulders and then filled my body up with cement. It took so much energy to move from the bed to the couch, and just the thoughts of doing even the smallest chore tired me out. The antinausea medications had something to do with my fatigue, I knew, and I hoped that once I was finished taking them that my energy would once again return.

While I was tired, my appetite was increasing, and I could not seem to fill myself up. As soon as I ate a meal, I was thinking about the next one and craved all the stuff that was no good. My clothes were already starting to get tight, and the doctor's warning that 50 percent of breast cancer patients undergoing the same treatment as me would gain weight played over and over in my head. While I knew that getting through the treatments was my number-one priority, I did not want to gain a ton of weight while doing it. Little did I know that this was the beginning of my thirty-five pound weight gain throughout my treatment journey.

> *Every day we are called to small things with great love.*
> ——Mother Teresa

Kelsey came by that weekend, and we did our annual flower planting; however, I was more of a spectator than a participant. We visited the greenhouses and selected plants, all the while I held onto her arm. I was feeling pretty weak but happy to be spending time with her and doing something we both loved.

Every year for as long as I could remember, Kelsey and I would roll around in the dirt in the spring, planting, potting, and moving around flowers. We both took such joy in the garden, and I looked forward to it every year. We both loved to pick out the flowers and then plant them among the perennials in the garden and then watch them grow, delighting in the colors as the season lengthened.

One year, we decided that we needed a big flower bed on our front lawn, so we pulled out the shovels and the wheel barrel and spent two days digging away at the grass, molding a flower bed to our satisfaction and then heading to the greenhouses to purchase plants to fill it up. As we planted the last flower, we stood back and admired our handwork. Then we painstakingly watered the bed for weeks until it started to take root and bloom. Every time I walked by it, I smiled.

Kelsey took lots of time cleaning out the flower beds, removing last year's dead flowers and cleaning up all the weeds before planting our new flowers. I sat on the deck, watching her for a while, and then moved to sit on the grass beside her and chatted as she went about her work with dirt on her cheeks and a smile on her face. It took her all afternoon to get everything planted to her satisfaction, and I settled back in the gazebo and closed my eyes as I listened to her watering the flowers before she put away her garden tools. This was the first year I wasn't the foreman, and I was proud of the job she did and knew that I would take a lot of pleasure in watching the garden flourish throughout the summer season. She kissed me good-bye, tired from a good day's work, and then headed home, leaving me with a smile on my face.

My bones were feeling like cement, and as I sunk deeper into my chair, I could hear Cliff vacuuming inside. It was still hard to believe that this was my life. Here I was, sitting outside, having watched my daughter do all my spring gardening for me in one day while my husband did the housework inside, and I was unable to physically help either. While I knew how lucky I was to have my family ready to help, I still felt like I was missing out, that there was a part of my life in which I was unable to fully engage. I could feel the warm breeze blowing over my face, and I took in deep breaths of the fresh air.

I am so blessed, I thought, but then I wondered how I could believe that when I had cancer. Was that not a contradiction on so many levels?

But I knew I was blessed and would have to keep that thought at the center of my mind in order to get healthy again. As I sat there willing myself to get enough energy to climb the stairs to the house, I knew my future would be bright and that thought would keep me going.

I did a quick check on the computer to see where my fund-raising stood for the Timberwolves' head shave, and I was astounded to see that it was now at $6,185. Six thousand dollars! Amazing. I was amazed at the generosity of people, and I took time to write thank you notes to all who had donated, hoping they would realize how much every dollar pledged meant to me.

One of the replies I received to my e-mail was from an old family friend named Eileen. I had babysat her children for years and had always felt a special bond to her. She had always been so kind to me and listened to me rant in my teenage years. When she found out I was diagnosed with breast cancer, she reached out to me through Facebook, following my progress, always encouraging me.

She wrote, *Kim, you never cease but to amaze me—from a wonderful little girl to an amazing wife, mother, and courageous young woman. I am cheering you on every day in my thoughts and my prayers. You put a smile on my face and hope in my heart more than you will ever know. Xo. Keep smiling.*

I was feeling a little guilty about not keeping up-to-date with some of my friends and took the time while I was at my computer to e-mail a few of them with whom I had not been keeping up. My dear friend Christine was one of those friends, and her reply came back quickly and to the point. She wrote,

Hey, don't you ever apologize again for that ... EVER. I know your love, and I know where you are at in this walk. I expect nothing. I love to get your updates and even that I know is hard to keep up with. Doin' better than I would at that! You are loved whether we are near or far, and never forget that. You bless me just being you. Can't wait to see you too! Until then, my friend:

*The Lord is my strength and my shield; my heart trusts in Him and
I am helped. (Ps. 28:7). O Lord, my God, I called out to you for help
and you healed me (Ps. 30:2).*

*Praise the Lord, O my soul; all my inmost being, praise His Holy
Name. Praise the Lord, O my soul, and forget not all His benefits—
who forgives all your sins and heals all your diseases, who redeems
your life from the pit and crowns you with love and compassion, who
satisfies your desires with good things so that your youth is renewed
like the eagle's (Ps. 103:1–5).*

I always said she was my moral compass, and she never failed to find
a way to let me know that God would love me through this more than
anyone else could.

Cliff and I went out for a drive that evening, and we had a good chat
as we cruised through town. He said that every time he thought of the
cancer, he got mad. Then he said, no, he didn't get mad; he just couldn't
believe it. He was struggling as much as I was with the acceptance of our
reality, and it was as surreal to him as it was to me. He just wanted our
lives to be normal again and for this to have never happened. Life had
been so much easier before breast cancer moved in, took over our every
thought, and became our reality.

Monday arrived and with it my best friend Juanita from Newfoundland.
I was excited as we headed down Highway 2 on route to the airport to
pick her up and even more excited that Cliff had let me go. He wanted me
to stay home and rest, but there was no way I was not going to be there.
Both Juanita and I had been waiting for this day since my diagnosis, and
I could not believe it was finally here. As we drove to the airport, I broke
down several times in both excitement and sadness. I was excited to have
her come but sad that it was on these terms. She kept saying that she had
no expectations and that she was coming to spend time with me, but I was
sad that this was not the visit I had always envisioned her making. I had
always thought on her first trip to Alberta we would visit the mountains,
drink on the deck, and shop. Now she was coming to accompany me to
the hospital, sit with me while I cried, and shave my head.

I tried to sleep on the way, but the excitement kept me watching the sights. Also, my head was starting to feel sore with little bumps coming out all over it. I knew to expect that, and it was the first sign that my hair was getting ready to fall out. I kept running my fingers through my hair, expecting to see a handful come away with my hand, but so far nothing was coming out. I was prepared to lose my hair at this point but was now nervous that it would start falling out before the head shave the following week. I wanted to be present and shave my head that day in response to all the money I had raised. I didn't want the cancer to dictate when my hair came out. I wanted control over that.

As we neared the airport, my stomach started to roll in excitement. I could not wait to see my friend, and Cliff was already prepared for what we all knew would be a big emotional scene. We took our place at the gate and waited. And waited. And waited some more. Cliff kept going to the monitors to check the arrival time and reported back that it had already arrived more than a half hour before. I started to get worried and jumped every time the doors opened, watching each face as it turned to corner to see if it was my friend. Texting her brought no reply, and I was fearful she had missed her connecting flight in Toronto, or worse yet, was lost inside the airport. Finally, I went and studied the monitor and realized we were at the wrong gate.

As we laughed, we took off running through the airport, knowing that by now Juanita had been waiting for more than forty-five minutes at the other end. As we neared her gate, we could see her walking toward us, dragging two suitcases, with a smile on her face and a stream of obscenities coming out of her mouth. We were laughing so hard as we hugged that tears were all forgotten. She wanted to make it perfectly clear that she had not been lost, that she had known where she was all the time, and that we just couldn't find her. We piled into the vehicle and headed back home, talking up a storm and catching up with each other. It was so good to have her close enough to touch. After a short timend I let her and Cliff do some catching up while I napped in the car on the way home.

I had hoped to have more energy for her, to be able to sit and laugh like only the two of us could, but the fatigue was winning the battle, and as soon as we got home I retreated to my bedroom to take a nap while Juanita and Cliff sat on the deck and caught up. Through my open bedroom window I could hear their voices talking quietly. I lay on my bed and wept, feeling sorry for myself and mad that I didn't have the energy to get up and visit. It seemed unfair that my friend had traveled a full day to be with me and I didn't have the energy to visit. Everyone was so healthy, and I didn't have the energy to move. As I drifted off to sleep, my pillow was wet from my tears.

When I woke up, I felt much better and made it to the couch, and Juanita and I caught up as Krista, Glen, and Tracy arrived to greet her and join us for supper. As everyone milled around, talking and laughing, I felt my body get hot, and my heart started to race. I could hear them talking but couldn't figure out what they were saying. I left the room, stumbled back to the bedroom, and lay on the bed, trying to slow my heart rate and breathing. I found it hard to take a good breath and felt like my head was going to explode. I was scared, not knowing what was happening to me.

Cliff came in to check on me and helped me get up, and we went to sit on the front step, all while I tried to catch my breath. He was worried, and as we sat there, he took my temperature and blood pressure. We started to laugh as he did this, but it made him feel better to be doing something. In hindsight, we know now that I was experiencing another panic attack. So much had happened that day with Juanita's arrival, our trip to Calgary to pick her up, and then having so many people around, and I had just become overwhelmed and tried to do too much too soon, thinking I could be the same as I was before. Everyone filtered out, and Juanita went to bed, exhausted from her day traveling. I was happy the day was over and hoped tomorrow would be a better day as I crawled into bed.

The next morning, I called the cancer clinic as soon as I got up and talked with one of the nurses about how tired I was feeling and how heavy my bones were. I told her it felt like I was getting worse instead of better, and she told me it was because I was in the low of my cycle at that time and that was to be expected. She told me to hang in there and it would get better as the days passed and to nap and rest as often as I felt I needed to. I felt much better after talking with her. Juanita and I sat and talked and shared some much needed tears before I headed back for a nap. It had been eight days since my treatment, which was the worst day for the fatigue and heavy bones, and as I drifted off to sleep, I thought about what Juanita had just said to me, that my vocabulary had totally changed since I was diagnosed. It was now full of words like *cancer, doctors, fatigue, chemotherapy,* and it would be like that now for at least a year, and I would have to find a way to cope with my new reality. She was so right.

When Kayla got home that evening, she showed us her new tattoo: *Family Is Everything.* It had been inspired by our family and was the best compliment she could have ever given us.

Cliff arrived home from work exhausted. He had been fighting me about my idea of me sleeping on the couch so he could get a good night's rest. Every time I moved during the night, he woke up and reached for me, asking if I was okay and if there was anything he could do for me. I felt torn between his need for me to sleep next to him and his need for a good night's rest. Even before this all had happened, Cliff hadn't liked sleeping alone and would not be settled until I crawled into bed with him. Many times in the past I had fallen asleep on the couch only to be woken up by him in the early morning hours as he guided me to bed and crawled in beside me. He did not want our lives to change now and did not want us to have separate sleeping arrangements, no matter how temporary, and he failed to acknowledge the toll the lack of sleep was taking on his body. So I tried hard to be quiet as I slipped out of bed, taking great care in trying not to wake him. Some nights I would just lay there and watch the shadows dancing on the ceiling, not wanting to move and risk waking him up.

Throughout the week, Juanita and I spent a lot of time catching up, going out for lunch, and sitting on the couch and laughing. She accompanied me to the hospital to see my nurses and took pictures of the clinic so she could show everyone home where I would be spending so much time that summer. As the days went by, my energy level started to rebound, and I found that I was able to be more active each day. We filled the days with laughter and food, sometimes having long conversations about what was happening but more often just chatting the days away like the two old friends we were.

Knowing that the following week we would be shaving my head, Juanita thought it would be a good idea to cut my hair short before that so that I could get used to it in stages. We set up a mini salon in the bathroom, and Cliff left the house before the first strand of hair hit the floor. He was having as much trouble with the idea of my hair loss as I was and was not yet ready to face it. I was nervous but happy to have Juanita be the one to hold my hand through this part of my journey, and I trusted her entirely as I watched the hair fall. We joked and laughed as I faced away from the mirror, not wanting to witness what was happening, but I was pleasantly surprised once we were done. It was short, but it looked good, and Cliff was relieved when he walked back in to take a look. He told me he had been afraid that I would read something in his reaction and be hurt, which was why he had left.

Tracy showed up just as we were finished, and she visited with Juanita as I swept up my hair and threw it away. Every time I imagined cutting my hair, I thought the worst part would be sweeping it up, but as I shook it off the dust pan into the garbage, I felt a little liberated. I had taken the first step and was taking control of the terms to losing my hair. Cancer was the reason I would lose my hair, but it would not dictate how or when.

Juanita came along with me to have my heart test done; it's a procedure where they measure your heart muscle. We arrived at the clinic at 7:00 a.m. They injected a radioactive dye into my vein and then had me lay on a machine that went up and down my chest. Juanita stayed in the room with me, and it was reassuring to see her out of the corner of my eye as she sat quietly doing homework while the machine did its work. I ended up falling asleep, and when I woke, the test was almost over. We went out to lunch to celebrate yet another hurdle completed.

As the week neared its end, I learned how to pace myself and nap when I needed to, which gave me enough energy to keep up with Juanita when we left the house during the day. She was very understanding with it all, and I never felt any pressure to pretend to be better than I was or to keep going when I needed to rest. It was as comfortable as a friendship should be.

One day, we met with Linda for lunch, and I found that my mouth was pretty sore. I was concerned that I was developing mouth sores. Another evening we met with a bunch of my girlfriends for drinks and snacks, and as I looked around the table, I was so happy to be surrounded by such amazing women. I longed for their innocence and wished I didn't have the health challenges I was facing. I wanted to be just like them again. But I knew I was so blessed to have them in my life and that while I wished I didn't have this awful disease, they wished the exact same thing for me. We all agreed on one thing: cancer sucks.

As we sat and caught up, I leaned back in my chair and watched everyone talking and laughing, and I reached up mindlessly and ran my fingers through my hair. I was shocked when my hand came away full of hair. Not wanting to draw attention to myself, I let my hand fall to my lap under the table while my fingers rolled the hair between them. I had known this day was coming, but I was not prepared. As I opened my fingers and shook the hair from them to the floor, my thoughts went to Monday when I would be shaving it all off. My face got hot, and I felt the lump come back to my throat. The hair on my neck stood up. Was I ready for this? How was I ever going to pull this off, I wondered. I looked around the table and realized that I had never before noticed how beautiful my friends were and how their laughter sounded like a song to my ears. I wanted to freeze that moment. I didn't want tomorrow to come because today I could be just like them on the outside. I hated that cancer was going to out me and make itself visible to everyone who looked at me. After Monday I would no longer be able to blend in; my bald head would scream *cancer*, and I wanted to scream back at it.

To take our minds off the upcoming scheduled shave, Juanita and I spent the weekend running around, going to the farmer's market, and doing some shopping. I wore a hat for the first time and was surprised that no one was looking at me. My energy was still low, but I wanted to make the most of my time with Juanita and pushed myself as much as I could. As the weekend wore on, my hair started to come out in handfuls. I found that I had an almost sick fascination with how it came out and how I could pull it out with no resistance at all. As much as I didn't want to, I kept touching my head, each time coming back with a handful of hair. I stood in the yard and shook my head back and forth, watching the loose hair blowing in the wind. I was so sad as I watched it fly away, taking with it my secret. Soon I would be bald, and I knew there was no turning back.

Cliff had been acting strangely for a few days, and I finally got him to talk about what was going on. He told me he wished I was not participating in the head shave and wished I would shave my head privately at home. He was concerned it would be too hard on me to do it so publically and that I was taking on more than I could handle emotionally. I tried to reassure him as best I could that I would be fine, that I needed to do this for me, that it was my way of fighting back at the cancer and taking control of when and how I lost my hair. I don't think anyone realized how important that was to me. There was so little I had control of anymore. Even though I was feeling anxious about doing it in front of people, I was proud that I was able to raise the money I had, and I wanted everyone to know that I was fighting this disease as best as I could. I felt that this was just one way of showing that I was not going to lie down and let it beat me. I knew this would not be the choice for many people, but it was my choice, and I was at peace with it.

Appreciate everything, even the ordinary. Especially the ordinary.
—Pema Chodron

On Sunday, Tammy came and picked me up and brought me to her friend's house to introduce us. Carrie had been diagnosed the year before with lymphoma shortly after her baby girl had been born. She had completed her treatments five months before. She had undergone many chemotherapy treatments, all while caring for a newborn baby girl. I was in awe of her strength and what she had been able to overcome. As I listened to her, I was amazed at her positive outlook and just how inspirational she was. We talked at great length about the loss of her hair, and I wanted to reach out and touch the beautiful short hair she had grown back. She told me how good it felt to feel it blow in the wind, and I found it ironic that while she was talking about hers blowing in the wind, the wind was blowing mine away.

I wanted to be where she was in her journey. One thing she told me that I will never forget was how she had not wanted to give her baby's first year away to her cancer, so she did everything with her; she just did it slower. To this day I still stand in awe of her strength and her courage and how she faced her illness and fought back with every ounce of energy she had. She gave me a bag of scarves she had worn after she lost her hair, and as we hugged good-bye, we cried together. I will be forever thankful to Tammy for introducing us, and Carrie will always hold a special place in my heart. She gave me such hope, and I found myself thinking about her lots throughout the upcoming months and kept telling myself if she could do it, I could too.

When we arrived home, Kayla was having a mini breakdown, unable to deal with all the emotions that were going through her mind and heart. She was confused and worried and said she just wanted it all to go away. She hated the cancer, she hated what it was doing to our family, and she hated to see me sick. My heart broke as I watched the tears roll down her face, over the freckles I have admired since she was a little girl. Her sobs mirrored the ones I was holding in. I wanted to take away her pain, make it all go away, and have our life return to where it had been before March 14. Would we ever be whole again, I wondered.

The morning of the head shave arrived, and as I showered and watched my hair swirl around the drain, I wondered what I had gotten myself into, all the while knowing that there was no turning back now. As Cliff would say, I was "pot committed." My phone buzzed constantly all morning with well-wishing from my friends. Each time I replied to one, another would come in, and it was nice to have something to take my mind off what was coming. I checked my e-mail and noted that several e-mails had come in during the night to wish me luck. I cried when I read the letter I received from Nancy, Cliff's nephew's fiancée. She wrote,

Hey, Kim. So today is the big day, or well one of them. I wish the best of luck to you. You'll be a beauty no matter what. And like everyone else says, now you can play with your wigs and try out new styles! Role play with Cliff! Lol.

Not a day goes by that I don't think about you. You are such a strong and amazing woman, and with the love and people that you have around you, there's no doubt in my mind that you'll come out of this JUST FINE! It'll just make you stronger. I was running errands

the other day, and was listening to this country song by Martina McBride, "I'm Gonna Love You Through It." Well, I had a bawl for you while listening to it. Gave me shivers all over my body. But the love that you and Cliff have for each other is strength enough to get you through anything. Just this the weekend we were up the shore having beers, and Katie and I were chatting and saying how we want yours and Cliff's love for each other. It's truly inspiring. We'd hit the boys and be like, "Rideout! Love me the way Cliff loves Kim!" Love you, Kim! Even though we are miles apart, everyone is still rooting for you! Go Team Rideout.

Nancy, there is no doubt in my mind how much Christopher loves you! When I had the time, I wrote back to her and said,

Thank you so much for taking the time to write me, Nancy. It went well on Monday but was a bit nerve wracking to say the least. I was so happy to have Juanita with me … Not sure I could have done it without her. The hair that was left is falling out like crazy now, and I am anxious for it to be gone now … It is just making a mess. I have a bunch of hats now and don't think I will ever wear the wig. Hats are so much more comfortable. You made me smile when you said that about the love Cliff and me share. You could not have paid me a bigger compliment. If it were not for him, I don't know where I would be. He has held me when I cried, and he has cried in my lap. He has done everything he could to make me feel safe, and when that wasn't possible, he has just been scared with me. When I curl up in his arms, I can hide from the world and let him take care of it all for me, and the days when he falls apart, I am strong for him. It has been a rollercoaster of emotions, but I have gotten this far because of him, and it is just like the song: we are gonna love each other through it. That is kind of our song now! Yes, you are right to demand nothing less. Life is too short! I am so thankful that we had such a wonderful family Christmas. What wonderful memories we all made! And I can't wait to make them again at your wedding! Love you too, Nancy! I feel all your love and encouragement every day! Team Rideout rocks!

Hugs to you all! Thanks for writing me ... I love getting e-mails from home!

Juanita and I sat and talked, watching the clock tick away the hours before we had to be at the school, and then Linda showed up with coffee for everyone as well as a beautiful inspirational book for me with an inscription that made me weep when I read it later that evening. As I got ready in the washroom, doing my makeup, Linda sat on the toilet lid and chatted me up, doing her best to keep my mind occupied. Shortly after she left, Tracy arrived to drive us to the school, and as we piled in, I popped an Ativan under my tongue and reached back to give Juanita one. Then I silently prayed for strength to get me through the next few hours.

When we pulled into the school parking lot, Cliff was already there waiting, and he looked sad. I knew he wanted to be anywhere but where we were. He still didn't understand why I was doing this and still didn't want me to, but he was committed to standing beside me, and I was grateful to have him there. As we walked toward the school, I looked up and saw a bunch of my co-workers standing by the door, waiting for me. I was touched and could not believe that they had shown up to offer me support. I fought back tears as we posed for pictures and exchanged hugs.

I grabbed Cliff's hand, and we walked into the school together. I was surprised at the number of my friends who had shown up and were sitting inside waiting for me. As I went and hugged each of them and thanked them for coming, more kept arriving. Kelsey and Kayla were there, both dressed in pink to show their support. My girlfriend's daughters Mackenzie and Shelby were there with the T-shirts they had made for the Relay for Life in show of their support for me. As we sat and waited for the assembly to begin, I looked left and right and behind me, and I was surrounded by friends and family. I was truly overwhelmed. Zac sought me out and gave me a big hug, promising to hold my hand as we did this together. Then he returned to sit with his friends. Cliff held my hand tightly, so tightly it started to hurt.

As the principal of the school called the assembly to order, she thanked everyone for coming and then introduced me and asked me to come forward. I was calm, and I remember taking a huge breath as I let Cliff's hand go and walked toward the front of the gymnasium by myself. As I took my place at the podium, I looked out over the sea of children, teachers, friends, and family, and I couldn't see a thing. I had forgotten to bring my glasses, but I thought at the time that was probably a good thing; if there were any faces full of pity, I didn't want to see them. As I started to speak, all I remember is how quiet it was. Everyone was listening to what I had to say. And this is what I said:

"My name is Kim Rideout, and I am forty-four years old. I have been married to Cliff for twenty-three years, and we have two beautiful daughters: Kelsey, who is twenty-one, and Kayla, who is nineteen. I have a life so rich in love, laughter, and peace that some days even I can't believe it. Many times my Facebook status is 'I am so blessed.' Simple as that.

On March 14 of this year, I was diagnosed with breast cancer. There is no history of breast cancer in my family. I was healthy and active with not a care in the world. I learned on March 14 that cancer does not discriminate. Since that time, I have had surgery and have already completed one chemotherapy session. I only have five more to go! I am anxious to get it done with so I can get back to living my life. And I have to say I still use the word *blessed* in my Facebook status many times.

I have been blessed with a beautiful, supportive family and blessed with the most wonderful group of friends any woman could ever have. Many of them are here today. The girl shaving my head is my best friend, Juanita, who traveled from NFLD to be with me today. Her mom is a thirty-year breast cancer survivor and living life to the fullest at seventy-two. My husband, daughters, family, and friends have walked alongside me from day one, minute one of my journey, and I look forward to crossing that golden finish line with them by my side.

Zac Walker and his family are very good friends of mine, and when I heard about him participating in this fund-raiser shortly after I found out I had breast cancer, I decided to join him and the team. If we can make some money for cancer research, let's do it! And I am so proud of how much we have raised! Because of fund-raisers like this, because of people like you, some day there will be a cure! I have breast cancer, but I am not going to die of breast cancer for two reasons: early detection and cancer research that has already been done.

I want the students here who are shaving their heads with me to know how brave I think they are. For me, losing my hair is not an option, as the chemotherapy will cause it to fall out very soon anyway. My reality is that if I didn't have cancer, I would not be shaving my head today. But you young men and women don't have cancer, and you are shaving your heads to fund-raise. You have taught me something about being brave and the impact that one person's doings can have one someone else's life. If you don't already, some day you will realize what a wonderful thing you have done today and what an impact on my life you have made by doing what you are doing and letting me be a part of it. At a time in your lives when physical appearances are so important, I am thrilled that you are putting aside any ego and vanity issues and doing something because you believe in the cause. That is my definition of bravery. I am so proud of you all. And for all the students here today, never stop giving to our community through charity, fund-raising, or volunteering in whatever capacity you can. Everyone benefits, including you. We can all make a difference.

I know I speak for any person or family who has been touched by cancer when I say to the young men and women participating, to the parents who support them, to the teachers and facility who helped make this day happen, and finally, to everyone who donated ... Thank you from the bottom of my heart."

When I finished the principal stepped forward to hug me, and when I turned around, I was being given a standing ovation! I was shocked and amazed, and I wanted to scream, "Take that cancer!" as I wiped away my tears. There was no room for tears today. The principal told me that Zac and I would start off the head shave, and I motioned Juanita to come up and join me up front. I walked toward the platform where two stools stood empty. *Here we go*, I thought. Zac and I settled on the stools, and he reached for my hand. We exchanged smiles as his classmates yelled out encouragement to him. Juanita snapped her cape around my neck, bent down, kissed my cheek, and asked me if I was ready. Then she said, "Here we go, chick."

I heard the clippers fire up, and I closed my eyes. As I felt the clippers run up the back of my head, I could not believe this was happening. It almost felt like I was standing in front of everyone, undressing. It was all so surreal. I could feel the cool air on my head as the hair fell to the floor. I could feel Zac's hand holding mine. I opened my eyes to look over at him and watched in disbelief as the girl who was shaving his head took all the hair in the middle of his scalp in one quick sweep. I quickly closed my eyes again and prayed for this to be over soon.

I was thankful Juanita started at the back first and then moved to the sides and left the front for last. I knew how hard this was on her, and I thanked her steady hand and her composure to do it. She quietly kept me up-to-date on where we were and how much longer before it would be done. There was no one else I would have wanted to stand beside me and take this step with, and I silently thanked her as the last of my hair fell onto my lap. As hard as that was for me to sit there and have my head shaved, I knew it was harder on her to actually do it, and I will be forever thankful that she stepped up and took on that task and did her best to maintain my dignity while doing it.

I opened my eyes and caught the stare of a child in the front row. She was watching me, eyes wide open and unwavering, holding her face in her hands. Her long hair fell over her shoulders as she watched me intently. I smiled at her, and she smiled back. What a beautiful smile. I exhaled, not realizing that I had been holding my breath.

Done. We were done. Juanita took the cape off, and I stood and turned to hug her. Then I turned and hugged Zac, and we made our way to the back of the gymnasium, where my friends greeted me with high fives as I walked by each of them. There was no sadness, just relief that it was over, tons of smiles, and lots of laughter.

I made my way to Cliff, and he stood up and hugged me. What a wonderful hug it was, full of relief as he whispered in my ear, "I am proud of you, honey."

I hugged Kelsey and Kayla, and we settled back into our seats and dried our tears. The floodgates opened once again when I glanced down at Juanita. She was crying into her hands; all the emotions of the day had finally caught up with her. I never loved her as much as I loved her at that moment.

Tammy was busy taking pictures for me that day, and I posed with as many of my friends as I could before everyone started to filter out and get back to their days. As I hugged each, there were tons of smiles, and it solidified for me that this was a celebration. For the first time I knew I had made the right decision. All doubts were gone. I had spit back into the face of cancer, stood on my own, and taken control, and did it ever feel good. There were lots of head rubs. Everyone wanted to feel the quarter inch of hair that was left and kept telling me how good I looked with short hair. While I knew they were all being kind, already I could not wait for my hair to grow back. I asked Tammy for her camera, and I scrolled back through some of the pictures she had taken. For the first time, I saw how I looked, and I was shaken. Was that really me in those pictures, I thought. Then I instantly pushed the thought to the back of my mind. There would be time for that later. Right now I needed to stay strong.

Thanks for your kindness, you're an angel!
—Author Unknown

When we got back into the vehicle, I sank into the seat and flipped down the visor so I could once again see my new style, finally letting it all sink in. It was over. I had gotten through it, and I was proud of myself. As we pulled away from the school, we decided to head out for lunch to celebrate this finally being over. Tracy, Juanita, and I settled in, ordered a round of drinks and tapped our glassed together in celebration. I was so relieved to have it over with and felt quite comfortable in my hat, blending in with the rest of the people around me. Conversation was light. The three of us decompressed and just enjoyed the company.

Cliff and I headed out for a walk that evening to talk about the day's events. I wanted to see how he was holding up, knowing how hard it had been for him to sit back and watch me lose my hair earlier in the day. He told me he had been so confused all day, feeling mad for what was happening to us and feeling sad for me. He hated to see me up there. He felt I was on display. He said he was proud of me and what I had done. He said he would give anything for our life to go back to where it had been before this all happened. He was stuck on the *why*, and I had no answers for him. We spent the last half of our walk in silence, holding hands tightly, each of us lost in our own thoughts but each as equally grateful that the day was drawing to an end.

An e-mail I received from Glen showed me that my intended message that day had been received:

I didn't get a chance to tell you when we left the gym today, but your message was fantastic. You are a great public speaker and are to be commended for making today's event that much more special and serious. I know the kids understand why they are shaving their heads but wonder if they sometimes truly understand the importance and significance. You set it all in its place today. Great job.

The following morning was my second appointment at the cancer clinic to see my navigation nurse and discuss my next treatment for the following week. As I showered, my hands were full of hair, and I knew it would not be much longer before I would have to shave off the little bit of hair I had left. I wore a little skull cap to bed, and each morning when I took it off, it was full of hair. While I wanted to shave the rest of it off, I wasn't ready to be completely bald yet, and I was concerned that it would be too much for Peggy to see. They were arriving in a few days, and I wanted to have a little hair left when I first saw her, not wanting to shock her too much.

As I prepared for my appointment, I was concerned because my mouth sores were still hanging around, although they were getting better. I received a bunch of texts from friends telling me that my story at the fund-raiser had been picked up by the local newspapers, and our picture was in one of them. We were celebrities for all the wrong reasons.

Cliff, Juanita, and I were shown into an examination room, and I was given a questionnaire to complete. As I filled it out, Cliff and Juanita chatted quietly next to me, and Cliff looked over my shoulder every now and again to see what I was writing down. The questionnaire was full of questions about changes in lifestyle and health, which I assumed they would use to gauge how my body was reacting to the treatment. My nurse,

Krista, arrived and pulled up a chair. I introduced her to Juanita, and we made some small talk before she looked at the form I had completed.

While she was looking it over, Cliff said, "Krista, Kim lied on question ten."

I started to laugh and almost fell off my seat as I reached over to playfully punch him in the arm. Question ten had asked if there was any change to sexual function, and I had answered no. It broke the ice for all of us, and we shared some laughter about it. Then she did spend quite a bit of time asking me why there was a lack of sexual activity.

Not only had cancer scared me, but it had taken away my ability to see myself as a woman, a desirable woman. I was feeling ill most the time, I was losing my hair, my bones ached, I had a big scar on my breast, I was gaining weight on a daily basis, I was experiencing panic attacks, and I constantly feared for my future. Sex was the last thing I had energy or desire for. On the other hand, I knew how important that aspect of our marriage was. At that point, Cliff and I had been together for more than twenty-five years, and we had always enjoyed a very healthy sex life. While he understood my lack of sex drive, I knew it frustrated him because in his mind, this was one more thing the cancer was robbing from us.

We both have always said that sex is only 10 percent of a marriage when it is good, but 100 percent when it is bad. For me, sex had gone to the wayside, yet I was thankful that Cliff still desired me, that he loved who I was inside, and that how I looked on the outside did not matter to him. At times I felt he never really looked at me because he kept telling me I was beautiful, and in my heart I knew that was not true! In my mind I looked more awful by the day, but Cliff never saw that; he just loved me.

Krista discussed this issue with us and told us it was a common problem with women who were going through cancer treatments and their spouses. I told her that I was afraid I could make Cliff sick when I had the chemo drugs in my system and that I was afraid to even kiss him, let alone have sex. I told her how I felt like I was radioactive, and I didn't even want my family to share the same bathroom as me because I was afraid they would catch something from me. Krista listened to my worries intently, taking notes and asking questions, and then assured me that these were common feelings, but she said I needed to educate myself and told me that while these were all common fears, they were unfounded. She asked us some pretty pointed questions about our sex life, or lack of it, and we shared lots of laughs with her and Juanita. Cliff kept us laughing with his answers. I think Juanita heard more during that session than she wanted to, and our laughter at times rang through the halls of the clinic. I was very happy Cliff had started the conversation in the first place and so relieved that Krista had thought it important enough to explore. Both Cliff and I were very relieved with her answers, and I was happy to have a forum in which I could talk openly, let Cliff hear exactly how I was feeling, and hear from someone else that those were normal feelings to have.

Krista was concerned about my mouth sores, and while I didn't want to make it a big issue, she said that the chemotherapy they had given me was too strong and was attacking my good cells too aggressively and in effect killing off too many of my good cells. We were learning that chemotherapy was not an exact science. She decided they would dial back on my next treatment a little so that it didn't happen again, and she gave me a prescription for a mouth wash and a cream to put on the sores. She did say they would look at it again before my treatment and there was a possibility that my treatment could be delayed if the sores were not cleared up.

Juanita only had a few days left with me, so we made the most of it, ate every donut within a five-mile radius of my home, had lunches out, and visited with my friends so she could say good-bye to them all. The night before she left, we headed to the ball field, and I played my first and last game of the season with the team. I struck out every time at bat, but we all had a ton of fun despite our loss. Then we headed to a local pub to share in a beer and some nachos before calling it a night. As Cliff left to bring her to the airport the next evening, we hugged tightly and promised to see each other again soon. It was not good-bye but "see ya soon." I was so thankful that she had come to be with me for those weeks and knew I would always remember that time with a smile on my face and love in my heart.

I had no time to get lonely, as Cliff's sister and her husband, Peggy and Dyrick, arrived the very next day from Newfoundland. As soon as I was diagnosed, Peggy had started to make plans to come and stay with us for a while and help out, and I was so happy the day had finally arrived. I met them at the sidewalk, and we hugged tightly. I was happy to see them, and I knew they were happy to be here, happy to do anything so they did not feel so helpless being so far away. As I held Peggy, I cried and told her I was so happy she had come to stay with me and that I was so happy to have family here. We spent the evening catching up and reassuring them that we were fine. We took great pride in showing them our home, as this was their first time visiting. Peggy kept saying how helpless she had felt the last two months and how happy she was to finally be here.

Again I was hit with how much this had affected everyone, not just me, and I was helpless to stop the hurt that so many people were experiencing because of it. As we sat and talked, I found myself wishing that everyone was just visiting on vacation and not coming to see me because I was sick. Cliff and Dyrick retreated to the garage, and Peggy and I sat on the deck, visiting with Kelsey and Kayla and catching up. I could feel hair falling down my back as it came loose. I knew the time had come to shave it all off. I had bald patches now that looked awful, but I was still reluctant to take the last step and shave the little bit of hair that was left. I was afraid of what I would look like. I was afraid of what Cliff would think of me when he saw me bald. I was scared.

Cliff knew the time had come to take the final step, so the next morning we agreed that he would shave off the little bit of hair I had left. He left to go to the drugstore to buy some good razors, and I got dressed and tried to mentally prepare myself while he was gone. First he clipped it with the electric razor and then went over it again with disposable razors. My heart was pounding, and I wanted to cry as I leaned over the sink and snuck peeks at Cliff as he went about the task at hand. He looked so serious, and as I watched the hair fall onto the sink and towel, I felt tears fill my eyes. Cliff sensed me tensing up and started to crack jokes, making me laugh in spite of my tears. I could not believe that Monday I had sat in front of hundreds of people and buzzed my hair down to a quarter of an inch and hadn't shed one tear, yet now I was crying in privacy of my own home as the one person in the world I was the safest with shaved off what was left. Maybe it was the finality of it; exposing my scalp was exposing my illness and, in part, my weakness. The sadness I felt at that moment was gut-wrenching.

I could not bring myself to look in the mirror until he was done, and when I finally allowed my eyes to raise and look at my reflection, I was shocked. How could this woman looking back at me be me? I touched my head from front to back, feeling the stubble and contours of my head I had never felt before. It didn't feel real. I was touching the skin on my own head for the first time. The skin looked pale, having been covered with hair since I was a baby, and it felt clammy. I kept thinking over and over, *This is not happening.*

I caught Cliff's stare in the mirror. He said, "If you had told me five months ago that I would be shaving your head today, I would have laughed and told you that you were crazy." Yet he had done just that.

I told Cliff to leave and I would clean up the bathroom, and when I was alone, I quietly closed the door and stood in front of the mirror. As tears flowed silently, I turned my head back and forth, looking at myself. I pulled a handheld mirror out of the drawer so I could see the back of my head and stifled a sob with my hand when I saw how I looked from behind. I quickly grabbed a scarf and tried to tie it like all the videos I had watched online had shown, but it looked ridiculous to me, like I was getting dressed up for Halloween. In frustration, I threw it down, opened the door, and went in search of my hat to cover my head. Feeling liberated would come later. Right then I just felt sorry for myself.

Tammy wrapped it up nicely in an e-mail I had received that morning:

Your feelings are so normal. Even the shave meant you still had hair, just less of it. This is a lot more revealing. It's like being self-conscious about your body and even having some thin semi see-through layer of clothing makes you feel better and more secure than nothing at all. But you did do it, and you are brave. Your hair will grow back, and while you see it as something that identifies you as having cancer, as the treatments finish and the hair starts growing back, you can start identifying each strand and each noticeable change in growth as symbol of beating cancer and kicking its ass.

Kayla came into the bedroom as I was searching for my hat and stared at me for a moment. Then she said, "Ma, you have a nice-shaped head." Kelsey arrived, and I was wearing my hat and told her I couldn't figure out how to tie the scarf. She removed my hat and tied the scarf in place.

As I looked into her eyes, I said, "Honey, I am bald." Her reply was simple: "So?"

I wondered if they were all not making a big deal out of it so I wouldn't feel bad, and if that was the case, I was thankful to them all. Peggy and Dyrick took a quick look and then continued on like all was the same, and Cliff told me over and over that I was beautiful. I took a deep breath and decided to make the most of the day, bald or not. It was time to put on my big girl panties, as they say, and suck it up. But man did it suck! I already missed my hair so much. We visited with Glen and Tracy at the lake and had supper with them, and for moments at a time I forgot what had happened that morning, and I was grateful for the distraction.

The Sunday before my treatment was a busy day with friends dropping by in the afternoon to see Peggy and Dyrick and to see my new "haircut." It was a great distraction for both what had happened the day before and what was coming the following day: treatment number two.

When everyone left, I poured myself a bath and had my first cry of the day. I was feeling overwhelmed with the love I had received that day and overwhelmed with the physical changes taking place for me every day. I allowed myself to hurt and cry and for a little bit wonder why. I didn't ask why, but I just wondered why. What was the reason all this was happening to me? Was it to teach me a lesson? To teach me to love and appreciate my life? I didn't think I needed a lesson because I already loved and appreciated my life so much. I woke up with thanks every day for all my blessings, and I celebrated my life always. Could it be that there was no reason and it just happened? Even today I struggle with that question. Even today I don't have the answer.

Cliff was watching TV when I got out, and I knelt in front of him and placed my head on his lap as he rubbed my back, not speaking. We were both lost in our thoughts. I heard before I felt a slap on the skin of my head. It wasn't hard, just a quick slap, not even enough to sting, and I raised my head and looked at him in disbelief. "What was that for?" I asked, and his reply was, "I just wanted to hear what it sounded like." We both started to laugh, our laughter growing louder and louder as tears rolled down our cheeks. "Just wait until you go bald," I threatened, so happy the mood had been lightened.

On my way to bed, I peeked in on Kayla, and she was still awake, so I lay down with her, and we chatted. She asked me if she could touch my head and then reached out and touched it gently with her fingertips. "Feels weird," she simply said.

Weird! Everything was weird!

Chemo day number two arrived, and we all milled about the house quietly, lost in our own thoughts. The cold sores in my mouth had not cleared up, and I was worried the clinic would not proceed with my treatment. For a short time I considered not telling them but knew I could not do that. We arrived at the hospital, and I got settled in the treatment room. While the nurse moved around and got everything prepared, she asked me how everything was. When I mentioned my mouth sores, she took a look and said that they probably would not proceed because the sores were still open and that administering chemo before the sores were better would just make them worse. She went to discuss it with my nurse Krista and then returned a short time later to say Krista had decided to postpone my treatment for a week.

Disappointed, mad, frustrated—I felt it all.

As we filed out of the hospital, I fought hard not to cry and could not wait to get home, go to my bedroom, and close the door on the world. I had been mentally prepared to have the second treatment completed and be one step closer to being done, but I was not prepared to have it postponed. I was disappointed beyond words. I wanted it over and didn't want to have to wait another week.

Within minutes of us arriving home, Linda showed up. She hugged me tightly and then pressed a silver coin in my hand; one side had a ribbon, and the other side said *strength*. She had been at a drive-through getting coffee on her way to the hospital to see us and was digging for change when she got my text that it was canceled. The change she pulled out of her purse at that moment had included the coin she was now giving me. As we hugged in the hallway and cried, Shawn walked through the door; he too had been on his way to the hospital to sit with us for a while during treatment. We visited for a while, and once everyone left, I retreated to my bedroom to rest. I was beyond disappointed and spent the afternoon sleeping.

That night when everyone was sleeping, I sent out an e-mail to update everyone on what had happened that day.

Thanks for all the e-mails and texts yesterday and today. Here is the update I promised.

Unfortunately my second chemotherapy session today was postponed until next Monday. I have been fighting mouth sores for about ten days, which is a side effect of the drugs and my body's way of saying that the dosage was too strong. As a result it killed too many of my "good" cells and is showing up in the sores in my mouth. I have been on a rinse for that since last Tuesday, and they are healing up nicely; however, it's not enough for them to want to go ahead and hit me again until I am fully healed. To go ahead now would be, as they put it, "an exercise in stupidity." My mouth would just blow up again but twice as bad. As disappointed as we are for the delay, I am also very thankful that they are taking the time to make sure I am healed before knocking me on my butt again.

For my next round, they will be decreasing my dosage to hopefully avoid this happening again, and I have also been given rinses and creams to use and will hopefully avoid a reoccurrence.

So that's that! June 11 is the next scheduled date, and until then, I will garden!

Love Me

My e-mail was much more upbeat than I felt at the time, but I also knew that it was better to be positive. No one wanted to hear me moan about how disappointed or mad I was.

I watched a video a friend had sent me; it was a song by Kal Hourd called "When Pink Is Just a Color Again." It was such a beautiful song, and toward the end there was a picture of a man walking, and the sign on the back of his shirt said, *My Wife Survived.* Tears, tears, tears. The floodgates opened. I wanted so desperately to see Cliff wearing that shirt in twenty-five years. I wanted to live. I wanted to survive.

I logged off, and as I walked away, the blue screen of my monitor cast my shadow on the wall in front of me and it stopped me in my tracks. I did not recognize my shadow. I could see a round head and ears poking out with no hair to hide them. I could not believe that shadow belonged to me.

As the week passed, Peggy and Dyrick kept busy around the house, helping out wherever they could, and my energy kept getting better and better as the days went by. I spent the first part of the week avoiding mirrors, and when I did glimpse one, I was still shocked at my appearance. But as the week progressed, I found myself getting more and more comfortable with my naked head and stopped wearing anything on it while at home. I always kept my scarf close at hand in case anyone dropped in, but for the most part I accepted my hair loss and enjoyed the freedom of not having to cover up at home.

As I slowly accepted my hair loss, I also noticed that the number on my weight scale was creeping up. I knew one of the side effects of the chemotherapy was weight gain. It seemed like a three-sided prong: the diagnosis, the hair loss, and now the weight gain. It was bad enough being bald. I could handle that. But fat and bald? That was another story. As much as I tried to watch what I was eating, the weight continued to pile on, and it was noticeable from week to week. I am happy that I did not know early on in my treatment that by the end of treatment I would be thirty-five pounds heavier; it was much easier to accept it five pounds at a time.

During the week, I found myself having some pretty serious pity parties by myself. While all my friends were as attentive as they could be, dropping by to visit, calling, and texting, they were still going on with their lives and enjoying the beginnings of summer. When they did drop by, I could not help but envy their health, their beautiful hair, their weekend plans, and their carefree attitudes. I hated those feelings, but as hard as I tried to stop feeling them, I couldn't. Then I would silently reprimand myself, feeling horrible for having those thoughts, feeling like a horrible friend. It was a vicious cycle. Some days I felt so lonely even when there were people around.

I wanted to put this all behind me and move on, fast-forward my life to a year from now. But even those thoughts made me anxious wondering what my life would be like in a year. I wondered if I would be well, cancer free, back to work, and engaged in my life once again. While I knew that my life was changed forever, I wondered what the new normal would look like for Cliff and me. There were so many unknowns, and I knew this was one of the reasons people told me to take it one day at a time and when that was too much to take it one moment at a time. I promised to enjoy every day as best as I could, to complain as little as possible, and to put as much energy into getting better as I could find. I did not want anyone to remember this period of time as one where I complained, moaned and groaned, or felt sorry for myself ... I wanted my fight to be strong and courageous, inspirational to any woman who found herself on the same path as me in the future. I set the bar high for myself, and some days it was hard to meet. Some days I failed miserably and let my worries and fears spill out onto whichever friend happened to be visiting that day, crying a river of tears. Cliff was on the end of many of those moments as well, but I always felt better after them, pulled my shoulders back, and got on with my day.

We all felt so much better when we met with my nurse, Krista, and she gave me the green light for my treatment to go ahead on the following Monday. We had a wonderful chat with her, and I told her how upsetting it was to me that my treatment had been delayed. She assured me that those were perfectly normal feelings and that it was understandable to be mad, sad, and upset all at once. She described having cancer as having a messy desk. Everything that happened was like adding a paper to the messy pile until you couldn't see the desk anymore, and in order to cope, you needed to file some of those papers away. By filing the papers away, she meant I had to deal with my emotions as they happened, and then they would be easier to handle rather than just stacking all the emotions on top of each other.

After our visit with Krista and our conversation, I felt my mood lighten and was able to enjoy Peggy and Dyrick's visit a bit better. The weekend was a lazy one, and I rested both my body and mind in preparation for Monday's treatment. People kept saying that because this was the second it would be easier because I knew what to expect. People kept saying that because they were cutting down on the chemo drugs this time around, it would be easier. But I was still scared. I was scared, and I didn't want to have to go back there again. I wished no one had to experience chemotherapy and the side effects it caused. I just wanted it to be over.

Cliff and I spent some time together, cuddling and sharing some tender words. He had been my rock for the past three months, but I knew how hard it had been on him. His heart had broken a million times over since this all began, but he had always managed to get a grip on his emotions and be there for me when I needed him most. When I cringed at my physical appearance, he told me I was beautiful. When I said I was tired, he covered me with a blanket, kissed my forehead, and told me to sleep. When I wanted to walk, he held my hand and slowed his step to match my turtlelike pace. He forced me to drink water when I didn't want it. He made sure I took my pills on time. He gave me space when I was feeling overwhelmed and held me tightly when I needed more warmth. As we talked, we looked back over the past three months and realized that when we looked forward three months, I would be done with chemotherapy. We both had a hard time concentrating and just wanted the second session to be over, one more hurdle over.

> *Don't fear the future, God's already there.*
> —Author Unknown

Two Down, Only Four to Go

The morning of my second treatment arrived cool and sunny, and Cliff and I lay in bed, holding each other, not talking, each lost in our thoughts. We finally got up, had our showers, and got ready for the day. I was feeling very agitated and stressed, and my nerves were standing at attention. As we drove to the hospital, I could feel the panic set in again, and I reached in my purse for an Ativan to help settle me down.

It was so good to have Peggy and Dyrick with us, and we kept chatting while we were waiting to be shown into the treatment room. Peggy had sat with her mom through all of her treatments years ago, and I knew this was unearthing some pretty painful memories for her, although she never once said anything. I watched her when she didn't know, and I could see on her face just how tough this was for her, and it only made me love her more. She was putting her pain aside to be there for me. I saw her swallow her tears a few times that morning.

By the time I was ready to be hooked up to my IV, the Ativan had kicked in, and I was feeling quite relaxed and settled. Linda showed up just as my treatment was underway, bringing coffee and a ton of stories to make us laugh and keep our minds off what was happening. It was so good to have visitors, and it made those hours spent in treatment fly by. I often marveled at how fast the time went as the IV was removed from my arm. That morning was no different, and before we knew it we were back in the car and on the way home. Just as Peggy was getting me settled for a nap, Tammy showed up for a visit. She had been unable to get down to see me that morning at the hospital, so she had decided she would drop by the house for a visit. Once she left, Peggy whisked me off to bed to sleep, and I feel asleep to the sounds of Dyrick working in the yard and the smell of food cooking in the kitchen wafting under my bedroom door.

As I lay there, I felt peace and comfort that one can only feel when surrounded by family. Peggy and Dyrick had done nothing but help and support us since they arrived, and I knew I was going to miss them horribly when they went home. For a short moment, I allowed myself to think what if. What if we had never moved away from home? I knew Peggy would be there for me every minute of every day if she could, and I knew she had played the what-if game many times in her heart, especially this year. But I also knew there was no sense in wishing for what we didn't have. I would let her love on me as much as she wanted while she was here and keep that love close to me when she returned home.

That evening, Tracy dropped in for a quick visit and to bring me over a card Juanita had left with her, and Bonnie dropped in to deliver a gift from April, another co-worker. It was a quiet evening, and the heavy feeling in my body started to settle in faster than last time. I managed to send out my second update to bring everyone up to speed on what had happened since treatment number two. Then I returned to bed.

Subject: Two Down, Only Four to Go!

Hello, everybody.

I hope you all had a good start to your week. Monday is over, so it is all downhill from here for you working-class peeps!

Now, time for an update on what has been going on since treatment number one on May 14. Thank you for all the e-mails and texts this morning wishing me well today. Your words of encouragement, prayer, and humor made the morning easier to face.

Here at the Rideout household, we have had a ton of visitors and lots of things happening. On May 21, my girlfriend Juanita from NFLD arrived to spend two weeks with me. We had a terrific time together, and it was so nice to have her here and spend some quality time with her. We did a ton of laughing, which was so good for my soul, and a ton of eating, which wasn't so good for my waistline! We shared our tears as well, but they were good tears, tears of recovery and hope. I will always be thankful for our time together. She is not just my friend; she is my chosen sista!

On May 28, we attended the Timberwolves Head Shave, and Juanita was at my side and shaved my head for me. It was a very emotional time in front of all those people for both of us. Before we began, Juanita leaned down, kissed my cheek, and whispered to me, "Here we go, chick." I sat next to my girlfriend's son, Zac, and we held hands as our hair fell to the floor. I saw it as another hurdle I have leaped over with as much grace as I could muster. At the end of the day I managed to raise $6,750 toward cancer research, and for that I am so proud as well as eternally grateful to my family and friends who were so generous in their support. The day saw almost forty of my friends and co-workers attend to support me, and I nearly burst with pride and emotion as I watched them file into the gym. To those of you who took the time out of your busy schedules to come and support me, thank you isn't enough. I felt the love, and the love is what makes every day easier. Our team raised a total of more than $21,000! How cool is that? Those kids are my heroes!

Juanita returned to NFLD on May 31 (with a promise to return next summer), and the following day Cliff's sister Peggy and brother-in-law Dyrick landed on Alberta soil. Peggy came into my home, gave me orders to rest, and has pretty much pampered me from then to now. She has cooked, cleaned, and everything in between. Dyrick has been busy being my lawn boy, jack of all trades, and chauffer while still managing to work on Cliff's Mopar and burn a few tires to the rims out on the country roads! My house has never been cleaner, and I am enjoying all the attention that goes with their visit! They have been a true delight to have with us, and we are going to miss them when they return home this Thursday. It will be the first time in almost a month that we will not have visitors, and our home will seem really, really quiet.

Last Saturday, Cliff took the initiative and told me, quite gently, that the time had come to shave off the quarter inch of hair that I had left. It was coming out in patches and was really looking awful, but I was afraid to take that last step. Up until then, I could wear a hat, and it just looked like I had a really short haircut. We made our preparations and went into our bathroom armed with shaving cream, towels, razors, and bandages (just in case). Cliff lathered up my head and then started at the back and worked forward. As he worked, I watched him in the mirror and marveled at the man I married. He is the most kind, loving, and gentle man, and I am so blessed to have him in my life. He has shown me that love goes deeper than hair, deeper than scars on my body and comes right from the heart. He caught my eye and said, "Who would have thought four months ago that I would be shaving your head today?" It took about half an hour and six razors to get it cleaned off, and it felt so good after. What could have been a traumatizing time for me was turned into a special day by Cliff, and I will always remember that day as being full of fun and love. I am so blessed. Amazingly I have easily adapted to my bald status, and every time Cliff or Peggy walk by me, they kiss the top of my head. Many times I forget to put on a hat while at home and only remember that my head is naked when company leaves.

Treatment number two went ahead today after being delayed last week because of mouth sores. They are almost completely cleared up now, and I am hoping that I do not have to experience that again. If I do, I am armed with the proper medications, ready to hit back at them right away, and hopefully they will not get as bad as they did last time. I didn't sleep much last night, still had butterflies and anxious moments all night. We arrived at the hospital at 10:00 a.m., and I was armed with my lucky charms in my pocket and around my neck. Peggy and Dyrick came, and we got settled in my treatment area as my nurse Taneal got me all set up. I looked at Peggy, and she winked back at me, and I said to Taneal, "Let's get this done." Cliff pulled his chair close and held my hand, but the difference this time was that we talked and laughed while the injections were being done.

Linda arrived halfway through with a round of Tim's for everyone and stayed until the last drug was almost finished. Today's experience was so different from the first one, and I know they will get easier each time. Only FOUR left!

We arrived home, and Tammy came to visit. After she left, Peggy ushered me into bed to relax and sleep. I fell asleep as soon as my head hit the pillow. What a wonderful sleep I had. I woke up several hours later to the distant hum of an electric drill (Dyrick was adjusting all the doors in my basement, which we didn't do when we installed the carpet in February. We can now close the doors!) and the smell of homemade soup wafting under the door in my room. Peggy sat me down and put a bowl of homemade chicken soup and buns in front of me and said, "Eat." It was so good! I have a bed and breakfast right in my own home!

It has been a quiet evening with a few short visits from Tracy and Bonnie.

It is now bedtime for me. I have been up for a few hours, and the chemo fog has rolled in again. I am very tired and feel like cement has been poured into my body, but I am not sick, which I am so thankful for. My next treatment is scheduled for July 3, the same day that Kayla leaves for Europe and Spain for a month. That will be a rough day for Cliff, and I may have to slip him one of my Ativan!

Thank you again for all the support in whatever form it has been offered. Taking one day at a time at times like this can be a pretty tall order, but knowing we have so many behind us has made our travel easier. Our family is truly blessed, and I look at each day with excitement knowing that I am one day closer to the end of this journey and getting back to living my life healthy once again.

I read the following quote yesterday and fell in love with it … "It may not be today, tonight, or tomorrow, but everything is going to be okay." Amen to that!

So, as Lloyd Robertson is famous for saying before he retired, "That's the kind of day it's been!"

Love you all.

Love Me

The morning after my treatment, I woke up at 4:40 a.m. and went to sit on the couch. Everyone in the house was still sleeping, and the sun was just rising, casting such a beautiful hue of colors over my living room walls. As I sat there I could hear the birds outside in the trees, singing their beautiful songs, and I wanted to sit there forever and listen. It was so peaceful, and I pulled my robe closer and sunk farther into the sofa, watching the rays from the sunrise dance across the walls. I checked my e-mails and felt the love in each I read.

My boss Sharon wrote,

Oh, Kim. Wonderful, amazing, real, Kim. Thanks for your update. Thinking about you always and praying/wishing you good thoughts. The chemo sounds like it just sucks, and I am proud of you for embracing your treatments with such kick-ass courage! I believe in you, as so many do. You are coming out on the other end of this thing an even stronger, healthier, more beautiful, crazier, more wonderful woman. I do love you. Take so much care.

And my dear Chicklet sent,

My prayers were with you extra today. I prayed for the strength your family needs, the strength and faith you need, the knowledge and expertise of the medical staff that tend to you and for you (and God) to know how thankful every one of your friends and family is for you. Thank you for sharing your heart and your story … You are such a gem. Rest assured you will kick this cancer, as God isn't done with your good works yet!

My Aunt Marilyn, who always writes everything in caps, wrote:

GOOD MORNING, PRETTY LADY. IT COMES AS NO SURPRISE TO ME HOW YOU'RE HANDLING EVERYTHING. YOU ALWAYS WERE A POSITIVE AND SPECIAL PERSON. TOO BAD I'M NOT CLOSER TO HELP YOU OUT, BUT IT SEEMS LIKE CLIFF'S FAMILY HAS IT ALL UNDER CONTROL. THANK GOD FOR THAT. I'VE HAD YOU ON THE PRAYER LIST IN OUR CHURCH SINCE THIS STARTED, AND WE PRAY FOR YOU EVERY NIGHT. I THINK OF YOU EVERY DAY. I WENT TO THE CANCER SURVIVORS MEETING IN GRANDBANK ON SUNDAY FOR YOU. WHAT A WONDERFUL AND UPLIFTING EXPERIENCE. I CHECK EVERY DAY FOR YOUR UPDATES. KEEP THEM COMING. LOVE YOU.

And my friend Juanita managed to make me laugh out loud with her e-mail:

Good morning, chick. Hope you have rested well ... I dearly love reading your updates ... You are my rock and a true inspiration ... If I had one wish (other than the one I always have that has not happened yet, that I was 5'9" and 120 pounds and blonde ... time to give up on that one I think) that would be that this never ever happened to you, and now that it has that I could be there right next to you holding your hand ... that is two wishes, isn't it ... Oh well ... Love you.

My friend Ruby, a sister breast cancer survivor wrote and said,

Kim, I could not help but shed a few tears when I read your e-mail. It is wonderful that you have such great support and an upbeat attitude. It makes your journey so much easier. Just continue to stay positive and take one day at a time. You are amazing and you're right, "Everything is going to be okay!"

And my dear friend Lori wrote,

Oh Kim! Thank you for the update. You are truly gifted at writing. I cried as I read about your hair-shaving experience at the school, and then I cried really hard when I read what you wrote about Cliff. (Damn, I'm crying again!) Isn't true love, unconditional love so beautiful? You are blessed with a wonderful man, and he is blessed by you. You are always in our thoughts. I pray you are feeling okay after treatment number two. Blessing to you, Cliff, and your girls and safe travels for Peggy and Dyrick tomorrow.

I felt warm from the sea of beautiful words. I didn't feel strong, inspirational, or courageous, but I felt loved.

The day got more beautiful as the hours wore on, and I sat outside in my gazebo and read while Peggy and Dyrick buzzed around the house, doing all they could do before they left to return home in two days. It was a beautiful day. I napped in the morning and woke up to the smell of fresh cut grass mown by Dyrick and the sounds of Peggy vacuuming; no dust bunny was safe when she was around. We ate on the deck for supper with the birds singing in the trees in the yard and the smells of the lilacs passing by our noses. It was a glorious, beautiful day, and I felt so good. I was nervous, afraid that I would be taken to my knees when I was least expecting it. While I was tired, I was not feeling sick, and the heavy feeling in my bones last night had passed again.

On their final day, I took them to lunch and tried to keep the mood light. Peggy was very emotional about leaving. She felt it was her place to take over for her mother and to be here and take care of me, but we all knew she could not do that. She had a life and family in Newfoundland that she had to return to, and I did my best to reassure her that we would be okay, that my chosen family here would be there if we needed anyone, and that she didn't need to worry about me. I knew she would worry, I knew she would fret, but I also knew she was leaving with a lighter heart having seen the wonderful network of friends we had to support us. As Cliff stacked their suitcases in the vehicle, we said our good-byes before we went to bed. Their flight left early in the morning, and we agreed that they would not wake me to say good-bye again.

The morning after they left, I woke up and walked out into a quiet, empty house. This was the first time in a month we did not have company, and I had mixed feelings. While I was happy to have some privacy once again, I missed tripping over people and having people around to talk to. I decided that the day would be a lazy day, and after a nice long bath, I crawled back into my PJs and settled in front of the TV. The next evening was the Relay for Life, and I wanted to try to conserve as much energy as I could so that I could participate. Cliff joined me on the couch when he got home. He'd had a long day, leaving at 4:00 a.m. for the airport and then putting in a full day's work.

> *Faith sees the invisible, believes the incredible, and receives the impossible.*
> —Author Unknown

The morning of the Relay for Life started with rain but then cleared up as the day wore on. My friends were busy all day out at the location, setting up the tents and getting everything that they needed for their team in order. The survivor walk was set to start at 7:00 p.m., so I rested all day with the hope I would be well enough to attend and participate in the walk. All day I wrestled with feelings of sadness, and I was very emotional thinking about the Relay for Life and the years in the past when Cliff, me, Kelsey, and Kayla participated and lit a luminary for Cliff's mom, my grandmother, and my friend Debbie, who had all passed away from cancer.

Never had I thought the day would come that people would be walking for me. Never had I expected to stop and see a luminary with my name on it lit on the side of the track.

I wished I had my family with me. I would have loved to have walked that walk with Mom and Dad at my side, my brother and his family, Cliff's family—brothers, sister, nieces, nephews. I missed them all so much. I did not want to walk with the survivors. I wanted to be like everyone else, wear the same color T-shirt, not a yellow one that clearly marked me as a cancer survivor. I did not want to stand out. My emotional struggle all day was exhausting, and I spent most of the day sleeping.

I didn't want to be a cancer survivor. I wanted to be someone who had never had cancer.

When we arrived at the relay, we sought out our beautiful friends, and I was amazed at all the preparation they had put into their home for the night. Adjoining tents had been set up, and there were heaters, beds, and chairs, along with a table with enough food to feed one hundred people. Cliff and I visited with everyone there, and I laughed when I saw all my little friends wearing their bras over their shirts. They were having so much fun and getting ready to start their full night of walking.

As the victory lap started, everyone pushed me toward the sea of yellow shirts and told me to join in. I was reluctant; I felt like an imposter. I didn't feel like a survivor yet. I was only at the beginning of my battle and still had not bought into the concept that a person was considered a survivor from the moment he or she was diagnosed. Cliff felt my hesitation, took my hand, and started to walk with me. As we rounded every corner, people cheered, took pictures, and smiled. I was so uncomfortable, feeling I shouldn't be there, not wanting to be there, and wishing I was just a spectator myself. I could feel the tension in Cliff. Once again I had pushed him beyond his comfort zone into a place where he did not want to be. We were both relieved when we passed under the finish sign. I did another lap with everyone, and as Linda tucked her arm into mine and smiled at me, I started to cry and was thankful that I had on my sunglasses.

Jen took my hand and led me over to the luminaries to show me the ones that were there for me, four in total. As Tracy and I stood there and looked at them, I whispered, "I cannot believe this is happening." She took my hand, and we finished the lap in silence.

After one hour, my energy was spent. Cliff and I said good-bye to everyone and thanked my friends for all they had done. As we slowly walked to the car, I cried, remembering all the hours I had spent walking on the track in the relays in past years, how much fun we'd had then, surrounded by our friends. This year the agenda had been changed, and it was my name being illuminated by the candles, and I was heartbroken. I was thankful for Mackenzie for starting the whole idea and for all my friends for joining in, organizing, and fund-raising. I knew how much work had gone into it, and I knew it was all done out of love for me. For the rest of my life I will always be thankful for that night.

> *Never, never, never, never give up!*
> —Winston Churchill

Over the next several days I dealt with more side effects. Constipation continued to be my nemesis, and I tried every remedy my doctor and nurses told me to try, and finally it started to work. It was hit-and-miss with the supplements they told me to take. It was mostly trial and error until I finally found the combination that worked without giving me those gut-wrenching cramps. As I fought with constipation, I also struggled with weight gain, and as each day wore on, I felt my clothes getting tighter and tighter. Some days the bloating was unmanageable, and I found it was just easier to lie in bed until it passed.

Some days when I looked in the mirror, I could still not believe the person looking back at me was indeed me. With my bloated face, bald head, and dark circles under my eyes, I did not look like me. The only thing I recognized was my eyes, but some days the sadness in them was too hard to look at, so I avoided the mirror as much as I could. I always said that to feel good on the inside you have to feel good on the outside, which also works the other way around as well. I didn't feel good on the inside or outside, so I really had to dig deep to feel good some days, and I couldn't wait for the day I could look in the mirror and feel pretty again. I asked Cliff how he could still find me attractive. His answer was, "I don't love you for your hair. I love you for *you*. And you are beautiful."

I started to feel really low and had read enough about cancer and depression that I didn't want to go down that path. I knew I needed to get a grip on my emotions, so I headed to the bookstore with the goal of buying something inspirational. I have always loved to read; biographies have been my number-one interest, and the book shelves in my den overflowed with books full of true stories. But I needed something new, something inspirational that I hadn't read before, something that had nothing to do with cancer or breast cancer, or even a woman.

While perusing the biography section, I picked up a book written by Trevor Greene called *March Forth*. At the age of forty-one, Trevor Greene, a journalist and a reservist in the Canadian Army, was deployed to Kandahar with the 1st Battalion PPCLI Battle Group. On March 4th, 2006, while meeting with village elders in a remote village in Kandahar Province, Greene removed his helmet out of respect, confident that a centuries-old pact would protect him from harm. Without warning, a teenage boy under the influence of the Taliban came up behind Trevor and swung a rusty ax deep into his skull, nearly splitting his brain in two.

Trevor's fiancée, Debbie, was initially told he would not live. When he survived, she was told he would never come out of his coma, let alone be able to move on his own. But Debbie never left Trevor's side, and after years of rehabilitation, setbacks, and crises, Trevor learned to talk and move again. In July 2010, he stood up at his own wedding with Debbie at his side and his daughter, Grace, carrying their rings down the aisle as their flower girl. It was a remarkable story of love told in two voices: Trevor's up until the attack that changed their lives and Debbie's as she worked tirelessly to rehabilitate the man she loved.

As I lost myself in the book, I was constantly amazed with Trevor's spirit and courage in spite of all the adversities he was facing in his rehabilitation. I started using him as my motivation to keep fighting. On mornings when my bones were aching, I thought of him not able to feel his legs but having enough determination to never give up the desire to walk again, and that made me get moving. When I wanted to stay in bed, I thought of him not able to get out of bed on his own, and I would swing my legs off the edge and get up. When I wanted to lie down and cry and feel sorry for myself, I thought of Debbie and how many times she could have given up, but she didn't.

While I would have many other periods when I was down, *March Forth* helped dig me out of a pit of depression and was just what I needed at that time. Once I completed the book, I sent an e-mail to the editor and asked that he send the note on to Trevor and Debbie Greene. I just wanted to let them know how much they had touched me and given me the courage to fight on. I was thrilled to receive a response from Trevor wishing me well. That book helped put my journey into perspective and taught me to never give up, because anything is possible as long as you believe.

Father's Day arrived, and it was a beautiful day. I called home and talked with Dad for a little while, wishing him a happy Father's Day and wishing I could have been cooking him dinner. The holidays were always the hardest time to be away from family.

When I checked my e-mails, I saw one from Carrie, and we corresponded back and forth throughout the morning. She wanted to know if she could come and see me at my next treatment on July 3 because that was her one-year anniversary. I told her I would love to see her that day and to celebrate with her. I asked her how she was doing, and she told me that since her diagnosis she knew herself better now and felt better about herself than she ever had before. She said that she worried less about little things and just tried to enjoy every day and that she was genuinely happy. As I read her words, I realized that while she was ten years younger than me, she was ten years wiser, and I was so happy to have her as a role model.

Throughout the day, I felt better and better and had so much energy. I spent hours in the garden, planting flowers and rolling around in the dirt. I felt like me again. While I was moving a lot slower than normal, I was moving, and I was having fun doing it. As I worked in the garden, where I have always found peace, I reflected on the events of the last couple of months and could not believe how far I had come. Through the ups and downs, I still always landed on my feet and still always managed to laugh out loud. Another strange thing I started to notice was my acceptance of my lack of hair. While I would never have admitted it to anyone, I was actually enjoying not having to worry about doing my hair on the days I wasn't feeling well. It was so much easier to tie on a scarf or put on a hat and go. Kayla had told me a couple of times that she thought I looked great and hoped that when my hair did come back, I kept it short. While I still could not wait to have hair again, I was accepting the lack of it right now, and that was okay for me.

That evening, Cliff and I settled in and watched a documentary on TV of a well-known Newfoundlander named Bill Kelly. Mr. Kelly had heart trouble for more than two years and talked about how in the beginning he was always afraid of dying. Then finally one day he got fed up with always been afraid and said, "Why am I living if all I am doing is being afraid of dying?" His comment took my breath away, and I realized that was exactly how I had been feeling: afraid of dying. Why was I doing all this—chemo and radiation—if all I was going to do at the end of the day was worry about what tomorrow was going to bring? Another light bulb went off for me, just like when I read Trevor Greene's book. I knew I needed to live in the day, the present day, and enjoy every minute of every day. Tomorrow would happen, and I would do it all over again until that day wasn't there anymore. And I knew that when the time came when there was no next day, I would be in heaven.

I wasn't ready for that day yet and didn't want it to come for at least forty more years. But until it did come, I would try to live every day to the fullest. I knew there would still be lots of lows, lots of days when I would want to just curl up and cry, lots of days when I would be mad or sad, but I knew that I would always have to pull myself up and that there was so much good to live for, so much life to live, and so much love to share.

Why am I living if all I am doing is being afraid of dying?
——Bill Kelly

Despite my newfound insight from the documentary, the next day found me feeling low and quick to anger. I was back on the rollercoaster of emotions. I remember feeling mad that everyone else's life was going along fine while mine was at a standstill. I wanted to feel the innocence of being healthy again. I wanted to feel that carefree feeling once again. I didn't want to be sick. I didn't want to have cancer. I wanted to be like everyone else. Rationally I knew that a lot of how I was feeling was amplified because I was feeling so tired and everything I did took so much time and effort. My days of just going out to browse through my favorite store seemed like years ago, and I wondered if I would ever feel well enough to do it again. I hated being sick, I hated being tired, and I hated the foreign things that were happening to my body.

I did notice that my head was starting to spring some peach fuzz on top, and just seeing those little signs of hair gave me hope. However transparent they may be, they gave me hope that my hair would indeed come back. At the very beginning when they went over with me the fact that I would lose my hair, they had also mentioned that there was a small percentage of people who experienced permanent hair loss, and I immediately started to worry that I would be in that small percentage. I guess I didn't have enough to worry about at the time!

I also continued to feel the burden and discomfort of the weight gain. I was only two treatments in, and already I felt like I had gained about ten pounds. All my clothes were tight, my hands were swelled up, and I was feeling very bloated. I made a silent promise to myself that as soon as I was feeling a little better, I would go and do some shopping for clothes that fit me, hoping that would help me with my self-esteem.

The worst feeling during this period was not the hair loss or the weight gain or even the treatments and side effects that went along with that. It was the loss of the physical intimacy with my husband. I have been in love with Cliff since I first saw him on the playground when I was eleven years old. We dated on and off throughout the years until we finally came together for good when I was eighteen. We built our first home and moved into it four months before our wedding when I was twenty-one.

Cliff and I have always been best friends and love our life together. We had our children when we were young; Kelsey was born two years after we were married, and Kayla followed twenty months later. We loved our family, loved growing up with our girls, and loved each other. Our children had grown into wonderful, responsible young women; financially we were stable; our careers were flourishing; we had a terrific circle of friends; and sex was great. We enjoyed that level of intimacy that comes from knowing someone for a lifetime, being with a person who knows you better than you know yourself, having no secrets, and knowing we were safe no matter what.

Suddenly that was all gone. Even though I was desired (I knew Cliff still desired me), I did not feel desirable. I would look into the mirror, notice how puffy and round my face was, my belly distended from constipation, and my bald head shining under the bathroom light. How could I feel desirable? I was so tired that a good majority of the days I would stay in my pajamas. How could I muster up the energy to roll around in the sheets? I had not felt pretty in months. I could not remember the last time I felt attractive. Sex was so far off my radar that I started to forget how good it felt to be in Cliff's arms.

Cliff was so patient. Knowing that my head was out of the game, he kept reassuring me how much he loved me, that it was okay, and that he would wait for me however long it took. There were lots of days that this took a toll on Cliff. The lack of intimacy was a small issue but huge at the same time. We went from engaging in an active, equally satisfying physical relationship to nothing. During the times Cliff was down or when he appeared to be mad or angry, I tried to show him the same grace he showed me. I knew he was struggling right along with me, but at times I was powerless to help him; it was hard enough to keep my own head above water.

On a particularly low day for me, my friend Krista dropped by to visit and brought a prayer shawl her mother had made for me. It was a beautiful shawl and the accompanying card said, *A prayer shawl is intended to be a reminder of God's loving presence and care. It is a gift for every occasion, joyful or sorrowful, chosen or unchosen. As you wear it, may you grow in your awareness of God's blessing resting upon you in all places and at all times.* Another beautiful act of kindness.

> *One person with courage makes a majority.*
> —Andrew Jackson

Again I started having that internal talk with myself. Who did I hurt by letting this get the best of me? I hurt me, I hurt my family, and I hurt everyone around me who loved me. No one benefited. It was time (again) to put on my big girl panties and step back up to the plate. No more feeling sorry for myself or being mad because my friends because were healthy and I wasn't. I would be healthy again. I would be strong again. I knew I would. I just needed to start believing that again.

It was also around this time that I started to think about what was happening to me on a rational level. Not only was I dealing with a cancer diagnosis, the chemotherapy, and the side effects of that and the fear that all that entailed, but I was also dealing with a hormonal imbalance. My periods had stopped upon my diagnosis (which I have come to learn is normal), and my body was thrown into a hormonal tsunami of about a 7.8 magnitude. How could I be anything but irrational at times, ready to crawl out of my skin? It was normal! These feelings were normal! All that I was experiencing was normal! It didn't stop the mood swings, the feelings of helplessness, the feelings of complete and utter sadness or fear, but it did help how I dealt with those feelings when they took over.

I tried very hard as well not to target Cliff when I was having a low moment. It is said that you hurt those you love because it is safe to do because they will always love you. I tested this theory time and time again with my family, and they always loved me through it. Cliff would often make himself scarce, spending time in his garage away from me when a mood hit, and Kayla would disappear with her friends, always waving the white flag before they came back inside.

One special thing we did have that helped us through those tough moments was laughter! After a meltdown, when everything was once again okay, Cliff would often call me a mean bald bitch. That may sound crass or disrespectful to some, but to us it was funny. I was mean, I was bald, and I was acting like a bitch. Call a spade a spade, people! We needed laughter, we needed joy, and we needed to know that things could be normal in the sea of desolation we often felt.

I also got really good at having internal conversations with myself over disengaging from my life. One night in particular, all the men went to the car show, which is their normal Thursday night routine in the summer. They drive their Mopars there and spend hours looking at all the cars that came and comparing each car to theirs. Then they head out to the back roads to drag race until the police show up and shut them down. On this particular night, after it got dark, they all headed back to Mark and Simone's and visited in the backyard, laughing and having a good time. I decided I would not go. I was mad that they were all having fun, and I was home not feeling well. I chose not to recognize that I had received several calls asking me to join them, to drop over for a drink, to share in the fun. Was there anything preventing me from joining them? No. Did they stop having a good time because I wasn't there? No. Who was hurt that I wasn't there? Me. Again I realized no one else's world was going to stop because I was sick. It was time to reengage or I was going to miss out on a whole lot more, and I would have no one to blame for that except myself!

My new mantra became, "Tomorrow is a new day. I plan to live it!" Looking back, I can see a direct correlation between my physical recovery and my mental state at the time. As time passed between my second and third treatment, my mental state improved, as did my physical condition. I had more energy, napped less, ate better, and laughed from the heart. Cliff and I shared more quality time together, and he started to relax more around me, not worrying so much about me falling apart at the littlest thing. He smiled more and looked more comfortable than he had in a while. We started walking every evening. He always held my hand tightly and let me set the pace and distance we covered, praising me if we walked farther than we had the night before.

As my physical and mental states improved, I found myself dealing with a new devil: boredom. As I got stronger and stronger, I had to accept that even though I was feeling better, I was still unable to do all the things I had done prior to my diagnosis. My body was still reeling from the effects of the onslaught of chemo, and it was nowhere near as strong as it had been in March. I had to give myself permission to relax and take it easy—not something I had done a lot of in my precancer life. When I felt at my lowest, some days I would reread the e-mail messages that had been sent to me. They always helped lift my mood and gave me the added strength I needed to get through the day, hour, or moment when I was feeling the weakest.

I met with several of my friends from work shortly before my third treatment. We went out for supper and then to a movie. It was so good to see everyone and visit, share stories, and catch up on everything that was happening at work. For a few hours I felt like one of the girls again. While we were there, Bonnie received a call from a family member to tell her that her cousin had just found out she had breast cancer. Even when we tried to forget about breast cancer, something was just around the corner to remind us of it. Despite the news, which she didn't share with me until the following day, we had a great time and shared lots of laughs. The following day, I received two wonderful e-mails from my co-workers that helped buoy my spirits even more.

My co-worker Jamie sent me a beautiful message:

It was really great seeing you again and heartwarming to see that you are doing so well. You look really terrific. Please know that I think of you often and send out positive vibes and wishes for a full and speedy recovery. You have the strength of a Greek god in you, and I have no doubt that you will pull through this like a champ! Keep up the good fight and know you have a ton of support in your corner.

And Bonnie followed up with the following message:

You looked so awesome last night. You have got to be one of the most upbeat women that I know. You truly are an inspiration to me ... to be more like you! WOW, I am getting teary eyed just typing this. You are a wonderful, beautiful friend, and I am so glad that you have come into my life.

Those couple of messages helped me get through the next day when I was feeling all low and sad because everyone was returning back to work while I stayed at home alone. Their words helped me prepare for my upcoming chemo session, which was just around the corner.

Supper with Tracy and Kayla a couple of nights later helped lift my mood as well. Conversation was light and fun and centered on Kayla and her upcoming trip to Europe. It also marked her last day of working before she left for her month-long trip, and we had a good time toasting to her safe travels. Later that evening, Tracy and I visited and talked late into the night. She was always there to help me unload, rationalize my fears, and hug away my terror. Everyone needs a Tracy in his or her life.

One morning after Cliff left for work, the air was filled with the sounds of sirens. They seemed to go on for hours. I called Cliff and my daughters to make sure they had all arrived safely to work and sent up a silent prayer of thanks that no disaster had fallen on our family that morning. We later learned that a thirty-one-year-old man had been killed at an intersection not far from our home. It gave me pause and reminded me how precious life really is and how it can change in an instant. For some reason, that accident impacted both Cliff and me, and we talked about it for weeks after. The man who had died was on his way to work, a day like the day before, never knowing that he would not return home that evening. Even though we did not know the man who died, we were both saddened that it had happened and felt such empathy for his family that we again promised to never take one day for granted.

The Friday before my next treatment, we had our usual visit to my nurse, Krista, at the cancer clinic to discuss my next treatment and have my blood work done, but at the last moment Cliff got called away for work, so I headed to the appointment myself. I felt vulnerable sitting in the examination room alone, as I had always had several people with me. As I started to talk with Krista, I broke down, much to my surprise. I thought I had been handling everything pretty well during that period and was startled that I lost my composure. Krista reassured me that it was normal to let your guard down when you were alone. We talked lots about the side effects of the chemo and how I was handling it emotionally and physically. I told her about the highs and lows I was experiencing, and she assured me that those were normal feelings to have and that I needed to allow myself time each day to cry if I felt the need. I will never forget her kindness that day, how she held my hand and cried with me, letting me know I was not alone in my fight.

After my blood work was done, I headed out to the cutline, where Mark and Simone were waiting. We had pulled our trailer out a few days before and were excited to have our first campout of the year. Cliff was to meet me out there when he was finished work that evening. We were playing cards, had the campfire lit, and were enjoying each other's company and laughing as loud as we could to make sure no bears came onto our site (my fear, not theirs!) when my cell phone rang. It was the hospital advising me that my white blood cell count was really low and that in the event it did not rebound by Tuesday, my treatment would have to be delayed for a week. As I hung up the phone, I started to cry, so frustrated with the idea that my treatment would not go ahead as planned. As I sat there weeping, Mark and Simone did their best to reassure me that all would be okay, saying they were sure my blood count would be up by the end of the weekend and that we should just enjoy the weekend, forget about next week, and have a good time. By the time Cliff arrived at the campground, we were all in a good mood, confident that everything would work out as it should.

We succeeded in not talking about the delay for the rest of the weekend and had a great time playing campfire games, board games, and keeping all the wildlife miles away from us by laughing like hyenas. We sat up until late at night, leaning back in our chairs and watching the satellites fly across the sky between the clouds. And while it was unspoken, I knew we all made the same wish upon the falling stars we saw during the evenings. When we did talk about cancer, it was always upbeat and about how this time next year it would all be over.

Much to Mark and Simone's delight, Cliff decided that weekend that we would buy a quad so that we could have fun in the woods when I feeling better. We went to a nearby community and visited some yard sales, stopped in a local florist shop to marvel at the beautiful flowers, and shared ice cream and pop from an old-fashioned corner store. It was a wonderful weekend with beautiful friends, and it helped me gain a ton of energy to get through the upcoming week and chemo treatment number three.

The day before my third chemotherapy session, I stayed close to home, not wanting to talk to anyone. I was so nervous that my blood counts would not be rebounded by the next day, knowing that if they weren't it would mean another week's delay.

Kayla and I lay on her bed that evening and chatted. She was nervous about her upcoming trip the next day. She was going to Europe to meet her friend and travel for a month. It was the first time she had traveled on a plane by herself, and she was nervous and excited at the same time. A wonderful adventure awaited her, and I didn't want anything to ruin it for her. She was nervous about leaving me, and I told her I would be okay and that I just wanted her to enjoy herself. I reminded her that when she returned in a month I would only have two chemotherapy sessions left to go. I was so excited for her and did not want her worry for me to ruin her trip in any way. I wanted her to go and have fun. To love life once again and not to worry about me all the time. And I would work on healing while she was away.

Every day we are called to small things with great love.
—Mother Teresa

Chapter 7
Three Down, Three to Go—Halfway There

The morning of my third scheduled chemotherapy session, I arrived at the hospital at 9:00 a.m. for blood work and then returned home to await the results. I was so pleased when I received a call an hour later to advise me that my blood counts had rebounded and exceeded where they needed to be. As Cliff and I headed to the hospital, I sent out a quick text to my family and friends, advising that we had the green light for treatment number three.

Just as I was getting settled in the treatment chair, Kayla showed with a bouquet of flowers for me. I didn't want her to hang around because I was afraid I would have some kind of reaction or something and that would be the last thing she saw before she headed to the airport. After some convincing, she finally agreed to head home to do her last-minute packing before her dad picked her up and drove her to the airport. Cliff stayed until the very last minute and then headed home to pick up Kayla. Linda arrived, bringing me lunch and keeping me company while the last of the drugs were administered. Just as we were leaving the hospital, the skies opened, and one of the biggest storms of the season hit us.

My sister-in-law had a charm waiting for me when I got home; it was called "Inner Strength." I loved getting these little packages and delighted in opening the charm she had picked out for me. Peggy made sure I had a charm for every chemotherapy treatment I completed and then a final one for my last radiation treatment. I always think of her when I look down at my bracelet.

The next morning I sent out the following e-mail:

Subject: Three Down, Three to Go! Halfway There!
Hello, everyone.

Happy July! Can you believe that it is July already? Time is just flying! And for me that means I am flying toward a healthy future once again!

All is well here at the Rideout household. Since my last update lots has happened. Peggy and Dyrick returned to NFLD the Thursday after my second treatment, and we were so sorry to see them leave. They left our house in tip-top shape and filled up our love tanks to keep us going for a while yet. Peggy continues to text on a daily basis to check in, and I have learned to text her back right away. She does not like to wait on a reply!

My recovery from my last treatment went well. I was knocked down for about twelve days this time, mostly with that dreaded fatigue. My blood count dropped quite a bit, and it caused my low to last longer than normal, and I really did hit rock bottom for a few days there. I am still eternally grateful that I do not have the issue of throwing up. I will take the fatigue over that any day. I have learned to be patient with myself and that perhaps it is not a good idea to try to get groceries when I am in my low … Took me an hour to bring them in and put them away one day, and by the time I was done, I was exhausted. Cliff is now getting very familiar with the grocery store and has even learned to look for the sales and takes great pleasure in showing me the receipt and pointing out his savings when he gets home.

On Friday past I had my appointment with my oncologist, and everything was looking great other than my blood counts. My blood work came back, and my counts were still only half what they were supposed to be, so I was told that if they did not rebound over the weekend, my treatment would be delayed another week. That caused me some anxiety, as every delay is a delay toward my full recovery. I am just ready to have this over with and to move on, but unfortunately this is something I have little control over.

So we headed out west with Mark and Simone and had a great weekend camping with them. It was our first campout of the season, and it felt so good to get out with our friends and enjoy ourselves. And guess what ... if you need to bring your white blood cell count up, I recommend a weekend of outdoor adventure, drinking cold Coronas under the sun, and laughing your ass off under the stars at night. Because on Tuesday when I went back, my counts were up more than where they needed to be, and my treatment went as scheduled!

I had to come home to wait for my blood to be evaluated, and it was a tense hour of waiting. Kayla was also leaving for Europe the same day, so it was a very emotional day for us. We got the call that treatment was a go, so we headed back to the hospital around noon. Then Kayla showed up with a beautiful bouquet of flowers for me. She stayed for a while and then headed home to get her last-minute stuff done. Saying good-bye was hard, but I know she is going to have a wonderful adventure over there. However, I am already counting the days until she returns home.

Cliff then had to leave about an hour before my treatment was completed to bring Kayla to the airport. My friend Linda (who has been with me for every treatment so far) arrived with lunch for me and to sit with me for the remainder of my treatment. About fifteen minutes before we were done, a storm moved in, and you could hardly see out the window. The rain, the hail, the wind—it was unbelievable. We stood in the entrance for a short while, and then Linda made a run for it to get the vehicle and bring it to the front door for me. I made it home cozy and dry, and Linda was soaked to the skin. Thanks, girlfriend! I love you to pieces.

When I arrived home, I tucked away in my nest and let the rain and *hail lull me off to sleep, and I slept until Cliff got home. He made us supper, and then I fell asleep once again. The days of treatments always offer the best sleeps. Glen and Tracy dropped over in the evening for a visit. I was in bed, so Tracy came and crawled into bed with me, and we visited while Cliff and Glen sat in the living room and watched car shows.*

Sleep evaded me most of the night as I waited anxiously to hear that Kayla had arrived in London safely. Her text came in about 3:00 a.m. and said that she was through customs and with her friend. Big sigh of relief. Then I feel asleep for a couple of hours before I had to get up to take my meds. I checked Kayla's Facebook page for any updates, and already she was making comments about the sexy English construction workers ... I didn't show that to Cliff; he is grey enough already! August 2 won't come fast enough for us.

Today we were back at the hospital for a booster shot. Because my blood is struggling so much with recovering, my doctors have decided that I will benefit from having this booster shot administered after each of my remaining treatments. The benefit of the booster is that it prevents your counts from dropping so low, which also reduces your chance of infection during your recovery time. The side effects of the booster are pain in your big bones (legs, arms, pelvis), but again it is a small price to pay. I am already pumped up on Tylenol to try to get a jump on it. In the future, I will administer this needle at home, so they made me do it myself today. It is a needle that you give in your stomach, and I was actually surprised at how easy it was. It gives me a new appreciation for all you diabetics out there, that's for sure. Cliff hovered like mother hen while I was doing it and was a little disappointed that it was administered in my stomach and not my bum ... I think was he hoping to get flashed!

So that is my update for this month. Thank you so much for the e-mails this week wondering where it was! It causes me such delight knowing that some of you actually look forward to reading it! I read somewhere this week that you cannot make it through an experience like this and keep it to yourself. You have to share it. So that is what I try to do each month.

And once again, to my dear friends and family, thank you so much for your ongoing love and support. As difficult as this journey has been, it is made so much easier knowing I have so many people I can count on. While many days I don't answer the phone and struggle to return your e-mails, please know that every contact warms my heart, and it helps to know you are thinking of me and my family.

I have climbed the mountain and am on my way down the other side now, and I am one happy camper tonight! Three down and only three to go!

Until next month, take care!

Love Me

It felt so good to be halfway there, and I felt like half the battle was over. My feelings of elation were intensified by the amount of peach fuzz that kept appearing on my head, and I thought I would burst when Cliff told me that the stubble on my head scratched his chin when he hugged me. I was fascinated each day when I rubbed my head and felt the newly grown stubble, but I also knew that the latest hit of chemo would probably cause that to fall out, with my eyelashes and eyebrows quickly following suit. I was worried about losing my facial hair. The faces of women without eyelashes or eyebrows always looked so vacant to me. I did lots of online research on how to draw on my eyebrows, but I was not looking forward to putting my newfound skills to use. It was easy to cover my lack of hair on my head with a scarf or hat, but there was no way to hide my face. I knew I would adjust just like I had when I lost my hair, but I was not looking forward to this next stage and having just one more thing taken from me.

The e-mails in response to my update started flooding in, and I was once again overwhelmed. I was secretly pleased with how well my e-mails were being received and loved hearing that people enjoyed reading them, because I had so much fun writing them. It had become something I looked forward to composing after each treatment, something for me to think about while the treatment was being administered. It gave me pleasure to know that even as sick as I was, I could still reach out and touch people and take them along my journey with me, just with words.

Lori and Bubba once again made me smile big with their e-mail:

You sound so strong. I know that there are times that you don't feel strong, but that's when you lean on those around you (another song just popped in my head—"Lean on Me"). You are kicking butt; I'm proud of you. Because you are open, everyone around you feels comfortable. I love how you are celebrating every step of this journey. Thank you for sharing. You are inspiring and helping people with your words, actions, and attitude.

My Aunt Marilyn set another seed to write a book with her e-mail: *Keep those updates coming. You will be able to write a book after this to support other cancer patients. Love you.*

My friend Angela wrote, *Thanks again for the update, Kimmy! I love that you are sharing, and it truly sounds like you are doing the best that can possibly be expected. I continue to hold you in my prayers, and I hope to see you soon. Mwah!*

And my friend and co-worker Bonnie wrote, *You have no idea how you have inspired a whole office. Your courage and fight to get better, your attitude, just everything. I have told you before that you are hero to me, and I wish I could even be a little like you.*

My friend Tammy A. wrote, *You are such an inspiration, Kim. For you to keep your spirits high as you go through this struggle warms my heart. I am so proud of you.*

And Linda simply wrote, *XXXXXXXXXXXXXXXX.*

The e-mails, full of words of encouragement, kept me floating through the dark days ahead. The week following my third treatment was rough. My energy level tanked like never before. I had a headache that would not let up, and my body felt like it was falling apart at the joints. As hard as I tried to stay upbeat, the more my body hurt, the lower my spirits became.

One afternoon, I decided a nice soak in the bath would help me feel better. I sat on the edge of the tub, pouring in the bubble bath and breathing in the steamy air, looking forward to the next hour of uninterrupted bliss with a good book and bubbles. Once I lowered myself in the tub, I looked over the edge to see my book on the counter, several feet away. I willed the book to move toward me on its own, knowing there was no way I had the energy to pull myself up and get it. As I lay there, my frustration turned into tears that ran down my face and mixed with the bubbles. I felt like a ninety-year-old. How was it possible that I was in the tub yet did not have the energy to get up? It was so hard to command my body to do something all the while knowing it did not have the resources to complete the simplest of physical tasks. I lay in the tub until the water started to cool around my body, and I started to shiver. As I tried to pull myself up, the water proved too heavy, and I remember thinking how I never realized before that water actually had weight to it. I felt like I was in quicksand. I slowly rolled over onto my stomach, moving so slowly that the water hardly splashed, pulled myself up onto my knees and hands, and then pushed myself up, feeling the sweat popping out from the exertion even while my skin was full of goose bumps from the cool bath water. As I slowly stepped out of the bath, I promised myself I would not try to do that again until I was better.

How could it be possible that a bath required more energy than I had? While rationally I knew this lull would too pass, just the past weekend I'd had a little spring in my step and enough energy to do some gardening. Going through the lull was the hardest.

I got through the following days, taking my antinausea meds, and while they did their job keeping the sickness at bay, they had side effects of their own that were difficult to deal with—the sleeplessness, restlessness, food cravings (and there was never a craving for a carrot stick). I crossed off the days on the calendar, knowing that as soon as the meds were complete, my body would once again start to get back to normal slowly.

Just when I would start to get really low, feeling sorry for myself or angry that this had happened, I would open my computer and get a beautiful e-mail like the one I received around this time from my friend Juanita: *Love you … love you … love you … I miss you so much … I miss our chats, our tears … our hugs and of course the donuts … I am so happy that you are halfway there, and I would give anything to be right there by your side … Rest comfortably, my friend, until the chemo fog passes …*

Kayla kept me busy texting me from Europe and telling me all about the stuff she was doing and how exciting it was. While the house felt quiet and vacant with her away, I was happy she was having a good time. I was so happy that she was away from me and the sickness, so happy that she had a month to be a kid and enjoy an adventure she had been looking forward to for so long. She was planning on visiting Spain and Portugal, and it all sounded like so much fun and a world away.

Toward the end of my first week of recovery, Simone treated us to a nice dinner on their deck, giving me orders to come empty-handed and just enjoy being served. My cousin Todd joined us, and I sat back and enjoyed the company, listening to Todd entertain everyone with his antics and breathing in the beautiful warm July air. I silently thanked God for giving me this beautiful day and these beautiful people in my life. As tired as I was, I was thankful to be able to enjoy the evening of good food and good friends. I settled into the deck chair, knowing it was going to be a long night as Cliff and Mark cracked open the bottle of Captain Morgan rum and poured themselves generous servings.

It was quite warm, and I was feeling the heat under my hat and scarf, so I decided to pull it all off and just let the air at my scalp. It was the first time I had done that around company, but I felt so comfortable with these people; they were family. Simone's daughter, Jessica, was sitting across from me, and as I pulled off my scarf, she looked at me and said, "Kim, you are so beautiful." I suddenly felt flustered, not knowing what to say while thinking, *How can this beautiful, healthy young woman think I am beautiful?* But as I looked at her, I realized she meant what she said; she was not saying it just to make me feel good, and it made me feel a little beautiful inside.

Difficult times have helped me to understand better than before how rich and beautiful life is.
—Isak Dinesen

The heat of July proved more than I could handle. The side effects of the chemo were amplified with the heat, and I sought shelter inside most days. I had to avoid the temptation of turning on the air-conditioning, as every time it kicked in, my nose started to bleed. I would go from room to room, trying to find the coolest place to rest, all the while praying for the cool days of fall to come quickly. While everyone raved about the beautiful weather and enjoyed the outside activities that went along with the sun and heat, I just wanted to find cool shade and stay there until November. The days seemed hotter and hotter, and the nights left me restless. The house only started to cool off in the early morning hours.

As the days grew warmer and warmer, my waistline expanded more and more. As everyone told me to deal with one battle at a time, I watched my face get rounder. My hands swelled so much that I was forced to remove my rings for fear of having to cut them off, and I finally understood the term "cankles." The higher the number on the scale got, the lower my self-esteem became, and my wardrobe choices came down to two pairs of yoga pants and three T-shirts. As I stood in front of the mirror, trying to find my waistline, I once again wondered how Cliff could feel any desire when he looked my way. All who were close to me knew how much the weight gain was bothering me, and everyone echoed the same sentiment: it was better to gain than to waste away to nothing. Every time I heard that, I wanted to scream. Personally I would have been more comfortable losing thirty-five pounds than gaining it. But that was just me, and I would find myself revisiting the weight issue throughout my entire journey, never finding any peace with the pounds I put on.

With the heat during July and between my third and fourth treatments, we had to deal with humidity like I don't remember having in many years. The evenings were so humid that the water would just pour off me. After my latest bath experience, having a cool bath was out of the question, so I kept the shower running at a feverish rate for several weeks. I took to sleeping in the spare room on nights when Cliff fell asleep before me, lying on top of the bed with a fan pointed at my head, only to wake up before the sun rose, shivering in the cool night air. It was those mornings that I would crawl back into bed with Cliff and snuggle into his warm back, drawing some of his body heat to warm me up, trying to be careful not to wake him up from the deep sleep he needed so much.

Around this time I found that I was losing track of the medications I was taking—some for headaches, some for nausea, some to help the aches and pains. The side effects of taking all those medications for me were feeling even more tired and sick. It took a while for me to identify that while I was taking medications to help me, it was doing the opposite, zapping my energy levels, which left me unable to perform the simplest household tasks and left me exhausted after walking the length of the hall or dressing myself. I decided that I would start to write down anything I took with the hope of seeing a pattern that I could reverse and get some energy back.

Some evenings when Cliff arrived home, we would try to go for a walk after the sun went down and the evening cooled off. I loved those walks, feeling secure with my hand in Cliff's, walking around the block, pushing myself as far as I could go. We would slow down when I tired and then speed up when I got my breath back again. I often tried to hide my fatigue, as I loved the praise Cliff gave me when I could keep up with him, loved the sound of satisfaction in his voice when he said, "Honey, you are keeping up tonight." He often pushed me to go to the grocery store with him, and I knew he loved the feeling of normalcy those simple chores brought him.

Our friends Shawn and Tammy arrived home from a trip to Europe, and we all gathered in Mark and Simone's yard one evening to listen to the stories of their travels and all the beautiful things they had seen and done. As I listened to their stories, my mind started to wander, and I couldn't help but feel a little sad, wondering if I would ever experience those things again, the excitement of a plane ride to a destination unknown to me, packing a suitcase, opening the door to a hotel room in a faraway place. At that moment it was hard to believe that I would ever feel healthy enough to enjoy those things again.

I sank back into my chair and watched everyone around me laughing and sharing cocktails, feeling sorry for myself as I choked back the ice water that was sweating in its glass on the table beside me and mentally working out when my next medications were due. Sometimes my life seemed so disconnected from those I loved, and at that moment I felt the disconnection grow despite my best efforts to beat it down. I knew I was loved and that I was as big a part of their lives as they were mine, and I tried hard to bring my best to the table, laughing when appropriate and adding to the conversation as best as I could, all the while wondering why they could not see my pain.

> *All the darkness in the world cannot extinguish the light of a single candle.*
> ——St. Francis

During the same week, I met with a local photographer, Tracy Kuhl. I had been thinking of having some professional pictures done for some time and finally reached out to her by e-mail one evening, giving her my story and asking her if she would be interested in doing my pictures. I had met Tracy a few times in the past and had been a fan of her work for some time. She had this ability to turn a simple picture into a work of art. At the time, I did not realize that Tracy had lost her mom to cancer three short years before and had been wanting to photograph someone like myself for some time but didn't know how to reach out and ask someone dealing with cancer if they wanted their pictures done.

I was anxious for our initial meeting, not sure how she would receive me, how she would feel about the weight I had gained, or even how she would camouflage it in pictures. She arrived at my home and after talking briefly with Cliff, we went into my bedroom so she could go through my closet to find something for me to wear for the pictures. As we sat on my bed, I told her about my treatments, my weight gain, and how bad I was feeling about myself, and she shared the story of her mom's struggle and how much she missed her. We shared some tears and a warm hug. Then she started to go through my closet and finally came up with a top that still fit, and we made plans to meet the following week for the photo shoot.

On days that were really hot outside, I passed them by sitting at my computer and staying in touch with the friends and family I didn't see much. I tried to never send an e-mail when I was feeling down, not wanting to sound depressed or sad. I always tried to be upbeat and put the best information out there. I saved the dark thoughts for my closest friends, saved them for a time when I could get a hug in person. Words are so powerful, and I was always aware to never send a message on the days that were my lowest for fear of making someone worry more than they already were. I didn't want the praise for how good I was doing to slow down, even when I knew I wasn't doing that well. That praise was what got me through some of my darkest days.

On days when it wasn't too hot, I met with friends for lunch and did some shopping in hopes of finding some clothes that fit me and didn't make me feel like a beached whale. As disconcerting as it was to find that I was up two sizes, it felt good to come out of the mall with a bag full of clothes that I hoped would get me through the next two months. In hindsight, it was a good thing I didn't know at the time that within a few short weeks those newly purchased items would also be too small!

One weekend Mark hosted a car show at the business he owned, and the guys had been talking about it for weeks. They were feeling pumped about bringing their Mopars and putting them on display. The day turned out to be another scorcher, and as I prepared to go, I briefly considered calling Cliff to tell him I wouldn't be coming. But I resisted, as I knew how disappointed he would be that I wasn't there. I put on my makeup and noticed my eyelashes were becoming very thin, and I wondered how much longer I would have them.

When I arrived, all my friends were already there, mingling around and visiting, and as I approached the group, I felt self-conscious of my head scarf and wished I hadn't tried to dress it up with a flower like I had. As I hugged Tammy, she said, "I love your flower." How did she know? Did she know? Did it matter if she did? She made me feel pretty at a moment when I was melting inside. We capped off that day with a visit and dinner with Todd, who once again brightened my day and left me with a smile on my face.

The glory is not in falling, but in rising every time you fall.
——Chinese Proverb

How do you keep rising when you continue to fall is what I wanted to know. But a break in the heat with a full day of cleansing rain answered the question for me. Just when you think you can go no further, just when you think you have nothing left to fight with, you find the strength to go on. The rain not only provided my garden with a much needed drink and knocked all the dust down, but it also seemed to clean my internal world as well, washing away some of my fears, some of my sadness. As I lay on my bed and listened to the rain hitting the tin roof of the shed outside my window, I took deep breaths, breathing in the cool damp air, and felt a peace settle over me. My body relaxed like it hadn't done in weeks, and I drifted off into a solid sleep, knowing that tomorrow things would be better and that I would be one day closer to being healthy again.

I was missing my work family terribly around this time as well and had been receiving e-mails from my co-workers asking when I was going to come in and see them, so I sent a message that I would be in on Wednesday. I had been putting it off, so worried that they would be shocked when they saw me, not wanting the stares or the uncomfortable moments from people I had not seen in months. The morning of my visit arrived, and I woke up anxious and nervous, already tired from the emotional stress. I showered and got dressed, changing at least five times, never liking the image that stared back at me in the mirror. When I left work in May, I had been twenty pounds lighter, had a full head of hair, and had enough energy to run around the office all day long, yet here I was returning bald and fat and with just enough energy to get dressed and hook my purse over my shoulder. As I drove across town, my hands were soaked in sweat from nerves and kept slipping off the steering wheel. I just wanted to turn around and go home. My fears were unfounded, as I was greeted with hugs and warmth from everyone I saw. No one seemed uncomfortable around me, and they didn't treat me any differently than they had in the past, and it felt so good to be back in the familiar environment again. While there were questions concerning my health, most of the conversation was light and fun, just like it had always been.

Prior to my visit, my friend Crystal from work had sent me an e-mail to tell me that she was organizing a team to put in the CIBC Run for the Cure in support of breast cancer in my honor. I was humbled, I was honored, and I was stunned. I could not believe they wanted to do this for me, and I made a silent promise to myself that I would walk with them. They wanted me to name the team, and for lack of anything more creative, I came up with Kim's Breast Friends. I saved the website and found myself visiting it every day to see how much money had been raised, and each time I opened it, I was even more honored to be loved by such a wonderful group of people.

During that week I also met and had coffee and a visit with my "cancer sister," Carrie, and we caught up on each other's lives since our last visit. Every time I saw Carrie, she inspired me more and more. Her story just amazed me and will continue to inspire me for a lifetime. I soaked up every word she said, knowing that she had been where I was, and she was looking so beautiful now, feeling great, and experiencing a love of life you only get when you have stared death in the face. Every time I thought of how she had completed her chemotherapy while raising a baby girl, not wanting to miss out on her daughter's first year of life, I marveled at all she did while going through her treatments. I told her I didn't think I would have been as strong as she was; it took everything for me to take care of just myself right now, let alone a baby too.

After our visit, we went to the parking lot, and she told me she had something for me in her vehicle. She pulled out a beautiful pink quilt she had made for me. Through my tears, I thanked her, knowing I would cherish this quilt for the rest of my life, and I tried to put into words how much her support and compassion meant to me. She had come into my life at a time when I felt so vulnerable and scared, and she had become my idol and will continue to be an inspiration to me forever. Yet another example of those earthly angels that are placed in your path at a time when you need them the most.

Kayla was having the time of her life in England, and we Skyped every few days. I was feeling quite bloated and unattractive, and I didn't want her to see me that way, so I came up with the ingenious idea of placing a Post-it note over the camera on the computer before I logged in. When she asked why she couldn't see me, I always pretended I didn't know what was wrong and suggested that perhaps we had a bad connection, all the while wishing I could put a Post-it note on other areas of my life. How easy it was to hide behind that little square piece of paper, play acting that all was well on this side of the pond when she could not see me. I missed her so much, and I soaked in her beautiful, healthy face and closed my eyes as I listened to her voice and heard the excitement in her words. I was very content that she was happy and having a wonderful adventure away from the trials of cancer, chemo, and sickness.

The day of my photo shoot arrived, and I paced around the house all day, wondering if this was a big mistake. I knew this was probably the worst I had ever looked in my life, and now that the day had arrived, I wished I had not agreed to it. I tried on my outfit several times throughout the day, standing and spinning in front of the full-length mirror in my room, turning away each time feeling less comfortable than I had the previous spin. Masie, the makeup artist Tracy had set up for me, arrived. We shared pleasantries as I asked her how she could work with my bald head and lack of eyelashes and eyebrows. She touched me on the arm and said I would be beautiful, and while I was apprehensive, I gave myself up to her and let her work her magic.

She opened up her makeup case, and her hands flew over my face, applying foundation, drawing in eyebrows, and feathering on some blush, all the while chatting to me about her work and how much she enjoyed it. Tracy arrived with her camera and beautiful young daughter, Sarah, and started to snap pictures, telling me to just relax. I was literally in the spotlight, and while I was not sure how I felt about that, I decided to let it happen and enjoy the ride.

Once my makeup was complete, we went into the backyard with Cliff, and Tracy started to take some pictures of Cliff and me. The more I relaxed, the easier it was to act natural. As Tracy snapped away, I prayed that we would get a couple of good pictures from the evening. It was so important to mark this point in my life, and I wanted to have something I could look back on and say, "Look how far I have come." But I wanted that "something" to look pretty because it had been so long since I felt anything close to pretty. I also wanted this to be a good experience for

Tracy, knowing that she had wanted to do a shoot like this for some time. I wanted her to be proud of the photographs.

After a short time in our backyard, Tracy, Sarah, and I jumped into her vehicle and headed downtown to another location where she wanted to take some pictures. We ended up next to a brick wall just off one of the busiest streets in the city. We parked the vehicle and walked to where she wanted to take the pictures, and as she set up, I watched the vehicles driving by. People were going on with their lives on that warm July evening, enjoying the last moments before the sun set for another day. I had driven by this place thousands of times, and I had never even noticed the little oasis tucked away in some trees. Now it would be a place that would forever be meaningful to me.

Tracy had me sit down, and as she took pictures, she gently asked if I would remove my head scarf. As I did, I noticed a young man in a passing vehicle that had slowed for the lights. He was looking at me, and I could almost see him thinking, *Why is there a bald woman sitting there?* His eyes seemed to search the area. With my hand on my head, I closed my eyes, listening to the sound of the passing traffic and the constant click of the camera.

This cannot be happening! Really? This is my life? I thought as I sat on the side of the road in the middle of town for the entire world to see. It turns out this was one of the most beautiful pictures of me I had ever seen. Tracy caught the raw emotion of the moment, and I will be forever thankful to her for the role she played in my life at that time.

A short time later, when Tracy posted the pictures she had taken on Facebook, the response to them was unbelievable. I could not believe it was me in those photographs and could not believe how she had captured everything I wanted documented, from the love between Cliff and me, to the joy I still had, to the pain and fear I felt, all while still making me look beautiful. She made me feel beautiful at a time in my life when I could not even spell the word let alone feel it, and I will be eternally grateful to her for that. She took a place in my heart next to my other earthly angels. I am so glad to have those pictures, and I am even happier to have chosen Tracy Kuhl to do them for me.

I did not realize the spin-off that taking the pictures would have on other aspects of my life, but I suddenly felt a sense of comfortableness about my physical appearance. Cliff and I went to the lake to have dinner with Glen and Tracy one evening shortly after, and for the first time I felt comfortable enough to go out without a hat over my scarf. Up to this point, I would put on my head scarf and then pull a hat over it, feeling that the more I covered up, the less people could see me, and I understood that I was using this analogy both figuratively and literally. I did the same with sunglasses, often keeping them on when I was inside a public place, thinking that if people could not see my eyes, they wouldn't see my pain. But suddenly I was going out without my hat and feeling comfortable taking off my sunglasses and meeting people's glances in the aisle at the grocery store, smiling at them, and getting a smile in return. I felt like I was coming alive again.

> *God made you as you are in order to use you as He planned.*
> —J. C. Maculay

Chapter 8
Four Down, Only Two to Go

Treatment number four loomed, and on the day before the treatment, we met with my nurse, Krista, to go over the new cocktail of drugs I would be given and the side effects I could expect. It is common to change up a patient's chemotherapy halfway through in order to give the best defense against any wandering cancer cells that may be left in his or her body. My new treatment regime was called Taxotere, and the list of side effects were scary, with bone and joint pain being on the top of the list along with weight gain (great!) and loss of remaining hair. It is funny that after all this time, those are the only three side effects I remember us reviewing, although now after looking it up I know there are many more, and I know Krista went over all of them with me. She gave me some good ways to deal with the side effects if they happened and once again gave me a renewed hope that I would get through this okay. I was scared going into this fourth treatment not knowing what to expect from the new cocktail of drugs, and once again I worried that I would have some fatal reaction to them. I was comfortable with my old cocktail. I knew exactly what to expect from it, and I was not happy about having to change.

Chemo day number four arrived, and Cliff and I headed to the hospital, once again traveling in silence, holding on to each other's hands tightly. For some reason Cliff was very nervous about the new drug, and while I didn't know at the time, he was terrified I was going to have a reaction. After the drug was hooked up to my IV, we settled in. As it dripped into my line, Tracy, Tammy, and my friend Colleen, who was visiting from Israel, arrived. The distraction was good for Cliff, as he looked like he was ready to pass out. He was so nervous that morning and kept checking my face and touching me just to make sure I wasn't getting hot. He called the nurse over at one point and had her look at me, convinced something was happening and I was having a reaction. She assured him that I was fine and that everything was going well, and the girls then took over and provided him with some distraction for the duration of the treatment. I was thankful they were there, making sure there were no silent moments.

When we arrived home, I assured him again that I was feeling okay, and as I crawled under the blanket on my bed, I told him to go on back to work and I would see him in a few hours. He was reluctant to leave, but I convinced him it was all okay, and as I listened to his vehicle pull out of the driveway, I was thankful he had the distraction of work to help calm his nerves.

I fell into a deep sleep and didn't hear him return home less than an hour later. I only knew he was home when I woke up and stumbled to the kitchen for a drink and saw him sleeping on the couch. He had arrived at work and then couldn't settle, knowing I was home alone, so he had returned home and lay on the couch, ready in case I needed him. The day and the stress had taken its toll on my husband, and he had taken all he could for one day. I let him sleep and returned to bed, comforted in the fact that he was feet away. We both slept until long after the sun passed over the neighborhood and cast comforting shadows over our home.

That evening I knew what to expect, knew that sleep would not come easily for me, so I sat down at the computer to answer some e-mails that had come in and sent off my forth update.

Subject: Four Down, Only Two to Go!

Hello, everyone!

Welcome to the end of July! Can you believe where the time is going this summer? It is just flyin'! But that is okay with the Rideout family because it means that my chemotherapy is closer to being completed!

It has been a quiet three weeks since my last update. Treatment number three kicked me down pretty good for about ten days or so. The booster shot I received did its job and prevented my white blood cell count from tanking, but it did cause me quite a bit of bone pain, but this was easily taken care of by pumping myself full of Advil every four hours. I am sure I now know what it feels like to be ninety years old. I moaned every time I tried to get up, my knees cracked every time I moved, and I often found myself walking hunched over, holding onto my back. All I needed was a head of grey hair and a cane to complete the picture.

Talking about hair, for those of you who have not seen me in a while, I am as bald as an orange (for lack of a better comparison). Not a hair to be found, except I still do have my eyebrows and eyelashes, which my oncologist nurse advised me yesterday will quickly become extinct as well after this new round of chemo kicks in. When I get mad, Cliff calls me a nasty bald woman. But soon I won't even be able to pull my eyebrows into a scowl because I won't have any!

Last week was my good week, and I spent every day out socializing, doing coffee, lunches, and dinners and catching up on everyone's life. (Side note: Thank you, everyone, for not forgetting me, even when I go underground dealing with the side effects of the chemo! It helps to know you will be there when the fog lifts.)

Our plans to camp this weekend got canceled when Cliff had to work, so on Friday night we visited the Western Fair here in Red Deer with Mark, Simone, and Tammy and had fun tasting the fair food. Deep-fried Snickers bars were interesting, but I would not recommend the chocolate dipped frozen banana. It is actually a frozen banana. Who would have guessed? (Not me, obviously; however, Cliff knew right away.) It is quite gross! We also took in the Nazareth show, and after a few songs I understood why it was free ... Those guys have seen better days and moved around the stage quite like the description I gave of myself in paragraph two above, except they did have the heads of grey hair.

Saturday night, we headed out to the lake to have supper with Glen and Tracy. What was going to be a nice quick dinner and visit ended up going until almost midnight, and Cliff slept all the way back into town, having spent quite a bit of time with the Captain over the evening, and I got to listen to Celine Dion on the radio while he slept! A win-win for both of us!

Last week I learned that my co-workers at FCC have placed a team in the CIBC Run for the Cure in my honor. I am humbled beyond words that these wonderful people would do something like that! FCC you rock! I am so blessed to work with such a wonderful group of people. The love and support that me and my family have been shown since the beginning of my journey is beyond anything I could have ever hoped for, and I will spend the rest of my life trying to repay all the kindness we have been shown. Thank you again.

Today was treatment number four, and I still cannot believe that I have four (count them—one, two, three, four) under my belt. Only two left to go. Today I started on a new cocktail of chemo, and I was quite stressed, as I was used to the old cocktail and wondered why they were messing with something I was already comfortable with. But they are the experts, so I once again reluctantly offered my vein to them. My friends Colleen, Tammy, and Tracy all came and sat with Cliff and me and helped make the hours go faster. Thanks again for the gift from Israel, Colleen. I love it. And for the iced cappuccino and donut, Tracy. I needed it. And, Tammy, thanks for thinking of giving me the purple scarf even though you left with it still in your bag! There was lots of chatter and laughter, and a few times I wondered if we were disturbing the other patients, but the nurses did not give us any warnings, so I figured we were good.

And finally, we are eagerly awaiting Kayla's return from the UK next week. She is having a wonderful time on her holiday and has visited Portugal, Spain, and Africa and is now back in England. It has shown us that we are not ready to be empty nesters quite yet, and we can't *wait to pick her up at the airport next week! It will be a happy day for us.*

So that's about all I have right now. The fog has once again rolled in, the pills have kicked in, and the computer monitor is starting to sway, so I think I will call it a night.

Enjoy the last days of July, and I will be in touch in August!

Happy summer, everyone!

Love, Me

I spent a restless night tossing and turning and finally fell to sleep just as the birds outside started to wake up and sing in the trees. I woke up long after Cliff left for work, and as I lay in bed I could hear the garbage truck in the back alley, stopping and starting, the brakes squeaking. I could hear the workers on the truck yelling to each other and the sounds of the empty tin garbage cans being thrown down to the ground. Life outside my bedroom window was going on as though nothing had happened, while my world inside had been turned upside down. I continued to lie there, watching the curtains sway in the slight breeze that was coming in the window, listening to the sounds outside, and daydreaming about my life before cancer. I started to cry, crying for all I had lost.

The days immediately after treatment were always the worst, and this round was no different except that I did find I was sinking lower than I had before. Flowers arrived, sent by Kayla—a dozen roses with a card that read, *Four Down, Two to Go. Love You.* But they did nothing to lift my mood. I was feeling really sorry for myself and had a huge pity party but invited no one. I continued to keep up the charade that all was well with my friends and family, and Cliff was the only one who saw the extent of my sadness. He was worried and tried everything he could think of to help me out of my funk, but nothing worked, and I lay on the couch and mindlessly watched whatever was on TV, not having the energy to get the remote control that sat on the coffee table, just outside my reach. Adding to my depression was the horrible bone and joint pain I was having. I had been warned it would be bad, but I hadn't expected it hurt that much. It hurt to move. It hurt not to move. There was no relief.

Mark dropped over to see me just at a moment when I was at my lowest. As I lay on the couch and looked at him sitting across from me, I could not hold it in any longer and started to cry. As I cried, I saw how much it hurt Cliff, and I saw the pain in Mark's face. Here were these two big beautiful men, so important in my life, who I knew would do anything in their power to help, but they were powerless. There was nothing they could do to help. It pained us all. I was hurting for Cliff; I knew he felt every pain I had. And I was sorry to let my guard down and let Mark see into the window of my pain. But it felt good to cry, and I didn't have the energy to even pretend to be okay at that moment. Mark hung around long enough to lighten the mood, and we shared some smiles and laughs after my mini meltdown. He followed it up with a text when he got home, assuring me everything would be okay.

My low continued for several days after that treatment, and I had a hard time shaking it off. The bone pain got away from me some days, and each passing day found me more and more exhausted. I was having a hard time functioning and just doing the simplest things. Walking to the kitchen to get a glass of water took more energy than I had stored. I lay on the couch, or in bed, moving as little as possible and counting the hours down to when I could take the next Advil, but as the hours and days passed, the Advil stopped working, and the pain in my bones just got worse. Cliff had started holidays and was home with me, trying to do everything he could to help ease my pain. On Sunday evening, five days after my treatment, I asked him to bring me to the hospital. The pain had been getting more and more intense all day, especially in my groin area, and I was getting no relief from it at all. I started to think there was something else wrong and knew I could not get through the night with the pain as it was.

We arrived at the ER around seven o'clock that evening, and I discovered that there is *one* advantage to doing chemotherapy: there is no waiting around in the ER waiting room. As soon as I registered at the front desk, they whisked me away to an isolation room because my immune system was so compromised. Cliff wasn't allowed to come back with me until after the initial assessment had been done, so he settled in for what we thought could be a long wait. I followed the nurse through the security doors and to the deep end of the emergency unit alone. As I lay in the hospital bed, staring at the ceiling, I once again felt so scared, and I could feel the tears running down my cheeks. I tried to fight the panic that was trying to erupt inside me. I needed the security of Cliff sitting beside me. I didn't want to be alone.

The nurse assigned to me was kind and did all she could to make me feel comfortable and relaxed. She told me her sister had been diagnosed with breast cancer when she was twenty-five, and she beat it, just had a baby, and was doing very well. I thanked her for sharing her story with me and relaxed in her care, knowing it would be all okay. We talked about all that had happened to me, and I told her how I had made a promise to myself to try to get through chemo without visiting the ER, how important that was to me because it meant to me that I was strong.

I wept as I told her how much pain I had been having all week, how there were times the pain would take my breath away, and how I tried to fight it on my own. I wept harder when I told her that I felt I had let myself down by giving into the pain, how I wanted to be strong and not let the treatments beat me up. When I looked over at her, she was wiping tears from her own cheeks. Then we laughed as she said she never cried with her patients. I asked if she would let Cliff come in, and she set off to find him. When she returned and pulled back the curtain, he was following her. Cliff exhaled and said this was the same room we were in when he took me to the hospital after we returned from Mexico a couple of years ago. I had been suffering from Bell's palsy then. I had thought that was the worst thing that could ever happen to me. Little had I known that it wasn't. What were the odds, I wondered. In two years, I had been to the ER twice, and both times I was put into the same room: room 23.

Upon assessment, the doctor decided he wanted to check to make sure I had no blood clots. He sent me for an X-ray, and when I returned from that department, they gave me some pain medication that worked almost immediately. Cliff pulled his chair up close to the bed and held my hand as I went for a little trip into never-never land, knowing he would take care of it from there. I was so tired. I just needed to sleep, and I was happy to not be feeling any more pain. The next day he told me that the doctor had advised him that there were no clots. He said the pain I was experiencing was from the chemo and the Neulasta shot and that it would get better in time. He gave us a prescription for stronger painkillers to help me over the rough days.

I slept most of the following day, waking only long enough to eat a meal that Tammy had cooked and brought over to us. It felt good to be taken care of, and I think the good meal along with the painkillers helped me turn a corner. The pain started to ease, and my mood started to get noticeably better. Cliff urged me to go out for a walk, and we strolled to the end of the street and back, both of us happy to see me vertical and moving around again.

The Lord bless you and keep you; the Lord make his face shine upon you and be gracious to you; the Lord turn his face toward you and give you peace.
—Numbers 6:24–26 (NIV)

As the week progressed, my pain eased quite a bit, and I was once again able to engage in my life, and that in turn took stress off Cliff. He returned to working in his garage with his radio blasting and him whistling away to the songs. When he did come into the house for something, his feet hardly hit the steps as he ran up them. It felt good to be feeling so good! I had lunch with Linda and Colleen one day shortly after my visit to the hospital, and after I left the restaurant I realized I hadn't once thought about my illness other than when we spoke about it at the very beginning. I was once again at a point where every waking thought was not consumed with the word *cancer*, and I was grateful to be at that place again.

As my body healed from the latest onslaught of chemo, it allowed me to do more physically. I found myself out in my flower beds, pulling weeds and trimming back the perennials that had taken over because of lack of maintenance. I sat back and smelled the fresh grass after I mowed it, drank gallons of water to keep hydrated in the heat of August, fanned myself with my hat, and wished again for an early fall. I must have looked funny sitting there on my lawn, all bald and smiling.

Kayla arrived home from Europe, and we were happy to have her back on Canadian soil. She looked healthy and happy as she came through the airport security door. I threw my arms around her and cried, so happy to have her safe and back in my arms again. On the drive home, she regaled us with stories of her travels in between the frantic texting with her friends, trying to bring us all up to speed at the same time. I finally settled back and smiled as her fingers did the talking, knowing we had lots of time to catch up later. Right now her friends wanted her attention.

The weekend following my visit to the ER, Cliff and I headed to the lake to spend the weekend with Glen and Tracy. Tracy's brother was kind enough to offer his lake house to us for the weekend, and it took me all day to pack up the vehicle with all the things we would need. I was nervous and excited at the same time: nervous about how our friends at the lake would act around me but excited to see them as well. We hadn't seen most of them since before I was diagnosed, and I didn't want anyone to feel uncomfortable around me. But those fears were baseless, and they greeted me with as much, if not more, love than ever. After the first initial questions about my health, things slid right back to where they had always been, and I just became one of the gang again, enjoying a game of poker, watching the sunsets with Tracy, and sitting around the fire and visiting with everyone. It was a great weekend.

During this time, the hair on my head really started to sprout again, and I now had a little covering of peach fuzz over my head. I loved it every time Cliff commented on how it scratched his neck when he hugged me. Each morning I stood in front of the mirror and tipped my head this way and that way, looking for some new growth and marveling at what was there already. I kept rubbing my head, thinking it would stimulate faster growth.

The privilege of a lifetime is being who you are.
—Oprah

The week before my second to last treatment I kept busy, meeting friends for lunches or suppers, enjoying the fellowship, all while trying very hard not to be envious of everyone's carefree life. What I finally realized during those last weeks of summer was that being sick when the weather was nice outside was even more painful because everyone was so active. That only highlighted my limitations even more. As much as I tried not to, I found myself resenting my friends' plans to go fishing or four wheeling or boating on the lake. I had the energy to do none of that, and I felt more and more removed from their lives and felt even worse that I was holding Cliff back from enjoying his summertime activities as well.

The year before my diagnosis, Cliff and I had purchased two Sea-Doos and had spent every opportunity we had on the lake, racing each other, cruising back and forth over the water, loving life. This year we had not even taken them out of storage because I could not be out in the sun, and I didn't have the energy to enjoy them. It just sucked! I wanted to be able to do all those things, and many times I lost sight of the bright future I would have, instead choosing to focus on the present and what I was unable to do.

One evening, we went out for supper with some friends and sat on the deck, enjoying a cold drink. Cliff ordered me a Corona, and it arrived icy cold with a lime wedge pushed down the spout. As I tipped it up and felt the cold beer run down the back of my throat, I felt like I was in heaven. I was so happy I had drummed up the energy to join everyone that evening. The sun was setting, and Tammy and Linda kept moving me every twenty minutes to make sure I was out of the direct sunlight. While I hated the spotlight of having people worry about the sun shining on me, I knew it was a small price to pay to enjoy the friendship and laughter. As I sat back and listened to everyone talk and catching up on their week, I watched the cars pass by our patio and people walking on the sidewalk. At that moment I was so thankful to be part of this beautiful, busy evening. I was blessed to be well enough to hold a cold beer in my hand, laugh at Shawn acting like a crazy man, and participate in wing night on a patio in the middle of downtown. For me the food tasted better, the laughter was deeper, the hugs were tighter, and the beer was sweeter! Life was good.

The following weekend, we packed up our trailer and headed out for a weekend of camping with Mark and Simone. The whole gang was coming out on Friday night, but the four of us decided to head out earlier and relax. After we set up camp, we lit the campfire, settled in with our board games, and cooked our meals together, all the while keeping the other campers awake with our laughter late into the night. We took a road trip one day and headed to the mountains to see a waterfall. It was a beautiful day; the weather was warm, and the company was perfect. We spent some time jumping on the rocks at the falls and had a nice picnic lunch. I tasted my first cucumber sandwich while the water roared behind us.

For a short time, we all forgot about cancer and just enjoyed the day. We stopped on the way back and enjoyed an ice cream, visited a local museum, and watched a black bear walking along the road. Simone and I sat in the back of the truck and laughed our heads off, driving Cliff and Mark crazy with our high-pitched laughter. They were happy to see the sign of the campground upon our return.

Over the weekend, three other families joined us, and we all managed to squeeze around the little campfire the provincial park provided. In the evening after the sun went down, we all sat around the fire, and as I looked around I couldn't help but reflect on how much these people had helped Cliff and me this year. Even on that evening, they were watching out for me, asking if I was drinking enough water, inquiring whether I was cold or tired, but never hovering and always being very subtle.

My legs had swollen quite a bit during the previous few days—another side effect of the chemo—and were extremely uncomfortable. Tammy kept after me to drink lots of water, telling me it would help with the swelling, and Linda pulled my feet up into her lap one evening while we sat around the fire just to keep them elevated. It doesn't take much to reach into someone's heart, and my heart was touched so many times. Even that weekend it was touched more times than I could say. Tammy making sure I was drinking water; Simone calling me an idiot and laughing at me, never treating me any different; Linda offering to massage my legs; Tracy coming to crawl into my bunk with me because I was too tired to come out—all that love in one day! How blessed I am! You don't need to do much, because it is the little things that really count.

We had a lobster boil on our final night. We cooked the lobster together, and then everyone gathered around and ate. It was such a great way to wrap up our weekend, and it wasn't long after the dishes were cleared away that the poker chips came out and a game was in the works.

The next morning as I made my way around to the campsites to say good-bye, I made sure I said, "I love you," to each person I hugged, hoping they would all know without me saying just how important they were to me.

To love without condition, to talk without intention, to give without reason and to care without expectation – this is the heart of a true friend.
— Author Unknown

Chapter 9

Five Down, Only One to Go

The day before my second to last treatment, I headed to the hospital to have my blood work done. Then we had an appointment to see my oncologist. My nurse, Krista, was away on holiday, so we had to see the oncologist. It was the first time I had seen him since before my treatments started. As we sat in the waiting room, there was an older couple sitting across from us, and the lady was very irritated and vocal, telling her husband how mad she was with the doctors and that she didn't care to have the chemotherapy. I was relieved when she was called into the room, and I caught Cliff's eye. He had been watching me watching her, and he was trying to gauge how upset it had made me feel. As I leaned into him, I whispered sarcastically, "She is a pleasant soul." Cliff replied, "She is just upset, honey," as he took my hand in his and squeezed. I thought, *I am upset too.* I had just stepped off the scales, and I wanted to crawl into a hole and hide. I could not believe that the weight continued to pack on, and I was so discouraged.

When we met with the oncologist, he advised me that all the side effects I was experiencing—the swelling in my legs, the pain in my bones, etc.—were all normal. He said the chemo drugs they were giving me were very hard on the body. I asked him if they could dial the chemo back a little so it didn't beat me up so much, but he said no, as he felt the drug in the full dosage was my best defense against the cancer reoccurring. He gave me a prescription for pain killers to help if the pain in my bones got unbearable again and said, "Hang in there, Kimberley. You are almost done."

Almost done. In four weeks and a day I would have my last treatment, and while I was anxious to get to that day, I knew I still had two more treatments to get through, and they were going to be tough.

Chemo day number five arrived. I woke at 5:00 a.m. It had been a restless night for me, and I kept waking up covered in sweat every hour or so. I was feeling very bloated when I got up and proceeded to drink several glasses of water in hopes that it would help. I sat at the computer and read the e-mails that had come in throughout the night and responded to them while at the same time responding to the texts that were coming in. Everyone was wishing me well and excited for me that after this day, I would only have one treatment left.

As I settled into the now too familiar treatment room at the hospital, Simone arrived and then Linda, Tracy, and Kayla showed up. Once again I was thankful to have visitors to help the hours go by faster. Some people would rather be alone during their treatments, but for me, the more people around me the better. If I allowed my mind to think about the poison that was being pumped in my body, I would have a breakdown, and the only way to prevent that from happening was with the distraction of visitors. I was assigned to my favorite nurse, Sonya, and she kept us all laughing throughout the treatment, telling us silly stories and keeping us entertained. The treatment went by without a hitch, and as the IV was removed, Simone said, "Kimmy, just one more." As I heard her words, I put my head on Cliff's chest and wept, not able to believe we were almost done. The end was so close now.

Cliff brought me home and settled me into bed, and I drifted off to sleep only to wake up to Kelsey climbing into bed with me, and we lay there and listened to the thunderstorm blowing overhead and talked quietly. We were soon joined by Kayla. I lay back on my pillow and watched my daughters talk between them, enjoying the conversation but not participating. It felt good to feel the warmth of their bodies next to me, and the sound of their voices was comforting despite the pain that was setting into my legs and the clouds that had already set in my brain. Later in the evening, I convinced Cliff to head to bed without me and planned to take up residence in the spare room for the night so he could get a good night's sleep. He protested but soon gave in, which confirmed for me just how tired my husband was. After he was settled away for the night, I worked my way into the den and sat at the computer into the early morning hours of the following day to compose my fifth update.

Subject: Five Down, Only One to Go

Well, family and friends,

I am just one treatment away from having completed this leg of my journey ... September 4 will see me completing my last chemotherapy session, and I can't wait for that day to arrive. It seems like a lifetime ago that I had my first session on May 28, and now the end is so close that I can almost taste it! Exciting!

Number four really knocked me down hard. This new treatment I am on for the last three sessions has some different side effects, one being bone pain. Unfortunately I was hit with the bone pain full force, and it took me down hard for about ten to eleven days. At one point, we ended up visiting the emergency room and spent seven hours there being assessed and finally pumped up with enough pain killers to take down a small horse. The only advantage I have identified to dealing with cancer is that when you visit the ER you get to skip the waiting room and are moved inside to isolation right away because your immune system is so compromised. However, it did make us feel so much better to be checked out, and when we arrived home I slept the rest of the night and most of the next day away. But that was my turning point, and I started to rebound slowly after that.

Cliff has been on holiday for the past two weeks (just returned back to work today), and it was so good to have him home with me. We managed to camp a couple of weekends ago with Glen and Tracy at Raymond Shores for two nights, staying in the luxury accommodations of her brother's lake house. It was so nice to see everyone out there and catch up. Last weekend we were with the whole gang at Gull Lake. Mark, Simone, Cliff, and I were there for four nights in total and took a day trip the Crescent Falls and had a nice picnic at the falls. Then we managed to spot a black bear on the side of the road on the way back. It was a great weekend full of food, fun, campfires, and laughter. Most of the weekend I was clutching my sides, which were sore from laughing. Thank you, my friends. You are the best medicine anyone could take!

Kayla also arrived home the first week of August, safe and sound, to our great relief. It was so good to see her walk through that arrival gate, and I cried for a full fifteen minutes after I got her into my arms. She had a wonderful time and made memories that will last her a lifetime. She visited London, Portugal, Spain, and Africa. How cool is that? Within twenty-four hours our home was full of her friends once again, and life has returned to normal.

Treatment number five went off without a hitch yesterday. Linda, Simone, and Tracy arrived to keep Cliff, Kayla, and me company. We chatted and laughed, and before we knew it the two hours had flown by. Again, thank you to my friends who just show up on treatment days … You don't realize how much your presence makes those hours so much easier and takes our minds off what is happening. I have the best friends ever. As they were taking the IV out, I heard Simone say, "Only one left." I got very emotional, and as much as I fought the urge, I started to cry, finally realizing that indeed I only have to go through this one more time; I could not believe that I only have to offer my veins to be flushed one more time. It is a good feeling.

We returned home, and I ate lunch and then retreated to my bed to let the rain lull me off to sleep. I was awakened by Kelsey crawling in bed with me and almost fell back to sleep as she wrapped her arms around me and kissed me on my bald head. It felt so good. We talked and listened to the rain and thunder. Then Kayla joined us, and the three of us snuggled for an hour or so before they left me to go back to sleep. What a perfect ending to the day for me.

Again, I have to say thank you for all the support. It gives me strength every day—strength to look at every day with positive thoughts *and strength to look at the future with excitement. And every day I continue to marvel at my luck to have Cliff walking beside me through this. He has been my rock of strength and determination, and he loves me through all the highs and lows that I face every day, feeling every pain I feel, and rejoicing in every hurdle I cross. How blessed I am. What more could a woman ask for?*

So on that note, I must head back to my nest and rest. The fog is rolling in, and my eyelids are starting to get heavy, so it is time to rest.

Enjoy the last weeks of summer, my friends, and when my next update comes, I will be done with chemotherapy! How exciting is that?

Love Me

> *Wherever you are is where you are supposed to be.*
> —Author Unknown

Wherever you are is where you are supposed to be? Am I supposed to be lying on my bed with so little energy that just a visit to the washroom requires an hour of lead-in time? I didn't think this was where I was supposed to be, but I was determined to get to where I thought my place was, and that was healthy once again.

The day after my fifth treatment found me very tired, but the pain wasn't too intense as I prepared to give myself the Neulasta injection. Today was a bittersweet day for my friends, as they were putting their dog, Patches, to sleep because of old age, and I wished I had the energy to go over and give Simone a hug or to bring them supper, anything to help ease their pain. They were the second family to have lost a pet since I had been diagnosed. As the day passed, I was flooded with e-mails from friends and family, wishing me well and giving me the encouragement to keep going.

I received the most beautiful message from my friend Joanne:

Hello, my Kim. Thank you for your update. You inspire me like no other person has. First with your beautiful, loving, and unique personality (and your laugh, which I wish I could hear daily). Then with your marriage. I have never witnessed a more incredible union between a couple. Such love, passion, and friendship. And now with your "fight." Because of your amazing strength and determination, you still shine as the beautiful person you are. You never let this cancer get the best of you. You still bring love, laughter, and smiles to all those around you while you are going through the toughest fight of your life. You amaze me … I think you are wonderful.

As I read her message, I cried. She had helped me to see that I was still the same person. Even if I couldn't see it, others did, and that was comforting.

From my angel on earth Christine came a simple message that said so much: *Love you so much … You are doing great! Catch up with you more when you are not foggy!*

Sending lots of love and prayers your way, wrote my sweet Squirt.

Messages came from home. David and Jennifer wrote, *Hi, Kim. We are so excited for you and your family that this is all coming to an end. Dave and I will be counting down the days with you, and we also can't wait for your last treatment. Enjoy the rest of the summer, and you truly are blessed!*

Each time I stepped away from the computer, I always had a smile on my face and a lightness in my heart, regardless of how I had been feeling when I sat down. The words people sent, the love they expressed, their cheerleading from afar, it all meant so much to me, and some days it was what got me through the day. It felt not that much different from a hockey team in the world series. Your team is two goals behind and feeling pretty low, not feeling very good about their game, and feeling bad for letting their coach down. Then all of a sudden the fans in the bleachers go wild, chanting, waving flags, standing to show their jerseys. And suddenly you get a new wind, start skating down the ice faster than before, and fight for that little black puck. Your game gets better, stronger, faster.

Kayla turned twenty the day following my fifth treatment, and Simone, Linda, and I took her out for ice cream after work and then headed home. Cliff had a bunch of company in the garage, and we all visited together before I had to beg off and head inside to rest. Kayla had a rough day. She was still struggling so much with my illness and was not dealing very well with me being sick. Despite my best efforts to put on a brave face for her, she was still very uneasy and worried that something else was going to happen to me. While some days it was exhausting to try to pretend that all was okay, I needed to do it for my family. Like Kayla, Cliff's mood was directly impacted by mine. If I was having a good day, he would too; if I was down, he would be too. It was a never-ending circle—a hamster wheel from which we could not escape.

As the week drew to a close, my pain got worse and worse. The aching circled my body, around my head at my ears, around my knees, and around my hips. I kept up a steady schedule of pain killers, which in turn made me very tired and sleepy. When I was alert, it was because the pain killers had worn off and I was experiencing the discomfort again. I was so tired of being tired, so tired of not feeling well, so tired of watching everyone around me do all the simple things that I had not been able to do since I got sick. I started to do a countdown to my final treatment, and while it seemed so far away, I knew it would be here before I knew it. I kept telling myself to hang in there, that we were almost at the end.

The week proved to be a very emotional low for me, and that snowballed into a low emotional week for both Kayla and Cliff. It was easy to hide my sadness, frustrations, and pain from the outside world, but time and time again Cliff and Kayla saw me at my lowest and reacted to it. As had been proven in the past, when I got to my lowest, Cliff sometimes sunk right down to the depths of despair with me, and both of us sat there in a funk, unable to shake the feelings of gloom off and unable to help the other. At this point, we were all so tired, tired of the fight, tired of the struggle every day, tired of cancer. I hated the word and cursed the day my name had been linked to it.

Kayla picked up the bad vibes bouncing off the walls in our house, and it made her sad, confused, and afraid. One night as we lay together, she told me how helpless she felt watching me like this, and it made her sad that there was nothing she could do to help me. I tried to reassure her that just by being there she was helping me, but I knew my words were empty and that I wasn't offering her much comfort. She needed to work through this on her own. I had been the one diagnosed with breast cancer, but it affected us all, and I hated seeing my family in such pain.

My fifth treatment had really beaten me down, and I knew this was to be expected. My nurse had advised me that the side effects would be cumulative as the treatments progressed. It would get worse before it got better. I recognized that I was not bouncing back as quickly as I had before, the heat was bothering me more, the hot flashes were getting more and more frequent, and I was feeling bloated more often. I was just praying for the time to pass quickly, for my last treatment date to please arrive, and for the fall and cooler temperatures to follow. I was tired of the heat and could not wait for the fall to arrive and bring the cool air with it.

The second week after my fifth treatment proved to be a low I had not experienced before. Maybe it was the combination of the heat and my physical discomfort from the bloating, the heartburn, and the lack of energy. I hit an all-time low. Simone recognized my lack of zest for life and came over and sat with me on the deck one afternoon, talking to me and asking me questions until I started to cry. Letting it all out, I told her how sad I was and how I was so tired of being sick. "I am feeling bitter that everyone's life has gone on while mine has stopped," I said. *There. I said it,* I thought. I was so afraid she would judge me after she heard my words, but she didn't. She nodded and reached out to touch my arm. She said she could not understand how I felt but that it was okay to be honest about my feelings. She asked me to never lose sight of the fact that this would be over soon and that I would be on the road to recovery. I felt so much better after our visit, and as I looked at her beautiful face and watched her sweep her hair out of her eyes, I knew she was right. One day I would be healthy again and able to participate in all the joys my life had to offer. I just had to be strong and get through the remaining months of my treatments.

As my physical strength depleted, so did my desire to do anything. I got so tired that one evening I poured myself a bath, sunk into the warm bubbles, and lost myself in the comfort. I lay there for perhaps an hour. The house was quiet on the other side of the bathroom door, and all I could hear was the occasional drip of water into the tub. I let my mind wander forward, thinking about Christmas and how special it would be. I could almost smell my Christmas cakes baking. I could see the lights sparkling on the tree and hear the laughter of my friends and family as they gathered at my home to celebrate another Christmas together.

As the water grew cool, I opened my eyes and slowly sat up, but that was as much energy as I could sum up. I sat there, willing myself to stand, but there was nothing. The water was too heavy. *Not again!* I remembered this happening before and could not believe I had found myself in the same predicament. The water was too heavy! How could that be? How could I be so weak again that I could not push the water off to get out of the bathtub? I pulled the plug with my toe and slowly rolled my body over so that I was lying in the tub on my belly and then pulled myself up onto my knees and hands. Then I slowly pushed myself up until I was sitting back on my heels. As the water drained, I slowly stood up and wrapped myself in a towel, promising again that that would be the last bath I would indulge in until after my strength returned.

As I was crawling into bed, Tracy arrived and crawled on the bed with me. She pulled the blanket up over herself, and we lay there and visited. The sun was setting, and the sunset was bouncing off the bedroom walls, creating a beautiful peaceful lighting. Tracy had always had a wonderful way of pulling out my deepest feelings, asking all the right questions to get the deepest of answers. We talked quietly, almost whispering, and I told her how sad I was that day for so many reasons, which she knew so well, and the tears started to flow. I couldn't stop. As Tracy hugged me, she said, "You are going to be all right, my friend. It is going to be okay. You are almost done." I could see the pain in her eyes. She hurt so much for me, but she also believed more than anything that I would beat this and be okay. I pulled on her strength, and that evening I knew once again that God had placed these wonderful people in my life for a reason, and right then that reason was to help me through this trying time.

When you are at your lowest emotionally, it is so easy to be negative, to see the glass as half empty. But hopefully you will be lucky enough to be surrounded by positive people, people who love you unconditionally, never judge you, and only want what is best for you. Even in my darkest moments, I always knew how blessed I was to have such beautiful people in my life, and my heart burst with love when I thought about them and all they had done for me. I didn't need much, just a hug, a touch on the arm, or to share a deep laugh, and that was delivered to me time and time again.

We headed out camping to the lake to celebrate Mark's fortieth birthday, a long awaited occasion we had all been looking forward to for years. Mark was the youngest of our friends and the last to turn forty. He was always unmercifully teased as being the baby of the group. Sitting around the campfire, I was once again so thankful to have such beautiful friends, ones who did not dwell on my illness but rather let me set the pace. If I wanted to talk about how I was feeling, they listened; if I wanted to laugh, they laughed with me; if I wanted to go to my trailer and lie down, they covered me with a blanket and told me to sleep well. It was comfortable. It was warm. It was family. The weekend was full of laughter and fun, visiting with old lake friends that I only saw during the summers, catching up on what was happening in their lives, and singing along with Garret as he played the guitar. As I sat back in my lawn chair under the stars one evening, listening to him sing "Toes in the Water" by Zack Brown, I really listened to the words for the first time and thought, *Yes, life is good today.*

As the weekend wore on, Cliff relaxed more and more and focused less on me, and I felt the weight of his hovering dissipate. It felt good to be able to go for a walk myself and just be, felt good to have him focused on something other than me, how I was feeling, and if I was having any pain. For periods of time over the weekend I forgot about my bald head, forgot about the cancer, and just had fun, blending in with everyone else.

One evening, I sat with Roxanne, Joanne, and Leanne, three sisters I had been introduced to years ago by Tracy. These girls radiated beauty from the inside out, and from a distance I had always admired their sisterly friendship, their family, and their lives. From the first moment I met them, they had included me in their fold during our visits to the lake, and I have many memories of good times spent with them sharing sociables, playing poker, and just sitting around the fire singing. On this weekend, we sat together, and they told me how proud they were of me for being so positive and how they loved to read my updates on Facebook or the e-mails I sent. I tried to tell them it wasn't always like that and that they only saw what I wanted them to see. I felt like such a fake to accept their compliments without explaining to them first that I was not always positive and that at times I was scared, tired, and deflated.

Rather than change their minds about how they felt about me, they insisted that it was all part of the journey and that it was okay to feel those things, but they were still inspired by my attitude, and in their eyes I was courageous. As I listened to them and shared some warm hugs, I thought that perhaps I did deserve those words. Again I wrestled with the idea that perhaps it was okay to be sad, scared, and maybe even mad, but that didn't mean I couldn't also be positive, inspiring, and courageous. Those three sisters, without even realizing it, helped me think a little differently and pointed me in the right direction. They helped me realize that despite all I was feeling, the side I was showing was helping and inspiring people. I suddenly felt stronger than I had in a long time and allowed myself to warm inside with their compliments.

The week before my final treatment was busy, and I was thankful that my energy levels were rebounding, especially after the weekend camping. Simone's daughter Jessica was getting married in February and asked if I would like to join her and her mother in Calgary as they shopped for wedding dresses. Knowing I would not be able to attend her wedding in Mexico, I was honored to be asked to tag along and spent the day before our road trip resting up so that I would have enough energy to keep up. As the curtain was pulled back time and time again to reveal Jessica in another beautiful gown, I watched Simone watching her and fought back tears. Simone was so proud of her daughter and so excited for her wedding and to witness her exchanging vows with her love.

I was happy for them and found myself fighting back tears, realizing that some of them were for me. A feeling of panic started to set in. I wondered if I would be around when Kelsey and Kayla got married, or would I have a setback before then? Would the cancer come back before I had a chance to see my daughters get married or before I could hold my grandchildren in my arms? What if this treatment didn't work? And where were these thoughts coming from, I wondered. I had not anticipated that day being as emotional for me as it was, and I realized that I was still very fragile. After we returned from our shopping trip, Mark and Simone joined us for dinner, and we relived the day with the men. I noticed Simone did not mention my tears, and I was grateful she had not noticed. I could not explain my feelings to myself and was thankful I didn't have to explain them to anyone else.

I hosted the girls from work one evening for a visit and spent the day cleaning my house. Chores that use to take one hour now stretched into three, and despite Bonnie's firm e-mail warnings not to do anything to prepare, I spent most of the day trying to clean my house and set up my deck for my company. I was happy they were coming over to see me rather than me having to go to work to see them. I was so self-conscious of the weight I had gained, my pale complexion, and my lack of energy that I had avoided going into the office to visit. I didn't want the men I worked for to see my like that, to feel pity for me. It was much easier to just avoid them. As the ladies arrived, I sat back and enjoyed listening to the stories and catching up on the news of the office and their personal lives. I loved my job and loved the people I worked with. I knew only too well what it was like to work in an unhealthy environment, and I counted my lucky stars every day that I worked in the positive environment that I did.

A couple of days before my treatment, I received a call from Kelsey. She was so excited as she shared her news that she and Sean had gotten engaged. I wanted to be happy for her, and my mind instantly flashed back to how I had felt as I watched Jessica model her wedding gowns. Would I now have a chance to see my daughter get married? Was this perhaps a sign that everything was going to be okay, I wondered. We chatted about her ring, and after she agreed that she would finish school before they got married, she promised to drop by and show it to us. As I hung up the phone, I reflected back and could not believe Kelsey was engaged. She would be turning twenty-two this year, but in my mind she was still my little girl. I remembered the day she was born like yesterday! Her head was all misshapen from the forceps, and I didn't think she looked very cute, but I loved her so much. We laughed every time we told her that story, and she always pretended to be so offended, but I knew she loved to hear it. Fast-forward twenty-two years, and there she was getting married. Married! My beautiful little girl was getting married! Life does go on.

On the Friday before my final treatment, I met with my nurse to review how I was doing and to go over what to expect for the final treatment. She could tell from just looking at me how beat up I was, but I was nervous to tell her the full extent of my fatigue. I was afraid that if she knew she would delay my treatment for another week to give me a chance to build up my energy again. I wondered out loud how people functioned when they had to have ten or twelve or fourteen treatments. So far I had only had five, and I was feeling like there was very little left for me to fight with. I asked Krista if that meant I was weak and not as strong as I thought I was. Krista assured me that I was strong, not weak, and that the chemo was just building up in my system and that all the side effects I was feeling were normal. She looked at my legs, which were swelled up so much they hurt, and again assured me that this was normal.

"Just take it easy," she said. "You are almost done." I hung on to her words. I was almost done.

Krista had been one of those constants in my life during that time, and looking back, I am not sure I could have done it without her. From the moment I met her, she put me at ease, answered my questions honestly, and didn't hold anything back, believing we make better choices when we are well informed. From the minute she closed the door, I knew I had her undivided attention, and I could take as much time as I needed to go through the list of questions I had for her each visit. She didn't just treat my body; she treated my mind, picking up on those subtle clues, the body language, the words not spoken, and knowing there was something else she needed to dig out.

One thing she did that was unique but endeared her to me that much more was to share some of her life with me. I didn't feel like she knew everything (and I mean everything) about me, but she remained a mystery to me. That helped me connect with her on a much deeper level and allowed me to trust her with stuff I would not tell anyone else. Before our session wrapped up that day, I tried to express to her just how much she meant to me and what a pivotal role she had played in my life over the past four months. I hope she heard me. She was my nurse, my doctor, my marriage counselor, my shrink, my mentor, my teacher, and my friend.

September long week arrived, and it was our last trip camping for the season and the final hurrah before my last treatment. As we pulled up to the campsite, everyone was already there, the campfire was blazing, the smell of the smoke was sweet, and there was chaos as there is always is when you throw four or five families in the middle of the woods. Quads and dirt bikes roared by, loaded with helmet-clad children. The men came toward us with drinks in their hands and offers to help guide our trailer into its spot. Simone opened my door, pulled me out, and folded me into a hug as she hopped up and down, squealing in my ear, happy we were there.

After we got settled and made it around the campfire, I couldn't help but remember back to the May long weekend when everyone had pulled out of town and Cliff and I had been left behind. I had been too sick to go. There I was, four months later, back with the group, enjoying the beautiful outdoors. It was such a good feeling, and despite my swollen legs, the heartburn that was constant, and the shortness of breath, I promised that I would enjoy the weekend completely.

The weekend passed in a blur of fun, and my favorite moments were spent sitting around the fire, looking up at the stars, and trying to identify the satellites that flew across the sky. A quick second favorite were my sleeps in my bunk, pulling the fuzzy blankets up to my chin and letting the laughter of the children outside lull me to sleep. As we packed up and headed home at the end of the weekend, I was very melancholy knowing that this was our last campout of the season and so thankful I had been well enough to participate.

We arrived home, and I spent the next couple of days taking my time to do some yard work, clean the house, and just relax. My energy was still low, and I was very anxious about how I would feel after Tuesday, knowing that I was going into the final treatment feeling so depleted. I tried to talk to Cliff about how I was feeling, but he just kept saying, "Only one more." He was seeing the light at the end of the tunnel, but I was very nervous that this last treatment would do me in, that I would struggle because I was so tired already.

I spent the day before the final treatment responding to Facebook and e-mail messages that were flooding in. Everyone was happy for me that I was so close to being done, and I drew on the love and support each message contained. Juanita texted throughout the day, telling me I would be okay, and my sister-in-law sent a message every day, telling me she loved me and how proud she was of me. I loved to hear my phone buzz, knowing another message had been delivered, another message full of hope.

On the eve of my treatment, Tammy forwarded the following message to me, so fitting for that moment:

> *Expect to have hope rekindled. Expect your prayers to be answered in wondrous ways. The dry seasons in life do not last. The spring rains will come again.*
> —Sarah Ban Breathnach

As I lay in bed the night before, I thought, *I have not been a victim to cancer, but I have been a hell of a good student.* I knew there would be no sleep for me that night, and as I watched the shadows dance on the ceiling, I replayed the events of the last six months over in my mind like a black-and-white movie. When I closed my eyes, I could see different events as they unfolded. I remembered the day we found out, how scared we were. I remembered waking up from my surgery, looking for Cliff, knowing that I would be okay once he was at my side, and then being scared when I saw his face. I remembered sitting in the hospital and receiving my first treatment. I remembered how my stomach kept rolling and how I kept thinking I was going to pass out from the fear. I remembered the joy of going to the airport to pick up my girlfriend Juanita and then again to pick up my sister-in-law Peggy and my brother-in-law Dyrick so thankful to have that little piece of home in our house for a few weeks at a time. I remembered all the hugs. I remembered all the laughter. I remembered all the phone calls, all the e-mails, all the cards, all the visits. I knew it would take me a lifetime to repay all the kindness that had been shown to me and my family.

> *Be strong and courageous.*
> —Deuteronomy 31:6 (NIV)

Chapter 10

Six Down, None to Go

I could not believe the last day had arrived. Already! Did I really say already?

While the last six months seemed like a lifetime, on the other hand it seemed like it was yesterday that this had all begun. I was excited as I showered and took a moment to look at the peach fuzz that continued to grow on my head before I covered it up with my chosen scarf. I collected all my good luck charms—my rock from Juanita, my strength trinket from Linda, and the angel trinket from Maureen—after I fastened my locket from Tammy around my neck. I felt like one of those women who go to bingo and line up all their troll dolls next to their spare blotters for good luck. But those items had been with me from the first treatment, and they would make their final trek to the hospital with me today.

> *You have the power to become the hero in your own life.*
> —Author Unknown

The plan was for Simone to pick me up, and we would meet Cliff at the hospital. When I opened the door, Mark stood next to Simone. He wanted to come and lend his support and celebrate the final treatment with us. We stood in the doorway and laughed and cried, hugging as we made our way to the car. When we walked into the hospital, Kelsey greeted me with a dozen red roses, and Linda was already there waiting for us to arrive. There were lots of hugs and tears of joy, and I didn't have time to get nervous as the door opened and in walked Cliff, followed by

Shawn and Tammy, who carried a helium "I love you" balloon. Kayla came through the door moments later.

As I settled in and the nurse put in the IV, I started to cry, knowing this was the last time I would have to offer my arm up for chemotherapy. The thought that this was the last treatment was overwhelming, and I didn't even try to fight back the tears that started to roll down my cheeks. I was almost done, and I was so happy. I watched the nurse push the chemo into my IV through my misty eyes and felt Cliff leaning on the chair behind me, watching everything that was happening. Tracy arrived carrying a tray full of coffee, and on her heels, Bonnie and Karen from work showed up to visit for a short while. The nurse scrambled, looking for chairs for everyone, and I was so overwhelmed with my visitors that I forgot about the toxic treatment dripping into my body.

There were so many conversations going on between my visitors that I was preoccupied just trying to follow them, and before I knew it, the nurse was saying, "Kimberley, we are done." *Done!* My last treatment had dripped into my IV, and I had almost not even noticed, because I was so focused on all the activity around me. *Done!* As she rolled her stool in front of me and prepared to remove the IV, I once again started to cry. When she pulled out the IV, she looked into my eyes and said, "You have graduated."

It was over! I was done! Oh my God, it was over! I was so proud of myself and so happy it was done! As I looked around the room, I noticed many of my friends were misty eyed, and that made me cry even more. I knew I could never have done it without these people in my life, in my corner, supporting me every step of the way, cheering me on. That day, September 4, 2012, was a milestone day in my life that I will never forget.

We arrived home, and I noticed that the phones and computer were eerily quiet. The night almost seemed anticlimactic to me. Chemotherapy treatments were over, and while that was a reason to celebrate, I now had to face radiation treatments. Cliff and I danced around each other that evening, so happy to have it over but not wanting to get too excited yet, knowing there was another big hurdle to cross before I was done.

Before I crawled into bed, I prepared my last update on my

chemotherapy to send out to my friends and family. I was excited to send this one, as it represented the conclusion of the hardest months of life, and I had won.

Subject: Six Down, None to Go!

Hello, family and friends!

It is time for my LAST update on my journey through chemotherapy, and I have been looking forward to writing this since I wrote the very first one on May 14! Where has the time gone? I know everyone was wishing summer would drag on and on, but for me, the end of summer marked a new beginning for me, and I could not wait for it to pass!

I am so happy!

My last treatment on August 14 beat me up pretty badly, and I have been pretty depleted for the past three weeks. The worst part was the bone pain and the lingering fatigue that were at times debilitating. This round really left me at an all-time low and was by far the worst round I have experienced. Emotionally it was also a very tough one on me, dragging me to a very dark place, and I found I was isolating myself from everyone, not wanting anyone to see. But it is pretty hard to isolate yourself for very long when you have a husband and circle of friends like I do, who give you a couple of days to wallow and then do all they can to drag you out of your shell. Tracy just crawled into bed with me when I couldn't get out ... Friendship knows no boundaries. I keep saying how lucky I am to have the family and friends that I do, who never gave up on me when I retreated to heal and who loved me through what has been the toughest time of my life. I will never forget your kindness and compassion. From the meals you cooked for us, to the cards left in my mailbox and the dozens of texts, to the kind voice mails you left on my phone saying no need to call back but you were just checking in, and to the e-mails that fill my in-box every day, you kept me going, and I thank you for taking the minutes out of your busy days to reach out to me. You will never ever know how much that meant to me. Ever. To Peggy and Juanita back home, who text constantly, just to say hi and to check in, thank you!

When we met with my nurse navigator on Friday, she decided that they would dial back the final dosage of chemo because she felt the dosage they were giving me was too strong, which would explain why I was having such a hard time recovering. She is hopeful that with the lower dosage, I will not get as low and will bounce back from today's treatment much faster than the last. I am keeping my fingers crossed that she is right.

Since my last treatment, Kayla turned twenty and started college. She continues to be one of my biggest supporters and one who makes me laugh every single day. I don't know what I would do without her and the late evening ice cream runs she makes for me. What a blessing she is. Kelsey's big news is her engagement to Sean on August 29. We are very happy for her and even happier that she promises to wait to get married until after she finishes college, which gives us at least a year and a half to get use to the idea! Cliff is still processing the information in his own quiet way, and I hope that in eighteen months he will be at least resigned to the idea!

Despite my side effects from the last treatment, we did manage to get out camping two weekends. We camped with the Thodys and Ullriches at Raymond Shores on the weekend of August 24–25 and celebrated Mark's fortieth (finally) birthday. It was a great weekend with lots of laughs and a great supper celebration on Saturday night when his family joined us. On the September long weekend we headed out for some cutline camping with the Ullriches, Zazulas, Heidels, Jeffords and Dodges. There were great visits over the campfire, crib, Catch Phrase, and cards under the shelter and walks to gaze at the stars at night. Cliff and I enjoyed our meals in the quiet of our trailer while looking out the window at our fellow campers dealing with their kids, guests, and dogs (and visiting cats). Naps in the afternoon in my bunk were just icing on the cake! I look forward to next summer and feeling well and able to get out and get involved with all the physical activities I have missed with camping this year. Next year is going to be a lot of fun!

Today feels like Christmas Day (without the cooking, cleaning, and snow), and I have gotten the best gift of a lifetime! After a long four months, chemotherapy is completed, and we are so happy in the Rideout house tonight! Last night I got very little sleep, and every time I closed my eyes, the last five months played like a black-and-white movie on the inside on my eyelids. I marveled at how far we have come and cried some silent tears for the innocence the cancer diagnosis took from us. It was a night of reflection for me and a night to recognize all the blessings I have been given and accepted over the course of my treatment.

Mark and Simone showed up this morning to drive me to the hospital, and we were joined there by Cliff, Kelsey, Kayla, Shawn, Tammy, Tracy, and Linda. I wasn't sure who would come, never asking anyone, and was so happy to see these beautiful people file into the treatment room. The nurses were so accommodating to my family and friends, running around and delivering all the extra chairs so everyone would have a place to sit. As I looked around, I found myself sitting in the middle of a circle, one that was filled with so many years of friendship. All that was missing was the campfire in the middle.

As the nurse prepared my arm for my final injection, I found myself crying, and as I looked at my friends, they were crying with me. How cool is that, to have that kind of love? My big surprise was when two of my friends and co-workers Bonnie and Karen showed up unannounced to sit with us for a while. I was so surprised to see them, and the tears flowed once again. Once my treatment was completed and the needle was removed for the final time, the tears flowed again, and hugs and expressions of relief were shared.

So now I have some work to do. Getting my strength back and getting healthy enough to start radiation in the best physical shape possible. We have to go to the cancer clinic in Calgary at the end of the month and meet with them to find out when radiation starts, and it is looking like it will be mid-October. I also have some work to do to get these thirty-three pounds off that I have packed on over the last five months as well. I am feeling like a dough boy, which in my mind is even worse when you are bald! I am looking forward to the day I can wear more than yoga pants and can run a comb through my hair!

What a ride, what a journey! So happy to be at the end of this leg and be able to say the worst is now behind us!

Once again, thank you so much for your continued support, your love, your understanding, and your help. I could never have gotten this far without it!

Love you all!

Love Me

The day after my treatment I stayed in bed for most of the day, not wanting to overdo it. While I was anxious to see if I had fared better than I had at my last treatment, I wasn't ready yet to push it. Kayla arrived home from school and crawled into bed with me, and we had a nice chat. She was excited to tell me about a presentation she was doing at school. It had to be about something that had inspired her, and she was doing it about me. I was honored and touched and so proud of my daughter. She had a dream, and she was pursing it with all she had.

A short time later, Simone dropped by, and Kayla told her I was in bed when she answered the door, so she came and crawled onto my bed with me, and we visited as we lay there. I was too tired to move and was grateful for the company. It felt good to have the kind of friends who would just crawl into bed with me. It was peaceful, and she stayed until the chemo fog started to roll in again and I got tired.

As the evening wore on, I managed to get enough energy to sit at my computer, and I soaked in the e-mails of support and love that filled my in-box.

My friend Chicklet wrote,

You are an amazing inspiration to all of us. I admire you for stretching for the positive, your appreciativeness of your loved ones and friends, your strength to crawl out of your holes along the way, and for also sharing your ups and downs. I have prayed for you and will continue to do that. Take care, Kimmy. Glad you got that last treatment under your belt.

Juanita wrote,

I so enjoy your updates, but I will be so happy that your updates will once again be like your Christmas newsletters and no longer about chemo, because as your friend it breaks my heart to use your name and chemo in the same sentence, and I am so happy not to have to do that anymore. You have come a long way since March 14. You have faced so much with all your strength, courage, and conviction. You are a true friend and a true inspiration. I am not one bit surprised of the love and support that has been shown to you. You are so loved, and I am so happy to have met your friends and to see how much they care for you Cliff and the girls, and I so look forward to next summer when we are all together once again to laugh and have fun when cancer is a distant memory ... I love you, my friend.

My beautiful sister Peggy wrote,

My heart broke when I knew in my heart what you were going through and not being there with you. We have felt so helpless so many times being so far away. You have a remarkable network of friends who have been there for you throughout, and I thank God for them. I love and appreciate them all for being there for you, Cliff, and the girls when we couldn't. The pictures in the treatment room of all your friends said it all. I couldn't hold back the tears when I saw them. (You know, big girls do cry sometimes.)

Peggy's e-mail summed up all that I had been feeling for months. While I was in a province with no immediately family close, my friends had pulled tightly around me and my family, treated us like one of their own, and loved us like they loved their own families. Time and time again we were included in their family activities and meals. My friends' parents checked in on me like they did their own kids. I was as close to my girlfriends as any girl is to a blood sister. I was so thankful and will be thankful for the rest of my life for my chosen family—my chosen family who embraced me, held me while I wept, cooked for me, entertained me, and assured me that I would be okay. I will always be thankful for those who "loved me through it."

Ingrid sent a message and once again watered that seed to write a book, saying,

> *Kim ... So happy this part of your journey is done! And if you ever want a career change, you really should be a writer ... I feel like I could reach out and touch you ... Your words bring to life your experiences, and I thank you so much for sharing with us. Remember we are here to help with the driving to Calgary for radiation ... And when you are up to celebrating, we're there for you!*

Audrey sent a beautiful note saying, *Thanks for the update, you leave us breathless each time with the reality of what you have suffered. Take care these next few weeks. Maybe the weather will cooperate and we can still sit on your patio one afternoon.*

And my angel on earth, Christine, took the opportunity to once again remind me that God loved me and didn't leave me during those trying times:

> *Thank-you for always doing your updates ... I have felt connected! Miss you tons and praying for this round to go easier on ya! Today's scripture seemed fitting:*

> *"Then Jesus came to them and said, 'All authority in heaven and on earth has been given to me. Therefore go and make disciples of all nations, baptizing them in the name of the Father and of the Son and of the Holy Spirit, and teaching them to obey everything I have*

commanded you. And surely I am with you always, to the very end of the age.'"

He has surely been with you and will continue to be, as he promises! Such a beautiful promise!

I had been struggling with my faith for some time, wondering what message I was supposed to learn here, wondering why God would put this on my shoulders and have me fight my way out alone. I wondered what I had done to deserve this kind of pain, this kind of heartache, and many times I questioned who I was. I rationalized that if I was as good a person as I thought, this would never have happened to me, so that must mean I wasn't a good person. I had always felt so blessed with my life. Even when faced with some recent challenges, I never let the day end without saying a prayer of thanks for all He had given me. Now I wondered if I was just going through the motions and if He knew that and this was His way of making me stop and take notice. Christine helped me to check back in, to realize that faith was exactly that: *faith*. I had to have faith that there was a reason this had all happened and that I might never know what that reason was. And that was okay. I was in God's hands, and He would take care of me. He had never left my side. I believed, even when my faith was shaken, that God would help me heal.

My dear friend Donna wrote,

Thanks for the update. Thought of you all day yesterday, and we are so HAPPY for you that this chemo journey is now over for you! Hopefully this treatment will not be as hard on you with the lower dosage … You did so well at writing this last update with just having gone through your treatment. Your updates are full of so many emotions. Have you ever thought of writing a book? Take care and remember you are always in our thoughts and prayers … Love you.

P.S. Donna, I wrote a book!

And my new friend in cancer, Audrey, sent me a beautiful note saying,

*I am so happy that you see the light at the end of that "dark tunnel."
When I was reading your e-mails, I felt for you deep down in myself
... feeling that tiredness and wanting to do more but not being able
to. So, girl, you are on the road to health and happiness. Is it not great
to have family and friends beside you as you travel into that unknown
space? But here you are! Do a dance around the kitchen, singing your
favorite song.*

She had been exactly where I was and knew how important that strong support network of family and friends was.

As the week after my final chemo treatment faded, I once again suffered through hot flashes that left me soaked in sweat and fighting for a breath of cool air. When they hit, the discomfort was unlike any I had felt before, and every crease in my body pooled up with water. Once the flash passed, I was overtaken with chills and couldn't warm up. There was no relief, and it was its own form of torture.

Heartburn also decided to rear its uncomfortable head, and I experimented with different antacids. My bathroom cabinet started resembling a drugstore shelf.

My final treatment was over, and I wondered why I was not feeling exuberant. Why wasn't I jumping up and down in joy that I had closed the chapter on that final, painful period in my life? Cliff was walking around with relief written all over his face, but I didn't feel the same and struggled with why.

My discomfort grew to a point that it was the worst I had experienced to date. Cliff and I went for a drive, and as we turned each corner, the gas and pressure in my body rose higher and higher. I asked him to please bring me home, and when we arrived, I stood on the sidewalk, bent over in pain, unable to straighten up and walk inside. I was so embarrassed, so mad at my body for betraying me. I was in so much pain. I started to cry, thinking how unfair this all was and wondering why I had to go through it, wondering if I would ever feel normal again. I cried as I slowly made my way to the house and then hid behind the locked bathroom door and continued to cry until there were no more tears left.

The fatigue I was experiencing was worse than I had dealt with previously. I knew it was because I now had six treatments cumulating in my body, but it was so hard to deal with. I was ready to feel better. I was ready to get my energy back and be myself again. I was tired of being sick. I was tired of being tired. I wanted to go to sleep and not wake up until I was better.

As the fatigue, hot flashes, bloating, and headaches raged on, my mental state plummeted to lower than I had been in a while. I was taken to my knees once again and didn't have any energy to pull myself up. At that moment, everything in my life hid in the shadow of my dark mood.

I was also feeling resentful toward those around me who felt that it was now time for me to resume my daily schedule now that treatments were over. I felt they did not understand that even though the needle had been removed for the last time it didn't mean that I would be instantly better. I know they knew that and were only willing me to be better. Their words were nothing but encouraging. But I chose to be resentful rather than grateful. I had been hoping to feel better much sooner, and I was getting impatient.

My faith was being shaken again, and I tried hard not to blame God for what was happening to me. I sat at my computer and played a song over and over, the lyrics speaking directly to me: "Every tear I cried, you held in your hand. Never left my side. Though my heart is torn, I praise you in this storm." Did he know my tears were my prayers? That tears were all I had?

I received a beautiful text from my friend Dean saying, *You are my newest hero. There has been enough tears, so now it's time to get back to living and laughing and loving.*

Newest hero? After reading that text, I crawled out of bed and made my way to the kitchen, and before I knew it I had made a lemon pie, chocolate chip cookies, and had bread rising and ready to go into the oven. It was time to get back to living, laughing, and loving! A simple test helped me turn the corner on a dark day.

I met Carrie for lunch, and we passed two hours chatting about our treatments and how people in our circles handled it. She had endured fourteen treatments, one every second week. We talked about our fears of it coming back and how we dealt with those fears. We talked about our hair loss and her regrowth; she had already had five haircuts. We talked about our husbands and how they had dealt and were currently dealing with it all. And we talked about the horrible weight gain and the struggles losing it posed. It was so good to talk to someone who knew exactly what I was feeling, and I was once again grateful to have her in my life.

As the days faded in and out, my energy started to increase, and I found myself doing more and more, much to Cliff's delight. My body was slowly healing. One evening he was outside, and when he came in I was in the middle of moving around the living room furniture. "Honey, you're back" was all he said, but the smile on his face told the whole story. He was so relieved to see me moving around again and doing things I had done before.

Once my energy started to come back, it came back with a vengeance, and I found myself cleaning out closets, drawers, and cabinets. Anything I had ignored over the last six months now got double the attention. With the newfound energy came increased hot flashes and bloating. I stayed close to home because I had very few articles of clothing that even fit me anymore. It was discouraging, but it was somewhat overshadowed because I was so happy to feel a little normal again.

It was around this time that my hair started growing in again, enough that I felt comfortable going out with just a hat on. There was just enough hair peeping through that with a hat on I could fool myself into thinking I looked like I had a really short haircut.

The heaviness in my legs started to subside. I didn't feel like I had weights strapped around my ankles anymore, and moving around got easier. Everything I had read told me that the aches I was feeling were all normal and would get better in time. And they did. After months of feeling a little better every day, it seemed like one day I woke up and they were gone.

I still struggled with my weight issue and attempted to go shopping in an effort to find something I looked nice in and that fit. My shopping trip ended with me in tears, returning home empty-handed. By the time I made it home, my sadness had turned into anger, and I lashed out at Cliff as soon as I walked in the door. That lead to a full-blown meltdown, and I could not stop crying.

I told Cliff I was so sorry, but I was tired of feeling ugly. "It is so hard to stay positive all the time when I see this person looking back at me in the mirror every day," I sobbed. "Is it really too much to ask for some hair, eyelashes, and eyebrows? I want the old me back. I am tired of looking like this. I want to feel like a woman again. I want to feel pretty and sexy again." Cliff just held me, knowing there were no words he could say to make me feel better. I hated the way I looked, and I hated being sad. I hated the gutter I was crawling around in.

One of the hardest and most challenging tasks is to make sure your self-esteem doesn't get washed down the drain with your hair. It was something I struggled with daily as I stood in front of the mirror, tied on a head scarf, and put on some makeup, drawing on my eyebrows and putting mascara on the three eyelashes that hung on.

"I am still me," I kept repeating. "I am still me." But so many times I did not hear my own words.

The end of my chemo opened a whole Pandora's box of emotions that I was surprised to face. I was suddenly scared, wondering where I went from there. For the past six months I had seen my medical team at least once every three weeks; now I was suddenly set free to heal before radiation started in about two months. Eight weeks. I was fearful. Shouldn't someone be monitoring me? Watching me? The correct answer was no, but at the time I felt I had been set out to sea without a life raft.

I also started feeling resentful. I was tired of all the compliments that were being given to me. I wondered why people couldn't see that I was none of that. "Hello!" I wanted to scream. "I am just a big fat farce." I just wanted to lie on the floor and kick and scream. I was mad. I was so mad. Where that came from, I didn't know. All I knew was that it was there, and it was not a good place to be.

I passed the resentment I was feeling on to my family, and once again Cliff and Kayla picked up the lion's share of my rants. After a particularly bad day, I spoke pretty rudely to Kayla, and she left the room without saying a word only to return several moments later to wrap her arms around me and tell me that she loved me. That small gesture brought me to tears.

If you imagine the worst case scenario and it happens, you've lived it twice.
——Michael J. Fox

Around this time, I was experiencing a pain in my hip that I had not had before. It was almost debilitating it hurt so much. If I sat down for any length of time and then stood up again, it would hurt, and I would walk with a limp for several moments until it worked out. I was worried. What if it was the cancer returning? What if it had now moved into my hip? I spent weeks worrying about it until I met with my nurse, Krista. She ordered a bone scan. It turned out it was nothing, just some arthritis—a common occurrence after chemotherapy. I reminded myself that in the vast majority of instances, pain was not a sign of a reoccurrence of cancer but of old age!

Cliff and I struggled. He was tired of dancing around me, afraid to set me off with the simplest comment, and I was tired of what I interpreted as his lack of understanding. We were so far apart that we couldn't see each other. We had pulled tightly together during my treatments, and now that they were done, we were both tired and started to come unglued from each other. While I knew we were solid, I still worried about that scary statistic of martial breakdowns that occur after a breast cancer diagnosis and treatment. Cliff was planning his bi-annual moose hunting trip to Newfoundland, and we were both silently relieved that we could put some space between us and let our emotions settle.

As he packed his suitcase, I watched from the sidelines. I prayed that when he returned we could light that spark again, that our marriage would survive the hell we had been through. I needed my husband back, and I knew he needed his wife back. We had to find our way back through the murky waters that had now become our reality or else our marriage was going to suffer even more.

The morning he left, I woke up and realized he was already gone. He was catching an early flight and had left without waking me up. I was suddenly hit with a wave of aloneness that I hadn't felt before and made a vow to do everything I could to make it better between Cliff and me when he returned home. I pulled his pillow to my face and breathed in his scent before I fell back to sleep again.

The week that he was away, we talked sporadically because of poor cell service. Every time we did talk, he sounded happy and relaxed, and I hoped he was having as good of time as he said he was.

Tracy and I took advantage of our husbands being away and spent the weekend at the spa, being pampered. It was a great weekend and one where we chatted about so many things that had happened over the past six months. She was a great sounding board for me, and our conversations were always so free flowing with no perimeters.

When we arrived home, I headed out to the garden and spent the afternoon cleaning the deck off and getting everything ready for winter. While I was working, I suddenly realized that I hadn't had one thought of being sick. I was working away like I had any other time before this all happened, doing the same things I had done before, and I didn't feel the limitations I had felt these past six months. I was getting better! I felt I was turning a corner, and it was such a great relief!

My relief was short, as the following day I found that just getting out of bed took all the energy I had. I knew I had overdone it the previous days and cursed myself for being so stupid. I knew from experience that this would set me back for days, and I was mad. I had been feeling so good and foolishly convinced myself that it was over. But it wasn't. They said it took months and months for the chemo to flush through your body, and here I was only days in. My arms ached so badly I cried when unloading the dishwasher, remembering how easy everything had been the day before. I decided to take it easy for the rest of the week and let my body dictate how much I was able to do, not my mind. It helped. The days flew by, and each day I felt stronger and had less pain in my bones.

To reach our goal, we must sail sometimes with the wind and sometimes against it. But we must sail and not drift, not lie at anchor.
—Oliver Wendell Holmes

Chapter 11

Radiation

On Friday, Angela and I headed out early to meet with the radiation oncologist in Calgary. Cliff's trip plans had been made long before my diagnosis, and I didn't want him to change those plans to meet with this doctor. Angela had worked as a radiation technician years prior and offered to accompany me to the appointment. We arrived a few minutes ahead of time and settled into the waiting room. I watched as Angela looked through all the pamphlets that were laid out, knowing her thoughts were with her dad at that moment. I knew how much she missed him every day and that walking into a cancer clinic with me had to be one of the hardest things she could do. I was thankful she was there with me, and I was sad for her at the same time.

We were called in and sat down as the oncologist reviewed my file with us. He told me that with my type and grade of cancer, the chance of a reoccurrence was only approximately six percent. Six percent! That was the first time I had heard that statistic, and I was so relieved. I looked at Angela, and we smiled together. Deep breath. Then he followed with more good news, informing me that I would only require sixteen radiation treatments and not the twenty-five I had been previously advised. Sixteen! I was so relieved! That was nine less than I had been prepared for. He had shaved almost two weeks of travel time off for me in seconds. I would have to travel to Calgary daily for those treatments, so that was almost 3,150 kilometers I would not have to travel. I was happy, and Angela reached for my hand as we both smiled so big I thought we would burst.

This doctor was very positive and informative and took his time, answering all the questions Angela asked while I sat back and ran numbers in my head and realized that they all had a six. A 6 percent chance— that was good! Sixteen treatments—that was better than twenty-five! Angela asked about when treatments would start and told him I wanted to have them done as early as possible in order to avoid the winter road conditions. He told me to expect a call within a week to give me my treatment schedule. As we shook his hand, I wanted to hug him and say, "Thank you for being so kind."

As soon as we reached the parking lot, I called Cliff to give him the good news, and he was as relieved as I was. It was a good day. Angela and I talked all the way home, and I learned some information from her that I had not heard. I was glad she had been with me and had picked up on the stuff I missed. I was grateful for her company. I was thankful for her knowledge and her friendship. When we arrived home, there was a message on my voice mail advising me that my radiation dates had been set, and my first one would be on October 16. Another six! Now I had a little more than two weeks to heal and recover from my chemo. I was ready to do the work to heal.

Peace comes from being aligned with the present moment. Wherever you are, you feel that you are home—because you are home.
—Eckhart Tolle

The following day, Cliff arrived home from his trip, and as we hugged, he whispered in my ear, "I missed you, honey." I knew then that we were going to be okay. It felt good to have him home and to be in the safety of his arms, to have his presence in our home again.

The day after Cliff arrived home, I was saddened to read that Raylene Ranklin, a famous singer of the Canadian band the Ranklin Family, had passed away after a twelve-year battle with breast cancer. As I read the news report, I thought how sad it was that another life had been taken, knowing that for every high-profile person reported on in the news, there were thousands of others who were losing their battles silently. It made me sad.

The day of the CIBC Run for the Cure arrived, and I was anxious to get moving and head to the field to find my teams. My co-workers had entered a team, Kim's Breast Friends, and my friends had entered a team called Kim's Udder Breast Friends. As we found everyone, it seemed surreal that all these T-shirts had my name on them and that these people had gotten together in support of me. That these people even had to get together to support me was still hard to accept. On the front of the shirts there was a space for the participant to say who they were running for. My name filled that space on so many, and I laughed at the comments on some. My boss Spencer's shirt said, "I'm not running." I still smile today when I look at that picture. Cliff's simply said. "My wife."

As I crossed the field to the survivor tent to get my pink shirt, I noticed how many pink shirts were in the crowd and marveled that there were that many of us. One in nine women will be diagnosed with breast cancer in her lifetime is the statistic, and the ratio of pink to white T-shirts seemed to support that. Once I pulled my shirt over my head, I noticed the other women wearing survivor shirts smiling at me. They kept my gaze and even touched me gently on the arm as they walked by. We were a silent sisterhood, forced into this club kicking and screaming, wanting to be anywhere but where we were. But now that we had been initiated, we were resolved and accepting. Ready to wear that pink shirt proudly.

The walk started, and everyone settled in for the long five kilometer walk. It was the second time in three months that I had moved within a sea of hundreds of people, easily identified as being different because of the color of my T-shirt.

Cliff, Kayla, and I took our time at the back of the pack, walking slowly as I watched Kelsey take off in a sprint tightly on Angela's heels. As we walked, holding hands and cheering on those who ran by us, I vowed that I would run the full five kilometers next year.

Having only made it partway, I tired, and Cliff noticed my fatigue and urged me to turn around. I wanted to walk the whole way but knew I would suffer for it in days to come if I pushed myself. I reluctantly turned around, noting that there were already people headed back to the finish line after having run the entire course. As we slowly made our way back, we cheered those on who ran by us, and I turned my head up to the sky and soaked in the warm midmorning sun.

It felt good to be alive. I was so thankful to be alive.

We sat on the sidewalk and cheered people on as they crossed the finish line, and I found my eyes filling with tears as each member of my teams crossed. How healthy they all looked. How happy. The corporate spirit award our team won for being the top fund-raising corporate team in the event was just the sweetest icing on the cake. As we walked up to receive the award, Crystal, our team captain, pushed me forward and told me to accept the award on behalf of the team. I think I smiled the biggest smile I had smiled in some time.

As I hugged everyone good-bye, I hoped they all realized just how much their participation in the event meant to me. When you are a cancer survivor, you can appreciate how much it means to have people support your cause, to rally around you, to show up. It was a great day.

The following week, I headed back to Calgary to have the CT scan done to prepare for my radiation. I was also advised that I would have to have four tattoos placed on my chest area and that they would use those tattoos to guide the radiation beam with each treatment. As we walked into the Tom Baker Cancer Clinic in Calgary for the first time, I felt like someone had kicked me in the stomach. Cliff's hand got tighter in mine, and I knew he was feeling it too. Our local cancer clinic had been much quieter than this big hospital, and as we walked through the halls, we saw a different face of cancer in every direction we looked.

Everywhere we looked there was someone who looked like me. Some people looked so sick, pushing IV poles in front of them as they shuffled down the hallways. Others pushed by us as they quickly made their way to their destinations, so comfortable with their bald heads that they didn't even wear hats. As we made our way to the radiation department, I heard Cliff suck in his breath several times. He was having a hard time with the reality of this cancer haven.

I noted that people looked sad, they looked happy, they looked mad, and some just looked vacant. But the smiles were beautiful when exchanged. I was amazed at the many faces of cancer I saw that day and would continue to encounter over my three weeks of treatments. Young and old, every race you could name—they were walking through the halls of that hospital. Everyone had a story, everyone had a life, and we were all linked together by this awful disease called cancer.

The CT scan was quick and painless, and as I lay on the hospital bed, I made small chitchat with the technician who administered my tattoos. As I lay back with my arm over my head, they adjusted me this way and that, getting the position exactly right before the ink was placed. It took some time, and I quieted their apologies for taking so long, saying I would stay there all day if it meant that laser beam stayed away from my heart and lungs.

I was left in the room alone for a short time, lying on the bed with my arm still extended while they took some measurements from behind the wall. As I looked up at the ceiling, I felt tears roll down my cheeks, and I wondered where they were coming from all of a sudden. I was so happy to be at this stage of my treatment. I was almost done. But at the same time I was still accepting that this had even happened in the first place. I shed the tears for so many reasons: happiness to be almost done, sadness to have gone through this, bewilderment that this had even happened to me.

Cliff stood as I rounded the corner and took me in his arms before he nudged me toward the changing room. He was as relieved as I was to have crossed another hurdle.

I now had two weeks to rest and heal and get as much strength as I could in order to face the grueling schedule of driving to Calgary and back for sixteen workdays in a row. That was a 350 kilometer round trip each day, and just thinking of it made me tired. My muscle and bone pain were still bothering me, but I found that it was a lot less bothersome if I moved around, so I tried to do more and more of that as the days passed.

October was Breast Cancer Awareness month, and while I was happy and thankful for the support it provided, I found that some days I almost felt assaulted by the constant ads in the media. Just when I was having a moment when I could forget what was happening, a commercial ran on TV. I would be driving and thinking about something else, and a commercial would air over the radio. Every magazine I picked up displayed a pink ribbon. There seemed to be no way to hide from it, to forget. I wondered

255

how I would feel the next October, being a survivor and having completed my treatments? Would I be able to focus on the good the campaign did for women like me, for the research, for a cure, or would it still be too raw?

Jesus said, "Your father knows the things you need before you ask him."
—Matthew 6:8

Thanksgiving. Where do I start, I wondered as I opened my eyes on the morning of Thanksgiving weekend. I was so thankful. First and foremost I was thankful for life. I was thankful that God spared me. I was thankful for my family and for my friends. I was thankful for all the beauty around me. I was so thankful.

Another first for my family this Thanksgiving was that I would not be hosting my annual Thanksgiving dinner. I was still feeling the fatigue and did not have enough energy to cook for a crowd, so we joined Linda and Darcy and their extended family at the local corn maze. Everyone brought a something for the Thanksgiving feast, and what a feast it was. As I let the sun warm me, I watched all the activity going on around me and again felt so thankful to be a part of it. What a wonderful day it was. We all stood in a circle as Linda's mom said the blessing before we ate, and I felt tears once again surface. *Thank you, Lord, for life.*

We spent the full day at the maze, and though I was tired and my bones were hurting, I did not want to give in; I didn't want the day to end. I sat there and turned my face up to the sun, surrounded by the sounds of children laughing and everyone talking. I was in heaven.

I spent the final week before my radiation started cleaning the house and yard, getting everything ready for when I didn't have the energy to do it. I had been told up to that point that radiation would make me tired and that I would have to rest lots. I was not looking forward to the daily commute but was surprisingly calm about the radiation itself. I was certain I had already faced the worst with chemotherapy and was prepared for whatever my next round of treatments threw my way. I was confident in my ability to handle it.

Our first snowfall of the season hit that week as well, October 10.

We woke up to snow on the ground, and I was instantly worried that this weather pattern would hang around for the next month. I had hoped that starting my radiation in mid-October would help me avoid the winter driving conditions. Little did I know at that point that the three weeks I would be on the road would be the worst three weeks of the fall.

The cold winterlike weather woke up something inside me, my need to nest and make my house a home. After the months of heat and humidity, I welcomed the hum of the furnace and the smell of cookies I pulled out of the oven. The crackle of the wood in the fireplace warmed my soul as I curled up in front of it and slept away the fatigue. It warmed my bones and helped ease the aches. Each day I would get up and light the fireplace and plan my day. My goal was for my family to be greeted with the delicious smells of home cooking as they opened the door after their days had ended.

Every day I noticed my hair growing back a little bit more. While I was dismayed to see it was growing back mostly grey, I was so thankful to see hair where I once only saw my scalp. I ran my fingers over it daily, imagining it when it was once again long enough to comb and style. I imagined the day again when it was long enough for Cliff to run his fingers through it. I knew how much he missed my hair.

As long as you have breath, someone needs what you have.
—Pastor Joel Osteen

The weekend before my radiation started, I hosted our ladies poker night at my house. As I prepared that day, I noticed a shift in my way of thinking. No longer was I worried that my house wouldn't be squeaky clean for their arrival. I was more looking forward to the conversation, to the companionship, to the hugs and love. There were more important things in life than a clean house.

As the girls arrived, they were all dressed in an article of pink clothing, and I was touched. What a beautiful gesture it was, and as I gathered everyone together for a group picture, I was once again touched with just how blessed I was. The night passed quickly, full of conversation and catching up with those we had not seen in a while.

The day of my first radiation treatment arrived, and it was raining so hard I could hear it hitting the roof of my house. Cliff pulled the car up, and I dashed to it, soaking wet from the sprint from the house to the car. Our drive to the hospital was filled with joking and silliness, so different from our drives to chemotherapy. There was jubilance in the air; we knew we were now on the home stretch and couldn't wait to be done.

As we walked through the corridors of the hospital, there was a little spring in our steps, and we smiled at everyone we passed. This was day one, and there were only fifteen days to go! Fifteen days! Once we reached the radiation department I changed into my gown and placed all my clothing in the locker provided, including my hat. As I walked out into the waiting room without my hat, I realized this was the first time I had gone out in public without my head covered. I sat next to Cliff and waited for my name to be called, waiting for him to say something. He never did. He didn't even notice. How beautiful it was to be at that stage where I could enter a public area and he didn't even notice that my head wasn't covered. And even if he did, it wouldn't have mattered.

I crawled up onto the table, and my wonderful nurses moved me this way and that, getting everything ready. They were so kind, took their time, and answered all my questions with patience and ease. They had done this countless times before but understood that I had not. It was not routine to me, yet it was surprising just how quickly it did become routine.

The radiation treatment itself took less than two minutes; it was so fast that it was over before I had a moment to get nervous. After I was positioned just right, my nurse told me she would be leaving the room and would return when the treatment was over. As she walked away, I could hear the beeping from the big steel and concrete door as it slammed shut, and I was left in the room all alone. The machine circled my chest and stopped twice, and I could hear a clicking sound, which I assumed was the laser delivering the radiation. I felt nothing and was in fact very relaxed. I closed my eyes, and before I knew it, the machine was returning to the resting position and my nurses returned to say we were done.

I was given a cream and instructions to apply it four times a day to the area radiated. I used it twice. I was one of the lucky ones and experienced no burning or irritation. I had read all the stories about the pain and suffering some women went through during radiation treatments, and I was worried that I would be one of them, but thankfully I was spared that discomfort.

Radiation made me tired. I was so very tired again. But it was unlike the fatigue I felt from chemo. I wondered if it was mind over matter for me at that point. I was so close to being done. My treatments were almost over, and I was feeling excited about being that close to being done and able to close this chapter. For whatever reason, radiation did not beat me up like chemo had, and I was thankful for that.

Each day that I returned to the Tom Baker Cancer Clinic for my sixteen treatments, my elation grew. I was anxious to get it over, and my daily trips to Calgary were almost made in a celebratory mood. On the days Cliff accompanied me, we had a routine we adhered to, and it was comforting. We held hands and joked as we navigated through the hospital corridors. While I changed into my robe, he checked me in at unit 8 and was always waiting for me when I came out of the room a short time later. We always stopped for a tea on the way home and smiled every time I crossed off another appointment on the schedule they had given me.

Even the poor weather did nothing to dampen my mood. Each day we drove it got worse and worse. Freezing rain, blowing snow, fog—you name it, we had it during those three weeks. One day I was forced to turn around because the driving conditions were horrible. That added another day to the end of my treatment plan, but even that was okay. I was so close to being done I could taste it.

My will was strengthened even more with an e-mail from my friend Christine, which read,

Kimmy, starting the last leg of this unbelievable chapter of your life, I want you to remember that even before this, I saw you as an incredible woman, mother, wife, and friend. You have leaned on the Lord through this, I know, and it takes a lot of courage to trust an invisible God. But He is real, and He is faithful! He loves you so much, and so do I! As a sideline observer of what you have been through, I

259

know that God is going to use this experience for His Glory, for it was His strength that pulled you through as He surrounded you with such love and support and comforted you in your hours of need. You will help others through their time, I know that full well. It will bless you as you lend support from a perspective only you could have, having gone through it. Jesus never wastes anything that we go through. Trusting Him, not just through this time but for the rest of your life, I pray that you will experience amazing times with Him and know how much He cares for you.

Those drives back and forth to Calgary were very healing for me, and on days when my friends accompanied me, I had an opportunity to catch up with them and have some one-on-one time. There were some pretty intense conversations that took place inside my vehicle on those days, and there was lots of love shared. I am eternally grateful to each of my friends—Tracy, Tammy, Linda, Krista, Simone, and Shawn—who took the time to come with me. I took great pride in showing them through the hospital and sharing a little part of the final leg of my journey with them. One memory that kept me smiling every time I thought about it was when Shawn drove me and we stopped to buy some candy in the lobby on our way out of the hospital. We ate about two pounds of the candy on the drive home, and by the time we arrived back in the city, we were both doubled over with stomach cramps from the candy. I haven't been able to eat a Jujube since!

During my radiation, we celebrated three occasions: the annual jambalaya gathering, Halloween, and my forty-fifth birthday. It was a busy social calendar for someone who was healthy, and I was far from feeling healthy. But I didn't want to miss a thing.

The annual jambalaya was a party our friends had been putting on for several years. It was just an excuse to get together really. Glen and Ed prepared a big pot of hearty jambalaya, and everyone gathered for an evening, laughed, played games, and had a good time. This year Glen and Ed decided to put a twist to it and raise money for prostate and breast cancer. My friend Chris, a prostate cancer survivor, and myself had been part of the jambalaya since the first year, and we were both honored that they would turn what was always just a social gathering into something much more meaningful. It was another example of how people pull together and help each other out in times of need. The night was a smashing success, and for the number of people that attended I was amazed with the amount of money Glen and Ed had raised and was so happy to be part of it.

As the days of my treatment passed, I noticed a marked improvement in the pain I was feeling in my bones and joints. It was getting easier to move around, and it didn't hurt nearly as much to walk up and down the stairs. After my long drive to Calgary and back each day, I did have trouble when I first got out of the vehicle, but after I moved around a little I found that it eased off. As the pain subsided, my fear that something else was wrong subsided with it. I was still struggling with the worry of every ache and pain being a sign that the cancer had returned, and I knew I would have to deal with that worry for the rest of my life.

As I prepared to go out for Halloween, I decided I would wear one of the wigs I had purchased so many months before. It was a long blond wig, and I did not recognize myself when I looked in the mirror. It had been so long since I'd had any hair that the person looking back at me was unrecognizable. I could not believe it was me and was not sure how I felt about the image looking back.

As we walked into the Tammy and Les's Halloween haven, I was once again in awe of Tammy's decorating skills and all the effort she put into her annual Halloween party. People showed their appreciation for all her hard work by showing up in the coolest costumes. She had turned Cliff's distaste for Halloween into an attitude of anticipation and enjoyment. As I we all mingled, I left Cliff's side and moved around on my own and was amazed at the number of people I spoke to who did not recognize me. It had been so long since I had hair that I looked so different now. My friend's daughter, Kendra, had come over that night and applied false eyelashes, and that made the change even more dramatic. When people recognized me, they immediately pulled me into a hug.

The best part of the whole experience was that I looked just like everyone else. Just another person dressed up for the occasion. There was nothing that singled me out, and I found I was more comfortable that night around people than I had been in some time. There was nothing to be self-conscious about. It felt so good to blend in. I spent the night catching up with people I hadn't seen in a while and sharing parts of my story with people who were curious and asked questions. It seemed that everyone wanted to know what was happening. Especially women. I represented one of their biggest fears, and they wanted to know how I found it, if it hurt, what had happened, how I was feeling. But they didn't know how to ask those questions or even if I would be receptive to answering them. So I always took their lead, and if they appeared to want to know more, I would tell more. I had no problem sharing my story; it was therapeutic for me to talk about it, and I also hoped that someday my sharing would help someone else.

If you get, give. If you learn, teach.
—Maya Angelou

As my treatments progressed, I felt better and better, but the tiredness caught up with me. I tried to relax as often as possible but noticed that it bothered Kayla to see me sleeping in the afternoon, and I knew she saw it as meaning I wasn't feeling well. So I tried to time my rest periods for earlier in the day if possible and reserved as much energy as I could for the evenings when my family was around.

My skin started to get a little irritated, but it was nothing unbearable. I didn't like the smell of the cream they had given me to use, so I put up with the little discomfort I had, promising myself I would use the cream if the burning started to bother me. I started going for massages, which helped ease the bone pain I was having, and I always felt good after one.

Hot flashes hit me at moments when I least expected them, and I took to keeping my house cool and my vehicle even cooler. I laughed when friends came to visit and brought their own slippers or immediately reached for the blanket draped over the couch and bundled up under it. I was never comforted by anything I read about the hot flashes, knowing I had been suffering them for some time now and there was nothing I could take to help ease them. The only salvation was that it was wintertime and I could go out on the step in -20 degree weather and cool off really fast.

The weekend before my last three treatments, I celebrated my forty-fifth birthday, and I celebrated it in style. We were picked up at our front door in a limousine and driven around the city for a few hours with twelve friends, toasting my birthday time and time again at my insistence, stopping for pictures, and being serenaded by the limo driver. That night also marked the first night I went out in public without anything covering my head. While I wished that my hair was longer, I felt so blessed that I was at this stage in my treatment and undoubtedly blessed to be sharing the night with such beautiful people. We indulged in many sociables in the limo before being delivered to the local casino, where we had a delicious supper and then participated in a few games at the tables. It was the best birthday of my life to date. I was alive. I was surrounded by people I loved. I was loved. Best birthday ever!

> *If you wonder what you are going to be like in five years,*
> *listen to what you are saying about yourself today.*
> —Author Unknown

Cancer gave me a gift, and while I was a slow learner, I finally got it. I am beautiful. I am loved. I am strong. I am a survivor. I am all of those things, and I will be around for many years to say the same thing.

The final week of my treatments arrived, and with it came anxiety and fear. I was not expecting to feel those things, but I was suddenly fearful of what lay ahead. After my last radiation treatment, I would be set loose on my own.

At that point I didn't see that as good news, only something to be feared. While I have come to understand now that being left on my own for months at a time is a good thing, at the time I felt like I was being set free in the ocean without a paddle. What if something happened? What if another lump grew? What if my appointment in three months was too late?

I knew I could not think like that. I knew I had to be present and live for today, not worrying about tomorrow, but it was difficult to do.

The night before my last treatment, I sat in front of the TV and watched as Barack Obama was re-elected for his second term. As I watched history taking place again, I wondered what my history would be. I worried that I had sheltered my family from my pain and worries too much. I often tried to pretend everything was okay, and then when they acted like everything was okay, I would be angry. They were only acting how I had wanted them to, yet it caused me to have such conflicting emotions. I was happy they were feeling that relaxed, and at the same time I was mad that they didn't see what I was hiding from them. Talk about a rollercoaster of emotions. No wonder it was a called a journey.

November 8, 2012

My final day of radiation arrived. The weather didn't improve, and it was once again snowing and windy. Cliff and I left three hours ahead of my appointment time and slowly made our way down the highway. There was no way we were missing this final appointment. We chatted and held hands on the way, so happy this was our last time to travel these roads for this reason, happy the day had finally arrived but still not believing that it had.

As we walked through the hospital for the last time, we held hands and kissed in the elevator. This was our last elevator ride to the basement, to the radiation department. As I went to change for the last time, Cliff took checked me in for the last time. I put my clothes in the locker for the last time and went to sit with Cliff in the waiting room. For the last time. My name was called, and Cliff stood with me, kissed me, and said, "Please, God, this is the last time we will ever walk these halls."

I lay on the machine as the nurses moved me around and got me lined up to the laser, congratulating me on reaching my final treatment. As I lay there and listened to the door close after they exited the room, I felt peace. Tears started to flow as the machine circled my chest for the last time. It was the last time for everything. I had made it. I counted off the seconds as the laser clicked away. For the last time.

Once it was over, I hugged my nurses and told them how much I appreciated their kindness, how they had made my daily trips that much more bearable with their smiles. They were truly earthly angels.

I changed and went to Cliff, who was waiting for me. He pulled me in close and kissed me. We held hands and headed to the elevator that would bring us to the main floor. We didn't speak on the way up, just held each other tightly. We had made it. We were going to be okay.

As we walked out of the hospital front door, we noticed the sun had broken through the clouds. The storm seemed to be moving south, and we were heading north. We smiled at each other as we made our way across the parking lot for the last time. Cliff opened up my door, and I reached in and pulled out a magnetic pink ribbon I had bought several months back. It was inscribed *Survivor*, and I now felt I had earned the title. Cliff took it from me and secured it to back of our vehicle. Then, after taking some pictures to mark the occasion, we once again shared a kiss. We had made it.

Cliff opened the door for me as I stood beside him. He bent down to kiss me again, relief written all over his face. As we pulled out of the hospital parking lot for the last time, he said:

"Honey, let's go home."

Epilogue

It is only when we truly know and understand that we have a limited time on Earth—and that we have no way of knowing when our time is up—that we will begin to live each day to the fullest, as if it was the only one we had.
—Elisabeth Kubler-Ross

Several months have now passed since my last radiation treatment, and I have begun the slow process of healing both my mind and my body. I feel stronger with each passing day and am so grateful to be blessed with a second chance. I have been given a second chance to engage once again wholly in my life and will never take one breath for granted. My body is healing faster than my mind, and I hope that one day my mind will catch up.

Cancer robbed me of not only my health for a period of time, but it also robbed me of that sense of security we all have before we are diagnosed with a disease like cancer. I have read that cancer survivors can experience post-traumatic stress disorder (PTSD), and I take comfort in knowing that I am not alone in my feelings and fears. There are so many women (and men) who have walked this road before me, and unfortunately countless more will follow.

Before March 14, 2012, I was the same as everyone else. Then everything changed. My life changed. No longer was I the same as everyone else. I now had a new title to go along with wife, mother, daughter, sister, and friend. I was now also a cancer patient, soon to be replaced with the title of survivor. Even the order of my titles have changed: survivor, wife, mother, daughter, sister, friend. I had to be a survivor first.

Life as I once knew it no longer exists, but thankfully it has been replaced with a life that is just as beautiful. My relationship with my husband and our marriage is stronger than it ever was before; we were determined to never become part of that marital breakdown statistic. We have almost twenty-five years of marriage under our belts and can't wait to celebrate another twenty-five! The love I feel for my children is deeper than I ever thought possible. I thought I had always loved them to the deepest of my core, but I have learned that love can go deeper again when you face the threat of losing it all.

The gratitude and love I feel for all those who reached out and helped me through the darkest moments of my life can never be expressed. My heart has burst a thousand times from the love. My fears of being alone and forgotten were chased away from the very first moments my life changed.

Nothing is worth more than this day.
    —Goethe

God bless.

CPSIA information can be obtained at www.ICGtesting.com
Printed in the USA
LVOW080731300513

336031LV00002B/22/P